This book is dedicated to my wife, Gladys,
who made survival possible

TOO BRIGHT THE VISION?

African Adventures of an Anglican Rebel

ARTHUR R. LEWIS

COVENANT BOOKS
London
1992

The Covenant Publishing Co. Ltd.
8 Blades Court, Deodar Road,
Putney, London, SW15 2NU

Printed and bound in the United Kingdom by
Staples Printers Rochester Limited,
Neptune Class, Medway City Estate,
Frindsbury, Rochester, Kent ME2 4LT

Contents

Foreword

By Bishop Anselm Genders,
of the Community of the Resurrection, Mirfield:
former Bishop of Bermuda

Fr Lewis and I first met in 1966 when I arrived in Rhodesia and inherited the audit of the Mandea Mission accounts, so we have known one another for 26 years.

The chapter headings indicate his wide experience, ranging from old-time mission days to contemporary Marxist régimes and the liberal establishment. He is a man of integrity who has not been afraid to skate on thin ice and speak his mind plainly about disconcerting trends and events mainly in Rhodesia/Zimbabwe but also in the Anglican Communion at large. Opponents have accused him of putting politics first and have labelled him racialist — a foolish charge to level against a man who has worked in Africa, among Africans, for 40 years. Arthur Lewis' first concern has been for Christianity and the Church and the people he served. He saw religion being used to grind axes made behind iron curtains and in liberal workshops. The phrase had not been coined or he would have been described as "politically incorrect" by those who think in that ridiculous term.

Inevitably Fr Lewis made himself unpopular in places, and sometimes provoked real hostility with his back to the wall in defence of his freedom of speech and his priestly ministry. But the Gospel bids us in such circumstances, "Rejoice and be glad, for so persecuted they the prophets before you." This is greatly to the credit of Fr Lewis, and you have only to look round to see that most of his criticisms and warnings were truly prophetic.

It is a pleasure to commend this book not only to those who are interested in missions and work in Africa, but also to those who are concerned with (and about) history in the making and the declining trends of recent years, which are in full flood and threaten to sweep away the heritage of Western Christendom.

Anselm Genders

House of the Resurrection,
Mirfield,
W. Yorks.

July, 1992

1. A Tropic Christmas

"PRIVATE Smith will report to the Commanding Officer," blared the tannoy, "FORTHWITH." A moment later it cooed: "Will Lady Hidebound kindly attend on the Captain at her earliest convenience?"

After forty-odd years — it was November 1947 — the actual names are blurred now, but the voice remains with me still. So does that ship. The *Empire Windrush* had been a German vessel that had gone to the bottom. It had been brought up and refurbished by the British, and was now in use as a troopship. On this voyage, from Southampton to East Africa via Suez, it was carrying a complement of civilian passengers. I had got a passage as the newest recruit of the Universities' Mission to Central Africa (UMCA).

In 1857 David Livingstone appealed for a mission to bring Christianity to East and Central Africa, and more particularly to rid the domains of the Sultan of Zanzibar of the slavery which he described as an "open sore." English Christians then took missions to non-Christians more seriously than most do now. In the following year the Universities' Mission to Central Africa was formed in response to Livingstone's appeal. It was an Anglican mission, indeed an Anglo-Catholic one, and would have puzzled the dour Scottish explorer-missionary a good deal. But it tackled the job by sending out enthusiasts, bishops, priests and lay workers, who forswore marriage for the duration of their service.

As the middle of the twentieth century approached the dedication of the mission was still high, though there were problems that were hushed up. Almost every young Anglo-Catholic priest in England at some time considered the possi-

1

bility of working for UMCA. We were told simply: "Go ye into all the world, and preach the Gospel to every creature." The Mission offered us our keep, thirty pounds a year pocket-money and home leave every three years. We had no other thought than evangelism.

The coastal belt of Tanganyika Territory, today's Tanzania, was my own destination. Ecclesiastically this was part of the diocese of Zanzibar, for it was from Zanzibar Island off the East African coast that Christianity had spread to the main-land. (The high altar of Zanzibar Cathedral still stands on the site of the whipping-post of the former Arab slave-market.) Politically Tanganyika, a backward territory, had been ruled in turn by the Sultan of Zanzibar, the Germans (from 1886 till its loss in the First World War) and the British. It was now a trust territory of the United Nations, under British protection.

The *Empire Windrush* was not visiting Tanganyika, so I disembarked at Mombasa in Kenya Colony. Palm-fringed beaches rose above the dark blue of the Indian Ocean, and the docks and the old Arab town shimmered in the heat. The temperature was in the nineties — we had not heard of Celsius then — and the sky was flecked with only tiny clouds. If Mombasa looked a tropical Eden, however, reality soon broke upon me in the form of the agent I hired to get my luggage off the ship. This Asian gentleman rooked me mercilessly. I had yet to learn the ways of the East.

A cable from the bishop read: "Make for Magila via Tanga." Magila was the oldest Anglican mission station on the main-land. At the shipping office I enquired about boats to Tanga. It was a Thursday. The Indian clerk said: "Next week." I said, "I can't wait." The clerk probably thought "You Europe-ans never can," but said very civilly: "I'm sorry, Sir. There is no boat till next week." He added: "Of course, you can go by rail. It's roundabout, but it will get you there. There are two trains a week, on Tuesdays and Fridays."

The following afternoon I got my baggage to the station of the Kenya and Uganda Railway and travelled upcountry on the Nairobi line to a tiny place called Voi. The single track wound at astounding angles and unlikely gradients through plains and hills and a couple of howling dust-storms. At

2

Voi some of us changed for a cross-country sleeper which meandered gently through the hills. By midday on Saturday it reached the chilly town of Moshi on the slopes of Kilimanjaro, the highest mountain in Africa. It made long stops at every station, when people got out to buy fruit from African children and to stretch their legs.

For the last stage of the journey, down to the hot coastal plain, it was necessary to transfer to Tanganyika Railways. On this line the sleeping arrangements were almost luxurious. It is true the mosquitoes were firmly imprisoned by the mosquito wire on the windows, without hope of escape, but an attendant came round with a flit-gun and provided a net for each bunk.

On the Sunday morning (it was December 14th) we awoke to find ourselves in a sunlit fairyland. The train was descending through hills and valleys of vivid emerald, with tumbling streams and huge forests. These were the Usambara Mountains. Their breathtaking beauty gradually gave way to lush lowlands, crowded beehive villages and the coconut palms which were the first signs of the distant sea.

We reached Muheza, the nearest station to Magila, soon after seven o'clock, with the sun already beating down from a brazen sky. Many hands lowered my trunks to the sandy ground, but there help ended. Months of study of Swahili availed me nothing in the babel with which I was surrounded. There was no white face in sight, and obviously no one to meet me from the mission.

In the end I worked my way through the press to the stationmaster's office, where I attempted my best Swahili. "Salaam, Bwana. Nimekuja . . ." I soon got tied up in knots, and the young stationmaster was far too polite to say that he could see for himself that I had come. He smiled, and said in English: "You must be the new priest for Magila. We are glad to see you, and I have a message for you. The people at the mission are sorry that they cannot come to meet you, but it is Sunday morning and they are all busy. They have sent a box-body for you."

The "box-body" turned out to be a spacious covered truck, with ample room for my belongings. With it was a jovial

3

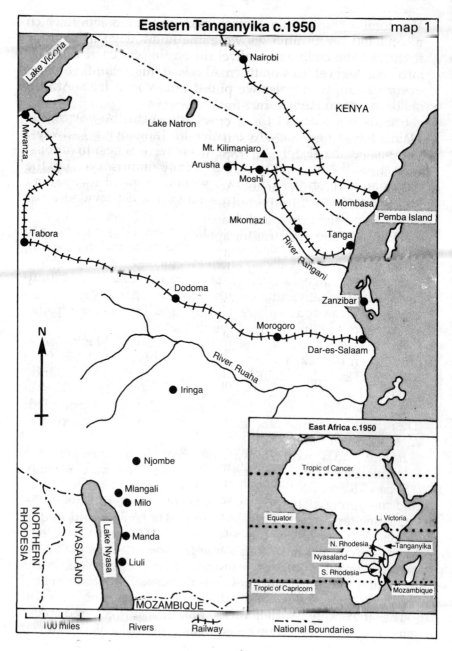

Eastern Tanganyika c.1950   map 1

Lake Victoria

Mwanza

Nairobi

KENYA

Lake Natron

Mt. Kilimanjaro

Arusha

Moshi

Mkomazi

Mombasa

Pemba Island

Tabora

Tanga

River Pangani

Dodoma

Zanzibar

N

Morogoro

Dar-es-Salaam

River Ruaha

Iringa

Njombe

Mlangali

Milo

NORTHERN RHODESIA

NYASALAND

Lake Nyasa

Manda

Liuli

East Africa c.1950

Tropic of Cancer

Equator

L. Victoria

N. Rhodesia

Tanganyika

Nyasaland

S. Rhodesia

Tropic of Capricorn

Mozambique

MOZAMBIQUE

100 miles   Rivers   Railway   National Boundaries

4

driver who spoke little English and pretended manfully to understand my Swahili. However he knew what to do, and soon we were on the red gravel road going back towards the hills. The few vehicles on the road raised huge clouds of dust.

After a couple of miles we pulled off on to what appeared to be an abandoned cart-track, where we bumped and bounced over the rocks and crossed a rickety plank-bridge. We halted abruptly below a square two-storeyed building with an upstairs verandah and a tropical garden ablaze with crotons and bougainvillaea. This was the clergy-house, at a small settlement called Hegongo. Across the valley, from Magila itself, wafted the unexpected sound of church bells. At the clergy-house the acting archdeacon, Canon Neville Nash, was waiting to receive me, full of apologies. "You will be tired," he said, "and will probably want to rest. But there is still just time to get to church if you wish . . ."

Magila was a quarter of an hour's walk across the valley and through the villages. You saw the church only at the last moment, since it was built on a knoll and hidden by scarlet acacias. The gothic structure, of rough grey stone, formed one side of a quadrangle, the other sides of which were occupied by the Convent of the Sacred Passion. It had been consecrated as long ago as 1886. Before you reached the church you saw the stone Calvary which gave Magila its other name, Msalabani or "the place of the Cross." I knew that long before the first missionaries arrived the German explorer Krapf had carved a cross on a tree here because he believed that this was where the first Christian mission should be built.

Outside the church I met the priest-in-charge, Father Thomas Dix, in his white cassock. There was time only for a brief hand-shake, since the service was about to begin. The Bishop was to hold a confirmation, and the church was packed. I squeezed in and was almost overpowered by the heat — even though the windows were unglazed and the birds flew happily in and out. The congregation sat on mats, the men on the right hand side and the women on the left, some with babies on their backs. Men wore shorts and open-neck shirts or, in some cases, the long white Arab *kanzu*:

women were dressed in coloured cotton sheeties. The familiar music was unaccompanied.

After the service I shook more hands than I had ever shaken before. Finally the clergy retired for coffee to the *baraza* or verandah of the sisters of the Community. Here I met not only the sisters and their Reverend Mother but Father Ernest Vuo, the much loved and respected African priest whose memory went back to German days. His younger colleague, Father Mikael Mayaka, was sick in hospital at Tanga.

Lunch back at Hegongo was served by Martin, the house-boy, in his red fez and white *kanzu*. There was cassava instead of potatoes, but otherwise it was an ordinary "European" meal, destitute of the stiff porridge which was the Africans' staple diet. Bishop Bill Baker proved a master of polite conversation and was looking forward to a Christmas visit to Government House in Dar-es-Salaam, the capital. Father Dix was full of his Swahili nativity play, to which I was dragged in the afternoon.

Hours later, before the short dusk, we stood on the verandah and watched the sun go down over the Amani hills in a blaze of gold. None of us were late seeking our beds after supper, for the oil lamps were dim and the mosquitoes whined incessantly. The beds had no mattresses: but it was a relief to dive under the mosquito-net into oblivion. I did not hear the bush-babies clattering on the roof.

* * * *

During the following days there was little time to look at the new and unfamiliar surroundings, but they thrust themselves upon me from morning till night. The birds which I had first seen flying into the church were of vivid blues and greens and reds. The African cuckoo sang all day, and the bottle-bird gurgled happily from the trees. I knew, and know, nothing of ornithology, but could hear for myself the bird which sang: "Put your feet up" and the little fellow who piped "Be quick! Be quick!" as I hastened to church before six in the morning.

There were owls in the church and bats in the privy. And

6

there were snakes galore. If in doubt you beat them with a stick. Cicadas sang in the trees day and night, and after dark the frogs made the night hideous with their monstrous croaking. Rats collected Father Dix's denture and deposited it in the roof.

Night, of course, was the time when the insects came into their own. Flying beetles made frontal attacks, and there were hornets and buzz-bombs and sausage-moths. My entomology was on a par with my ornithology, but these creatures named themselves. The praying mantis looked at one greenly over the edge of the table, with sad eyes. Termites ate the mats in church (and everywhere else), sprouted wings and immolated themselves in the lamps and in the soup. The lizards, however, were on our side: they scampered up and down the walls and ate every insect within reach.

Of course, I did not spend my first days in Africa studying its natural history. My priorities were to get to know the people and to make some headway with the language. I had been working at Swahili for months, with grammar books and vocabularies. But the Africans spoke at an enormous speed, and it was weeks before I could make out what they were saying. The position was not eased by the fact that they mixed it up with the local vernacular, Bondei, "the language of the valley." Swahili is the *lingua franca* of the whole of East Africa, but there are dozens of local languages and dialects as well.

On my first Wednesday I struggled through the Swahili eucharist in church, and the next day attempted a sung service for the boys' school. No one seemed to mind the most heinous howlers of the *Mzungu* or white man. From then onwards I celebrated the eucharist every day and sometimes officiated at the sung service on Sundays. Within three weeks I was preaching, with every word written out and memorised.

At the end of the school term the headmaster, Mwalimu (Teacher) Martin Kiama, invited us all to a sort of outdoor "speech day." The pupils performed uproarious skits on the *Wazungu* (Europeans), lapsing into Bondei for their more outrageous comments and burgeoning into English when they wanted to impress us. Afterwards Mwalimu Kiama took me

7

to his home, where, unlike the other teachers I had visited, he actually introduced me to his wife. He was a good head master and a good Christian: yet his house was as bare and apparently poverty-stricken as those of most other Africans, including the teachers. The salaries of teachers, clerks and the like were sufficient to enable them to have pleasant furnished homes, but they had not yet broken with the tradition that money was not spent on that sort of thing. Gramophones were a different matter. It was beginning to be the fashion to have both a gramophone and a record.

The clergy and teachers took me visiting in the nearby villages, where one sat outside the round huts to chat and make the acquaintance of the local people, especially the Christians. The often windowless huts were dark and smoky as a forge, for cooking was done inside them on three stones. The men did most of the talking, the women being busy with mortar and pestle. Along the pathways everyone greeted one another, and I soon learned that it was the younger who greeted the elder.

As well as Christians there were Muslims and the people we described (without offence) as pagans. These were animists or ancestor-worshippers, the followers of the most ancient religion of tribal Africa and indeed of primitive peoples everywhere. They were steeped in witchcraft, and we heard their drums at night.

By this time Christmas was almost upon us, and the priests were busy in church or travelling to the outstations to hear confessions before the festival. This work kept them busy for a week or more. I helped with the marking of communion cards. With large numbers of simple people these cards enabled us to keep a record of communicants.

On Christmas Eve there was a festive air everywhere, and men were returning to their homes from work in distant places. Christian houses were garlanded, outside, with palm branches and flowers, while the church was decorated both inside and out. All day people were arriving on foot from the further outstations to spend the festival at the mission. By now the flaming acacias were at their most brilliant. They were called "Christmas trees."

8

At the midnight mass the church was crowded to the doors, and the familiar carols were sung with enormous gusto. The church was lit by hurricane lamps. On previous years there had been some rowdyism, people having come to church after overmuch jollification, so communion was not administered. This year, however, there was no trouble, and indeed there was much evidently genuine devotion. It cannot be denied, however, that all African Christians, devout or otherwise, thoroughly enjoy a festival.

During the night the rain came. It came in a solid grey wall. You could hear its whoosh-whoosh over the valley before it reached the mission, where it hammered and drummed on the corrugated iron roofs and dribbled into the church and made pools on the cement floor. By the time of the early morning service the roads and paths were streams of bright orange. But the Christians came from all directions, including the normally lazy ones. Many a smart suit or bright frock, bought for the occasion, was woefully bedraggled before its owner sought a dry patch in the church. Some, not to be worsted, arrived in old rags with their finery in bundles on their heads.

As I sang the Solemn Eucharist it seemed to me that this was popular devotion at its best. It cost something — it cost monogamy and some effort and sacrifice — and it brought joy and meaning into the lives of unsophisticated people. Christianity in the areas served by the Universities' Mission was unashamedly sacramental, and was aimed at building a Christian society as well as converting individuals. It did not use "born again" terminology, but it brought people to Christ even if there was a long struggle with witchcraft and paganism on the way. The Christians of Magila were happy on Christmas morning because Christ was born and because they belonged to the world-wide fellowship of His followers.

The rain passed as quickly as it had come, the sun blazed torridly from a brilliant sky and the countryside was dry within hours. After church the festivities went on till the afternoon, when all except those who lived nearby began to drift back to their homes. There was no Evensong in church, for the books had fallen to pieces, but there was a small crowd

9

in church for the informal popular service which took its place. A football match rounded off the day, and the referee tactfully arranged a draw. Then we white priests walked back to Hegongo for a traditional Christmas dinner.

* * * *

In February Father Dix went on leave to England for six months, and I, to my horror, was left as acting priest-in-charge. Father Ernest Vuo was indeed past his most active years, but Father Mikael Mayaka was back from hospital and I felt he was more suitable for the job than I. He was a young man of courage and ability: nobody's yes-man, yet with the unenviable task of interpreting white to black and black to white. Yet he had no ambition to take on the responsibility, and in the case of a large mission everyone in those days assumed that a European would remain at the helm. Whites were usually better administrators.

My companion at Hegongo was Archdeacon Stephens — "Steve" — who had just returned from furlough. He was diocesan treasurer and educational secretary, and possibly a saint. His was the most formidable burden of work in the diocese, yet he was never heard to complain. He seemed to be at his desk all night, but in the daytime he had a constant stream of visitors, all with mundane problems. Bishop Baker (who lived in a separate bungalow) was away "on safari" most of the time. When at home he dealt with correspondence with his own hand, having no secretary. Cynics said that he never wrote unless he was fairly sure the problem had gone away!

During Lent we departed from our usual practice of confining church services to the daylight hours — the electricity reached no further than Muheza — and held an informal devotion on Wednesdays at eight in the evening for local Christians. It was soon my turn to give the talk. Immediately after breakfast on the Wednesday morning I sat down to write it, for I had not had a free moment in the earlier part of the week.

"*Hodi! Hodi!*" It was someone outside, on the verandah,

10

calling for admission. I had soon discovered that people did not knock at doors, which were usually open if the occupant was in; they called *"Hodi!"* There was only one answer to that: *"Karibu,"* or "Come in." It was the cook, coming to talk to me in my capacity as housekeeper. He said (a) that the woodman was on strike for more pay, and since there was no firewood there could be no more cooking; and (b) that we had just used the last of the butter and flour — so what?

It took some time to sort this out, inspanning old Yohana the gardener and calling the grocer at Tanga twenty-six miles away on our antediluvian telephone. The call was delayed an hour and a half, but I got through before the exchange closed for lunch.

At last I was in hopes of getting on with my talk. But it was not to be. For outside, on the verandah, half a dozen people were patiently waiting. *"Hodi!"* called one of them, and at my *"Karibu,"* they all trooped in. There were four men and two women. It appeared that the younger of the women was called Mariamu or Mary, and she was the cause of the visit. The spokesman was her father, the older woman her mother (she was silent as a mouse) and the rest were relatives.

I asked what was the news — *"Habari gani?"* — for this was the normal opening of any conversation after the standard greetings. *"Njema"* was the reply: good. There could be no other. Only then did the spokesman pour out a flood of Swahili, like waves battering on a sea wall. "Stop!" I pleaded. "Say it all over again, and twice as slowly."

It appeared that Mariamu originally belonged to Magila, but last year she had contracted a Christian marriage with a young man called Tomaso and gone to live at Mkuzi, the next parish. Tomaso had recently taken to drink, and had begun beating her. What was more, he had started carrying on with another woman who was not a Christian. Mariamu had put up with this as long as she could, but last night Tomaso had come home mad drunk and set about her, and she had had to flee for her life. She had gone back to her home, and now her father wanted to return the *lobola* or "brideprice" received from Tomaso's family before the wedding in order that the

11

marriage might be broken and Mariamu get another husband. Everybody knew perfectly well that Christian marriages were for life, but it was popularly believed that the Bishop could set them aside if he wished.

Cases of this sort were always brought to the clergy, for it was recognised that the tribal courts had no jurisdiction in matters concerning Christian marriage. This gave the church a valuable opportunity to work for reconciliation, and every priest used this opportunity to the uttermost. A huge amount of time was spent, and well spent, on marriage problems.

I listened as well as I could, expressed my sympathy and said that obviously I had neither the experience nor the linguistic ability to deal with the matter myself. What I could and would do was to arrange a meeting tomorrow with the African clergy, neither of whom was immediately available, and attend it myself. I wrote a letter to Tomaso requesting him to come to this meeting, and I had a good deal of confidence that he would, in fact, turn up. He would not wish to put himself in the wrong. Then I asked them all to pray. We shook hands, and the party went away.

By this time a considerable queue had formed on the verandah, though "queue" was perhaps not the right word. It was certainly not a case of first come first served. I mentally postponed the talk until after lunch.

The lad who came in next said that the news was good, but his father had just died. I composed myself with suitable gravity and said how sorry I was. "Father," of course, was a term which included almost any senior relative. "Will you please come and bury him?" asked the boy. "He was a Christian."

This raised problems. Burials were in the villages, not normally in the churchyard. And because of the heat they had to take place on the same day, within a few hours of death. The service was normally read by the local teacher, but this boy came from a place up in the hills where the teacher had been withdrawn. Neither of the African priests was on the mission, so obviously I ought to go. "You will have to come and fetch me," I said, "for I don't know the way. What time?" We agreed on two o'clock, and the lad went his way.

The next section of the queue consisted of mothers seeking baptism for their babies. I soon discovered that in no case was there any prospect that the children would be brought up as Christians, and other priests had told the parents that they should wait till the children were older and then send them for instruction. The mothers were trying their luck with a new priest.

After the mothers a young couple pitched up with their families, to "write up" their marriage in church. Of course, they should have made a prior arrangement, but they had taken a chance that one or other of the clergy would be on the mission. Since everyone was present who should be I thought it wise to press on. Frequently someone quite crucial would be missing.

"Writing up" a wedding was a fairly lengthy business, but not beyond my capabilities since the main thing involved was the filling in of a large form. The objects of the form, which the priest completed in the presence of all concerned, were to ensure that there was no impediment to the marriage, that the man and woman knew what they were undertaking and that the wedding took place with the full consent of both the families. The last point was essential, and the agreement was sealed by the *lobola* or "brideprice." This latter usually consisted of cattle, and was not a price at all. It was compensation to the girl's family, in a patriarchal society, for the loss of her labour as she joined the family of her husband. It made for the stability of marriage, and the Church went along with it.

After the formalities I chatted with the elders, blessed the young couple and arranged for the marriage instructions to be given by an African priest. When it was all over and we had shaken hands on the verandah I saw with a sinking heart that the queue had grown rather than diminished. This was one of those days.

Next in was the woodman, who having despaired of a rise was in hopes of a loan. Having been warned of the disastrous results of giving loans — they tended to evaporate in an alcoholic haze — I disabused him of his hopes and indicated the door. He was followed by a series of hard-luck stories of

13

quite astounding ingenuity, all intended to extract cash from me. My heart melted several times, but I had been told firmly by the archdeacon never to part with money without referring to him first. "The alternative," he pointed out, "is the financial collapse of the mission. And no peace for you or me ever again."

But I was defeated in the end, by an old man with a rigmarole about a duck. His plea turned out to be a hard-luck story with a difference. He was actually prepared to sell me his duck. I was about to send him off when I remembered that all our ducks had been eaten by a marauding animal, and Steve had suggested that I replenish it. "How much?" I said, cautiously. "Seven shillings," was his reply. "If the cook says its worth that much," I conceded, "you shall have it."

The wily old man sent his boy with the duck after lunch when the cook had gone home and there was not a soul about. It was an excellent duck, and I learned much later that it might have been worth three shillings. There was nothing for it but to pay up and tell the boy to put the duck in the pen, where I promptly forgot all about it. (The following day at table the archdeacon mentioned the subject of ducks, and my conscience smote me. Steve was a great lover of God's creatures, and, when I told him the story, said: "Poor thing, it will be starving. We had better let it out." We did, and it was never seen again.)

The boy from the hills who was to take me to the funeral turned up at half past three, not two o'clock. I consoled myself with the thought that people did not have watches. It was a hard hour's climb in the heat to the village, which was crowded with relatives and friends, some of whom had walked long distances at short notice. At one end of the sprawling group of huts the menfolk sat together, chatting and smoking. At the other end the women wailed. A handful of men stood about an embryonic grave, one digging with a hoe and the rest watching. It was obvious that the preparations were far from complete, and there was nothing to do but sit and talk with the men. After suitable condolences I suggested some digging, and pointed at the sun. They got the message.

When the burial was over I fled with scant ceremony, leaving the wailing behind me and arriving at Hegongo as the last daylight faded. The Lent service in church at eight was well attended. It should have been a spiritual opportunity, but my talk had perforce to be extempore. The congregation was superbly charitable, but to this day I do not know if anyone understood a word.

*   *   *   *

That Wednesday was neither unique nor typical. But months passed before I could seriously get down to the work of being a missionary. The real opportunity for that came after the priest-in-charge had returned from his furlough in England and taken up the administrative work again.

Then I could spend days walking the footpaths through the bush, visiting the villages and sometimes sleeping in one of the safari huts near a thatched church or school: or even, occasionally, a church or school with a corrugated iron roof. One stopped to greet people on the way, and a Christian name — Petro or Davidi or Salome or Elizabeti — would often betray a Christian who had lapsed from his religion. Such Christians would frequently come to church afterwards to talk over their problems, and, in spite of all the pressures, some would put their marital irregularities right and come back to church. The pressures were evident enough. Polygamy was widespread. The signs of witchcraft were everywhere, and drunkenness drained the life of the village communities. The sap of the coconut palm made a potent African beer, and at all hours men were to be seen shinning lithely up the trees to tap it.

A priest who slept at an outstation would always celebrate the eucharist the following morning. The altar would often be a blackboard on a school cupboard, and in wet weather it had to be placed in the driest spot. Christians from the surrounding villages would leave their fields to come to the service, though as harvest-time approached — in the fertile Bondei country there were two harvests a year — children would be left behind to chase away the birds and the monkeys from the crops. Communicants usually made their confession before the service, and afterwards the priest would be detained for hours listening to marriage problems. School started late on these days.

From the church point of view the mission teachers were a mixed bag. Some were keen on their religion and cared for the Christian families in their area, using their schools and churches as evangelistic centres. Others were Christians for convenience' sake and took the line that their job was simply to educate children.

The toughest part of the parish was a string of primitive villages, up in the mountains, called Manga Juu. You reached it by a tortuous ascent, crossing a river below a spectacular waterfall. At one point the stream was so narrow that you could leap across from one rock ledge to another, though there was a slippery twenty-foot scramble up to the path at the other side.

Manga Juu had been evangelised years ago, but the people had subsequently moved away to the palm-oil plantation at the top of the mountain and the mission had no choice but to close the small school. By now, however, there had been a drift back to the dilapidated huts, and one child even walked daily down to school at Magila. The lapsed Christians were swamped by the pagans with whom they were surrounded and the men had mostly taken several wives.

At first the villagers, especially the women, were suspicious of a stranger, and even hostile. But on my third visit I befriended a lapsed Christian who was prepared to show me round and introduce me to the headman and some of his people. The hostility began to fall away, and concealed Christians gradually appeared. Eventually I was offered the use of a hut as a temporary church, and thirty people turned up for a service. Only a handful could receive Communion, and most had to leave after the sermon: as in the early Church Christians in grace were the only ones allowed to remain for the Eucharist itself. But those who left did not go far, and we had a long discussion afterwards about the future of the Church in Manga Juu. There was talk of building a church,

16

and a few poles were cut. It just was not practicable to start a school again.

As the months passed I often climbed the hill to visit the Christians of Manga Juu, and the non-Christians too. I would sit for hours outside their homes, surrounded by the goats and the chickens. Sometimes it seemed that Christianity might make headway in these unpromising surroundings, but it was uphill work: and monogamy was very unpopular. It was evident that people could only be weaned slowly from the old ways, and in any case it was not our job to destroy stable relationships where they existed. What was needed above all was someone who could go round the villages regularly over the years, preparing the way for the future Christian community and teaching the "hearers" — potential converts — and the catechumens or baptism candidates.

In the adjoining area of Bombo an aged catechist called Mwalimu Hugh looked after a little church and taught a dozen children. This gaunt old man, almost destitute of formal education, was an outstanding character. In an unaffected way he just loved God and people, and he worked uncomplainingly for the pittance the mission could offer him. His life was spent, when not teaching the three Rs, in instructing people in the catechism and visiting them in their homes. He was regarded with reverence and affection and not a little awe.

One day I was sitting under the thatched eaves of his home, where the poultry squawked loudly, and talking about his people. I happened to mention Manga Juu, but he knew all about it already. "I will go," he said simply.

And go he did, every week, though it was a long and tiring journey over gullies and streams. He was readily accepted, and Christians living in open sin began to promise to sort out their lives. In fact very few accepted the public penance which was the outward manifestation of a real change of heart. This usually meant separating — prior to Christian marriage — from a casual or pagan partner and attending church for a period without receiving communion. Today this discipline, modelled on that of the early Church, may seem hard. In fact everyone recognised that, in the circumstances of the place and time, Christianity and Christian family life could not have been built up without it, and indeed Christianity would not have been taken seriously at all. The alternative would have been not Christianity but a sub-Christian syncretistic religion.

I left Magila in 1949, but was called back again there as priest-in-charge at a later date. Mwalimu Hugh was still visiting Manga Juu, and one by one, or sometimes two by two, the lapsed Christians came back to their religion. There were new Christians too, and the transformation wrought by Christianity in the villages was something which everybody could see.

Two questions, however, were already rising in the minds of all of us white missionaries. Paternalism was the order of the day: it was not only taken for granted but was actually demanded by the vast majority of Africans. "You are our father," people would say. How long could this go on? Moreover, though relations between the races were good, there was no question of black people and white people being treated in the same way. This simply was not practicable and was wanted by nobody, least of all (apart from a minuscule minority) by the Africans themselves. But could this state of things persist? And how could a bridge be built across so vast a cultural gulf?

2. Eden in the Hills

ZIRAI by moonlight was perhaps the most beautiful spectacle I have ever seen. It was far up in the Shambala Hills, a thousand feet or more above the central mission-station at Kizara and remote from any road or town. The church was of thatched wattle-and-daub, and the little "safari house" adjoining it, where I was camping, was acutely uncomfortable. But the view was breath-taking.

It was almost like daylight. On every side the peaks rose glittering into the shining sky, and cast dark shadows across the valleys below. In this world of whiteness the forests and the grassy slopes stood out brilliantly, with only occasional rocky outcrops and pinnacles. The night was alive with sound; the roar of the distant rivers and the cry of nocturnal animals. And everywhere, always, the beating of drums and the haunting songs which accompanied the Shambala dances. Doubtless many of the dances left a lot to be desired morally, for the whole countryside was riddled with witchcraft and most of the people were primitive: but the Shambala songs were unforgettably lovely.

In the morning I was up before first light, and the Christians were already making their way through the shadows of the forest to the church. The sun rose gold and crimson through a gap in the hills and the birdsong and the chattering of the streams filled the fresh new world.

Before the service several dozen of the people waited to make their confessions. In this way, if in no other, the priest was able to talk to them individually about spiritual things: and some who first came perfunctorily caught a vision of

19

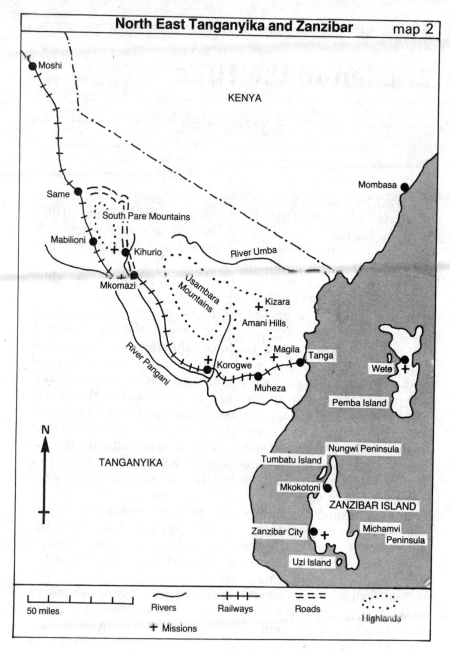

a better life and sincerely strove to put their religion into practice.

The service in church was simple and quiet, apart from the howling of the babies on their mothers' backs. There were, however, more men than women. I talked simply, too, without notes and without a pulpit, about the God who made us and loves us and how Jesus can change our lives. Unhappily it had to be in Swahili, with only a word of Shambala here and there. The African headmaster led the singing, and one of the teachers acted as server at the little stone altar.

Afterwards, of course, I greeted everyone, and those who wanted to talk waited behind. The "shauris" — or, more accurately *mashauri* — were almost always marriage problems. The whole concept of lifelong monogamous marriage was very hard for even the faithful Christians, but many tried and there were some triumphant successes. The small Christian communities had built over a dozen centres such as Zirai throughout the scattered "parish" or mission-district of Kizara: and the work of winning and encouraging new Christians was at each of them the same.

We mission-priests, of course, did not suspect that the moral standards we were urging on the African people — without which there could be no Christian family life and no Christian civilisation — would shortly be abandoned even by many church leaders in the supposedly Christian West from which we came.

By midday I was clambering, with Kristofa the houseboy, down the steep track to the mission at Kizara. But the mission was only the centre from which, day after day and week after week, "safaris" such as this were made on foot to the furthest corners of a far-flung, lonely and sparsely populated district.

*   *   *   *

New priests in UMCA were sent all over the diocese by the bishop, partly to gain experience but more often to fill in the overseas furloughs of the longstanding members of the Mission. A priest-in-charge would be away from his "parish" or mission-district for six months or more, and his work had

21

to be done. Kizara was the parish of Father Harold Smith, and I had been sent, in May 1949, to spend a week or two with him and then to take over.

The journey by lorry from Korogwe to Kizara had taken me through tinder-dry savannah and cactus country, along a "main road" with spine-jarring bumps and pot-holes. We made a stop at an outstation called Kwata, which was on the fringe of Kizara mission district. From there it would have been possible, by a four-hour walk, to reach the mission up in the hills. Instead we battled onwards and upwards, round the mountain and along a steadily deteriorating track, till we reached a village named Kwemkole. Here the track became a rocky footpath winding steeply up a fissure into the hills. No vehicle could get any nearer to the mission at Kizara, but the remaining climb was only forty minutes. My possessions had all been packed into head-loads.

We had arrived within a few hours of the agreed time, and Father Harold was there to meet us with the school drum-and-whistle band and a group of porters. "I hope," he said as we began climbing, "you have brought your warm winter woollies. It is going to be cold." Father Harold was a character. He was a dedicated missionary, a loner, a prodigious walker and, when he had the opportunity, a prodigious talker. His voice was stentorian, and he spoke a variety of Swahili which, some years later, was to die with him. Decibels had to make up for syntax.

"Wear two pairs of stockings if you don't want blisters," he told me. "And use a long stick. It will save you a lot of falls." His advice was to stand me in good stead. He then outlined a programme of work which would reduce any normal mortal to a state of collapse within a week. I agreed heartily with everything he said — he would brook no demur — and mentally determined that when he had gone I would do as much as my puny physical condition would permit and no more.

Kizara was another Eden. The mission was set in a garden of roses, spider-lilies and bougainvillaea, and was surrounded by dazzling emerald hills. The sound of streams was everywhere. Sometimes one would wake to find the world shrouded in mist, but much of the time the weather was like an English summer. From the guest-hut in which I lived till Father Harold left one could glimpse through the fissure up which we had climbed the Umba plain and Kenya to the north. This was uncharted land, inhabited only by the primitive Wakamba. Long after dusk had settled over Kizara the evening sunlight flamed on this wild country.

The mission church at Kizara was a long, low building with a corrugated iron roof and unglazed windows. Inside it was Franciscan in its whitewashed simplicity. The priest's house, built by Father Harold, was a rectangular three-roomed mud bungalow, thatched with palm-leaves: its windows too were unglazed, and in spite of the chilly climate it had no fire-place. A few hundred yards away was the ladies' house, occupied now only by Miss Beatrice Hart, who had joined the mission in 1924. She was to be my only white companion, and an energetic and saintly person she was. Her job was to supervise the schools, and she still climbed the mountains with goat-like agility. Beyond her house were the school, the dispensary and one or two teachers' villages. The teachers turned out to be a grand crowd.

Life on the mission was, however, something short of idyllic. The problems started in church on my first Sunday. The congregation was small in comparison with that of Magila, for Christians here were few and scattered. That I had expected. What I had not expected was the cantor — and the dogs. The cantor, who led the unaccompanied singing, was tone-deaf and, in full cry, sounded not unlike an old bull being sawn in two by a chain-saw. You could hear both the bull and the chain. Father Harold was too spiritual to notice such things, and Miss Hart too saintly to bother about them. I was neither, and mentally vowed action.

Even more horrifying were the dogs. There were three of them, and they devoutly went to church. One belonged to Father Harold, and was tied to his stool. Since the stool was light and Father Harold was usually at the altar this proved no restraint. The second belonged to Miss Hart, and was tied to *her* stool. The ownership of the third I never determined, or have perhaps forgotten: it was unfettered and had an amorous roving commission between the other two. Before Evensong the three conspired to invade the vestry, toppling the smoking censer and scattering the servers. They then swept down the centre of the church, sending the worshippers fleeing in all directions. Finally, during the chanting of the Magnificat, they set up a howling such as I have seldom heard before or since.

Before joining the Mission I was told by an older member: "We all become odd. Soon enough you will too." I tried to make allowances, but felt angrily that the wrecking of public worship in this way — and the apparent assumption that no one minded — was more than a bit much. Needless to say, the Africans never thought of bringing their dogs to church. The only practicable course was to wait until I was in charge and then to reason with Miss Hart. She laughed and said: "Of course, you are right," and did her best to banish the dogs from the church. The animals themselves, however, had minds of their own and put up a stiff resistance.

The best I could do with the cantor, even after Father Harold had left, was sheer flattery. Could he not see that his musical acumen had attracted disciples, and there were younger teachers who yearned for the opportunity of putting into practice the skills they had learned from listening to him? It was a dishonest ruse, and I am ashamed of it. But it worked.

Apart from the services the priest's work at Kizara consisted almost entirely of safaris. As well as the regular journeys to the outstations to preach and administer the sacraments there were emergency calls to the sick and dying — brought by runner. There was never any way of estimating the urgency of these calls. Sometimes I arrived in time to pray and administer the last rites. Sometimes I was too late, though the local teacher would usually have said what prayers he could. On one or two occasions, when I had dropped urgent work and walked for hours, it was to find the "sick" Christian hoeing his field.

Burials were usually the task of the teachers, but sometimes I was asked to take them even in very remote places. The energy of the *Mzungu* or European was thought to be unbounded. One teacher sent me a note, which reached me at midday, asking me to come at once to officiate at the funeral that afternoon of a much respected and faithful old Christian in his area. A quick calculation showed me that even if I had started at dawn it would still have taken me nine hours: four hours to walk there, an hour to do the job and four hours to get back. "Dear Teacher," I wrote back, "Please bury him yourself."

Another kind of "safari" was when the people came to the central mission for instruction. They slept in long thatched dormitories near the church. First they came as "hearers," who were taught the very basics of the Faith before being admitted as catechumens or baptism-candidates. They were given a cross and then sent home for eighteen months' instruction by their own teachers before returning for further instruction by the priest and anointing with the oil of baptism. (This was an ancient custom, restored in UMCA.) After a further six months they would come back for yet more teaching and would be publicly baptised in church. They wore white robes and each carried a lighted candle, and before the service they fasted and maintained silence. The robes were worn until the end of the Eucharist, after which there were great rejoicings and congratulations all round. There was a separate service for the few children who had been baptised in infancy, but unquestionably baptism in the teenage years or in adult life made the greater impact.

There were two more periods of instruction by the priest after baptism, the first to teach sacramental confession and the second to prepare for Confirmation by the bishop.

Teaching in the Shambala country was a difficult job, for the people (children and adults alike) were very simple and almost wholly lacking in abstract ideas. Moreover most of them had never seen a train or a town or the sea, and anybody who taught was permanently hunting for illustrations which were intelligible. The people were unaccustomed to pictures, and could only "see" them after detailed explanation. Here I had one great advantage over the school-teachers: I had Father Harold's magic lantern or *sinéma*. Basically it consisted of a four-gallon oil-tin and a kerosene pressure-lamp.

Until recently the mission teachers, grant-aided by the

government, had received a small salary which was adequate for their lifestyle. Most of them had no ambition to live like Europeans, and it would have been sensible to link salary increases with the acceptance of higher standards of living, such as the use of domestic furniture. In fact at this time the government thrust an enormous salary increase on them, leaving the youngest of them far wealthier than a priest who had been working half a lifetime. This was the result of a commission which had visited the capital, Dar-es-Salaam, and got no further. In some areas the result was little less than catastrophic, but at Kizara we were spared the worst excesses. In fact I cashed in on behalf of the underpaid African clergy.

As I paid out the salaries at the monthly teachers' meeting I talked about sacrificial giving — the church collections in those days were pathetic — and asked for spot cash for the black priests. When I said I would only accept notes the teachers laughed incredulously. But most of them got the message in the end, and there were even some cases of genuine generosity. The biggest obstacle to Christian giving was, however, the universal and apparently unshakeable conviction that the Mission and all white people had unlimited wealth.

*　　*　　*　　*

It was on a Tuesday morning that I decided to make a day-trip to a village called Kwemtindi, which I had not yet visited. As usual this meant climbing the mountain above Kizara and making one's way through the forest. Kristofa accompanied me, but I was familiar with much of the way and readily memorised the last leg of the journey. I was at Kwemtindi in a couple of hours. "Thanks, Kristofa," I said. "I can cope now. Go home and have an extra half-day off."

I spent some time in the head teacher's house, talking with the teachers and urging them to organise Sunday worship. Then the Chief turned up, and we discussed the school at another village, Kuze, a few miles away. I had been to Kuze more than once and had to tell the Chief that his school there was in imminent danger of closure owing to lack of pupils.

26

"There are plenty of children," I pointed out, "but most of them don't come."

The Chief was suitably alarmed, for if he lost the school at Kuze none of his children there could become teachers or clerks. I pointed out, too, that his sub-chief at Kuze had been thoroughly unco-operative. The teacher had in fact written asking me to go there and discuss the problem, since he himself had hurt his leg and he could not come to me at Kizara. I had a note to him in my pocket, explaining that I could not do justice to Kwemtindi and get to Kuze in the same day.

After looking at the school at Kwemtindi I went to greet the local Christian families: both of them. Normally I would have gone to greet the non-Christians, for civility's sake. But it occurred to me that I need not send that note to the teacher at Kuze after all. I *had* time to go there. That was my mistake.

The teacher at Kuze was delighted to see me, but the churlish sub-chief, to whom a message was sent, took his time to come. Face to face his attitude changed, and ultimately his efforts and mine sufficed to save his school. But when our business was done I noticed with some horror that it was after four o'clock. That meant two hours' hard walking before darkness fell. A child led me to the edge of the forest, and then I set off alone up the very steep slope.

The footpath was a tenuous affair which sometimes disappeared altogether in the gathering gloom of the forest. I had no compass and only a vague idea of my direction. Soon I was quite lost, and was bitterly regretting Kristofa's extra half-day. There was no stream to follow, and since it was imperative to get out of the darkness of the forest I just had to work my way through the tangled undergrowth towards what light remained. It took me three quarters of an hour to regain the path, but I joyfully recognised it as the one I had travelled in the morning.

I thought of returning to Kwemtindi and trying to sleep the night in the school. But it was light outside the forest, and I reckoned that with a superhuman effort I could get to the lowest river above Kizara by dusk, even though it meant re-entering the forest, and then find my way along the stream's bank in the dark. Of course I should meet no one on the way, for only on the rarest occasions did people travel in the forest at night.

Then it started to rain: cold, lashing rain. Through the rain I caught a glimpse of two squalid ramshackle huts in the wrong direction. Should I make for them? But I could imagine the stench and the goats and the vermin, and the long cold night in soaking clothes. There would certainly be no lamps in those huts, nor any possibility of sleep. I pressed on.

By this time I was tired and very footsore, and had frequent falls. However, I crossed two streams, on stones, in the last glimmering of the light, and thought I was going to make it. Then the path disappeared completely, and in a few moments it was totally dark. The rain became a driving, almost horizontal deluge.

I knew fear then. The danger of exposure was great. So was that from leopards and hyenas. I prayed, and prayer staved off panic. It would have been folly to have moved further from the path, even if it had been practicable to move at all through the dense undergrowth. Common sense suggested it would be wise to try to climb a tree, but in the storm and in the Stygian blackness even that was not possible.

The rain slackened at last, and I began to call. A faint echo came from a distant hillside, but that was all. There was a glimmer of light, but it was only a firefly. All was silence now but for the dismal dripping of water from the trees. I was shivering, and the night seemed interminable. Hunger and dizziness added to my misery.

Then at last, as I continued to call, I thought I heard a very faint answer. After a few minutes there was no doubt about it. Suddenly voices broke the silence, startlingly near, and there was a flash of lamps among the trees. When the search-party reached me I was only a dozen yards from the path, and the time was not yet eight o'clock.

The party was led by Kristofa and Yustino, the cook. They had set out on their own, before Miss Hart had raised the alarm. One of them was later to turn out to be a thief and the other an adulterer: but I never ceased to be grateful for

28

their prompt action that night. It was to be the first of several occasions when I owed my life to Africans.

It took over half an hour to reach the first of the villages near the mission, where I was received with choruses of friendly concern. The rain had started again, and at Kizara it was clattering on the roofs like a mad thing. I soaked in my old tin bath, and a hot supper and some bandages worked wonders. I was up at five as usual the next morning, a little sore and weary but none the worse for my experience. After saying "thank you" at the altar I made ready to receive the baptism candidates who were to keep me busy for the rest of the week.

I had learned my lesson. We missionaries were, and always would be, dependent on the people we had come to serve. Going it alone was a recipe for disaster.

*   *   *   *

A question which concerned me much during my first years in Africa was that of direct evangelism. We preached in church and visited people in their homes and ran Christian schools and hospitals. We tried, however imperfectly, to show Christianity in action, caring for people. Gradually we were laying the foundations of an indigenous Church in which men and women could find their way to Christ. But what *direct* appeal did we make to their minds and hearts? Did we make an appeal at all to the uninvolved and uncommitted? Perhaps the Anglo-Catholic Universities' Mission was not very strong about that. Truth to tell, the missionaries — priests, teachers, doctors and nurses — were all desperately over-loaded: and as the numbers of Christians grew so did the burden on the expatriate staff. Evangelistic zeal was not unknown among African Christians, but neither was it common.

In England you could bring a parish to life by holding a preaching mission with an eloquent visiting preacher. Here this was not possible. Outside preachers were a rarity, the language barrier was formidable and the people were scattered. That really settled the matter. I must run a mini-mission myself. A good place to start would be Kwata, the biggish

29

outstation four hours away on the "road" to Korogwe by which I had first travelled to Kizara. The head teacher there, Mwalimu Frank, was a keen Christian whose help could be relied on, and there was a considerable surrounding population. Within a month of the idea's birth the preaching mission had taken place.

The church at Kwata was dedicated to the Holy Cross, and in 1949 Holy Cross Day, September 14th, fell on a Wednesday. The plan was to have hymn-singing and addresses in church in the late afternoon on the preceding Sunday, Monday and Tuesday, throwing the church open to all comers, and to conclude with the Eucharist on the Wednesday morning. At this Canon Nash, now at Korogwe, agreed to speak, so on that day we would have that rarest of luxuries, a visiting preacher. As a bonus there would be a lantern show on the Wednesday evening.

It was not practicable for me to visit in the Kwata area beforehand, and in any case we only gave people a few days' notice. They did not keep diaries. However, the church elders at Kwata entered into the spirit of the thing and went round the local villages a day or two in advance.

Meanwhile I produced a large poster in colours, to be attached to the church door, and a number of smaller bills. These would undoubtedly attract attention, for most people would never have seen a poster in their lives. At that stage even Coca Cola signs had not appeared. I then hid myself all day in a remote hut on the mission and worked like mad at my sermons. Everyone could see plainly that Father was not at home that day: he must be on safari.

The magic lantern was safely transported to Kwata on the Friday, on the head of a porter who swung up the hills and over the single log bridge without batting an eyelid. I followed on the Saturday morning. The second half of the journey, beyond the mountain, was along a motorable track through hot savannah country. A Sikh who lived at the beginning of the track sometimes saved me over an hour by giving me a lift in his lorry, but today I was out of luck. The lorry had broken down.

This proved a blessing, for that morning there were lots of

people along the road and I told them all about the preaching mission. At Kwata itself there was a crowd on the verandah of the "hoteli" or tea-shop, and I was granted permission to put up one of my bills. The crowd immediately grew, and I had a ready-made congregation for my first talk. The local Arab shop-keeper, a Muslim, extended the same courtesy to me and I explained to the assembled folk that anyone could come to the mission to listen to what we had to say. I then went off to the local labour camp to put up another bill and repeat the act.

When at last I reached the church I found that my large poster had been up for some time and was attracting a stream of interested viewers. I immediately gave another little impromptu talk, and excitement was obviously growing. Throughout the rest of the day, whenever a group had collected at the poster, I left my safari hut to talk about it. By now I had plenty of willing helpers, for those who could read were explaining the wording to those who could not and were telling them all about what was going to happen.

The Sunday morning Eucharist was well attended by the Christians, but no one was accustomed to coming to church on a Sunday afternoon and it was impossible to know what sort of turn out there would be. Initially it was disappointing: the church would hold two hundred, but it was less than half full. But as we sang one popular hymn after another the number of people increased, and there was a good crowd by the time I gave my talk — a simple evangelistic message for people who knew little or nothing about Our Lord and what He came to do. The congregation included two Muslim chiefs (a third came another day) and, wonder of wonders, an Arab. The Muslims sat with their hats on, but that was a mark of respect.

It is the hardest thing in the world for Muslims to change their religion: but our approach to them was primarily intended to generate goodwill. This might lead to their children being allowed to come to our schools and to choose their own faith in the future. The people we aimed to bring immediately to Christianity were the simple animists and the lapsed Christians. In these circumstances the reaction to the

31

service was entirely favourable, but of course this did not mean Christian commitment. It meant that people were prepared to listen — and talk. Throughout the nearby villages they talked about the Christian message late into the night.

Most of the people who came to the mission were men, so I spent the following days visiting the women in the villages. This was not difficult since nearly all the menfolk were at work at the sisal plantations. The direct invitation brought many of the women to the evening services, and the church was packed on the next two nights. At these services I tried to get down to the nitty-gritty of Christianity. Mwalimu Frank gave his own little talks in the local language with considerable passion and eloquence, and made a deep impression.

It has to be admitted that the size of the congregations on those evenings was not unconnected with the lantern show to be held on Wednesday night, for which tickets could be obtained only at the services! We were at pains to explain that "these pictures do not walk" (i.e. are not movies) but this in no way diminished the enthusiasm of virtually the whole population to see them. Moving pictures would indeed have been far too fast for teaching purposes, making explanations impossible.

Canon Nash turned up on the Tuesday, and the festival on the Wednesday was celebrated with much enthusiasm: but it was the *sinéma* in the evening for which people were waiting. Mwalimu Frank and I made enormous efforts to ensure that only ticket-holders should get in. We even had scouts to control the groups who would undoubtedly be peering through the glassless windows, and others to maintain quiet and order. We had announced repeatedly: "The church is a house of God. We must always be quiet in it."

Our efforts were in vain. The performance was scheduled for seven o'clock, but the people were arriving at five. When we opened the door a solid mass of humanity forced its way in, and the racket had to be heard to be believed. Eventually I obtained a relative quiet, and stated in the voice of a sergeant-major that everyone must go out and we would start again, with ticket-holders only. When it became apparent that the pictures could be seen on no other terms the folk filed out and those with tickets (and some without) filed in again. Finally all was peace and order. But only within the church. We had reckoned without the drunks from the nearby plantation, who surrounded the church and started a monstrous caterwauling. If they could not see the pictures they would make sure no one else would either.

It was some time before I could make myself heard in the church, but when there was a lull I announced that we were very, very sorry, but there was nothing to be done except cancel the *sinéma* and ask everyone to go home. The audience was angry and disappointed, but saw the obvious sense of this. Within a few minutes the church was empty. But people were slow to go away.

Then I had an inspiration. Some of the drunks were moving off, so I made a further announcement. "I am sorry about this. Obviously we cannot have the pictures, but I don't want to leave Kwata without thanking you all for attending the mission. If you would like to come into church for a little farewell address, come in now." Quietly the folk made their way back into the church.

By this time my mind was in a whirl, and I had been badly shaken by a fall while trying to adjust the screen. But somehow I managed to extemporise a ten-minute talk. I have not the faintest idea what it was about. Then I suddenly called to the teacher at the door, in English, "Have they gone?"

"Yes," he replied, "they have gone."

"Fine," I said in Swahili. "Now we can start the show."

And we did, an hour and a half late. My mind was no longer lucid and my Swahili was definitely sub-standard. But for another hour and a half the people watched and listened. Half way through I said: "It is getting very late. Would you like me to stop here, or to go on to the end?" They answered: "Go on." And I did.

The attention during the pictures of Our Lord's Passion was such that one could almost hear people breathing. In some places it is not possible to show pictures of the Crucifixion to simple non-Christian folk. They merely laugh. But it was not like that here. Rather there were tears. The pictures brought home to people what Christianity is about, and were remembered for a long time.

It is difficult to judge the success of a preaching mission, for there are not any obvious standards by which success can be measured. But the lives of some people were changed: lapsed and lazy Christians came back to church, and some who were living scandalous lives quietly started putting things right. It was just one of those occasions (every priest experiences them) when the good God takes over and does the job Himself.

Father Harold was delayed in England by a dock-strike at Southampton, and I stayed at Kizara till just before Christmas. I never went back again. In my last days there I had a bicycle given to me by a member of the Mission staff in England. It could not be used at Kizara and up in the hills, but it proved a gift from heaven in the lower areas of the parish.

Christmas itself I spent with the white people at the agricultural research station at Amani, seven hours' walk from Kizara. The son of the African priest there had just been killed in an accident in which a lorry went over the edge of a plank bridge, and the bishop asked me to help out with the Swahili services over the festival. The white people were hospitality itself, but I could not get a quorum for a service in English. However, they gave me a lift to Magila, where I worked again for a year before returning to England for my first leave. The bike became a splendid asset in my old haunts.

*   *   *   *

It was not easy living with Europeans again, especially missionaries who were labouring under extreme pressure. Bishop Baker still obstinately refused to talk about the work, and flew into tantrums about trifles. I do not suppose my own temper was of the best, though I was almost always happy out and about amongst the Africans.

For the first time the material poverty of our own lives, and lack of simple luxuries, began to take its toll. A few members of the Mission had private means, and the bishop had a tolerable stipend. Most of us had neither. We could buy very

34

little and could do nothing to help our families, apart from sending an occasional post-war food-parcel in the days of English food-rationing.

As the tension at Hegongo increased the question arose in my mind: Should I come back after my leave? We were expected to do at least a second three-year tour. But would it not make sense to live a more normal life in England and do something for my mother and father? During the long lonely evenings at Kizara the thought of home had never been far away.

I had had a happy enough childhood at Solihull in Warwickshire. The grinding poverty of the twenties and thirties and my father's long periods of unemployment were made bearable by Christian parents who fought back against every adversity and whose Christianity was infectious. I had won scholarships to Solihull School and to Oxford, and my parents had backed me up when they knew I wanted to be a priest and a missionary. At an age when my contemporaries on our council house estate had been bringing money home for nearly a decade I was still at theological college. During my two short curacies in England I was little better off. Did I not owe my family something now?

My thoughts about the future were very confused and my motives mixed. But I had begun to have a vision of a Christian Africa. And even as I sailed back to England I knew that Africa was becoming home. And I knew that my parents and the rest of my family would say: "If your work is there, go back." Those, in fact, were their very words.

3. Sandstorm

THE upcountry train from Tanga to the Tanganyika hinter-
land, with which I was already familiar, had been known
to baulk at the steeper hills, retreat gracefully to the bottom
and try again. It was said occasionally to have run out of
steam altogether. Passengers then had to get out and cut
firewood for the boiler.

On the day in May 1952 when the train took me up to
Korogwe, after a brief stint on Pemba Island in the Indian
Ocean, no adventures whatever befell it. These were in store
for me in my new — and at last permanent — mission district
of Kihurio. Kihurio was a young mission pioneered by the
ascetic Father Neil Russell, and no white priest had as yet
lived there. I was to make my base for a month or so at the
big mission at Korogwe, and it was the task of Archdeacon
Sydenham of Korogwe to introduce me to my new job.

Herbert Sydenham, otherwise known as Sorbo Syd, was a
character. He was loud and jovial, and something of an
autocrat. The power behind the episcopal throne, he was
essentially the man who got things done. Throughout the
diocese no missionary but he had a car and a driver (the car
was the usual "box-body") and these conferred on him a
status equal to that of the bishop, who had neither. Arriving
at a mission he had only to honk his horn — or rather to tell
the driver to honk it — to ensure that everyone came to
attention.

Sorbo Syd sat lightly to the ascetic traditions of the Universities' Mission. He had built what seemed to the rest of us a
magnificent European style house, suitable for a government
official: it had a corrugated iron roof, ceilings and, the ultimate

37

luxury, glass in the windows. He insisted that there was no merit in squalor and poverty, and that missionaries should be raising the standards of Africa, not stooping to them. The whole diocese gasped when he installed an enamel bath and a refrigerator, and rumour soon had it that beer was to be found in the latter as well as butter. One missionary protested that Mission rules forbade the keeping of alcohol on mission premises. With a winning smile Sorbo retorted: "I don't *keep* it."

The ultimate outrage was the electric toaster. As soon as the power lines reached Korogwe Sydenham had had electricity installed at the mission, and the toaster followed hard on its heels. News of it spread far and wide in the diocese. At the diocesan synod Father Spurling of Tanga — an advocate of the simple life — had to be restrained, almost by force, from proposing a motion prohibiting the use by missionaries of electric toasters.

I myself found the archdeacon a little formidable, but pleasant and business-like and eager to give me all the help he could. Over tea (made with an electric kettle) he told me the basic facts about my new sphere. "Kihurio mission district covers the Pare Mountains, beyond the Usambaras, and the surrounding desert country. The Pare tribe is the most backward in the diocese, and I shall be surprised if you can get them to do anything at all. We will drive up tomorrow and have a look."

The main "road" upcountry followed the railway much of the way, and parts of it were unspeakably bad. As we skirted the Usambaras the plain became barer and barer, and drier and dustier by the mile. Scrub and thornbush were the only vegetation, and villages were few and scattered. It was along this barren road that we came across two tall Masai tribesmen walking with immense dignity, apparently into nowhere, with their spears. They thumbed a lift, and the archdeacon beckoned them to jump into the back.

Shortly we came to a fork, and there was some debate as to which track was the main road. We were making in the direction of Same, the district headquarters of the Pare country. One of the Masai leaned over to the cab. "Excuse me,

Sir," he said in startlingly cultured English, "I believe it would be an advantage if you bore to the right." It transpired that he had been educated at Oxford, but had reverted to his tribal dress.

As we left the Usambara Mountains behind, the huge pile of the Pare Hills loomed ahead of us, barely visible in the shimmering heat-haze. After a dozen miles of waterless and uninhabited desert we came to the little settlement of Mkomasi, the beginning of our mission district. But for the absence of camels it might have been in the Sudan. The railway station was a handful of tin huts near the line. Somewhere among the thatched mud dwellings was a church, but we pressed on without looking for it. There was no tree in sight, no blade of grass, no shade from the blistering sun.

After that we might have been travelling on the moon, were it not for the corrugations made by the vehicles and a little suspension bridge over a dried up river. We had left the railway, which went south of the mountains, and were following the road to the north-west. Quite suddenly we reached a kind of man-made oasis, with houses and palm-trees. It was watered by irrigation furrows which brought water down from the hills. Kihurio mission was on the further edge of this, and we were held up by a flood until some of the furrows could be diverted.

The mission was built on a rough quadrangle of red earth and consisted of a rectangular church, the African priest's house, a small primary school and half a dozen houses for the teachers. All were roofed with thatch and had the inevitable earth floors. The air was filled with flying clouds of fine red sand, and the wind moaned like a creature in pain. The sand got into one's hair and nose and eyes and ears, and after exchanging greetings with the African priest-in-charge each of us attempted a bath in a basin of red water. The archdeacon occupied the little safari house while I put up my camp-bed in the school.

Father Rafael, the African priest, and the teachers gave us a delightful welcome. The priest was frank about his desire to hand over the reins as soon as possible. "I hope you can do something with these folk," he said, referring to the Pare tribespeople. "A few of the Christians are the salt of the earth. For the rest, they do nothing unless you push. And they do precious little if you *do* push." The teachers, a friendly and forthcoming crowd, all came from other more advanced tribes. I felt within minutes that I was going to be able to work with them.

We had Evensong in church by the light of hurricane lamps, and a Sung Eucharist the following morning. The candles on the altar would have blown out had they not been protected by lamp-glasses. The Communion wafers had to be contained in a vessel or anchored down with a weight: otherwise they would have flown away in the ceaseless, restless wind.

As we later drove away, back to Korogwe, we saw the irrigated lands of the local people and the relatively attractive area in which their villages were built. "Why on earth did Father Russell accept such a hopeless site?" I asked the Archdeacon. "So far from the furrows water must be a desperate problem." "Father Russell's sites are notorious," was the reply. "Water is the problem on most of them. Maybe he thinks others enjoy discomfort as much as he does. Or perhaps he just takes whatever is offered. People are not keen to give us good land."

I looked back and saw that the mission was almost blotted out by flying sand. It was not a place fit to live in, but I could not wait to get there. It was a challenge and an opportunity, and this time I was not likely to be transferred before I could get to know the people or do any worthwhile work. The bishop had been clear about that, and, mistakenly, I trusted him.

Sorbo Syd had a genius for finding money. "You won't be able to live in that house," he said. "It will need a new roof and a cement floor and some real windows. And you had better go off to Tanga to buy pots and pans and bedding and all the other things you will want." He paid up on the spot.

At the beginning of June he drove me to Kihurio again, and a further fifty miles to Same, the administrative centre. We returned by the track south of the hills, along the railway, reaching our furthest outstation. This rejoiced in the name Mabilioni, and its tiny thatched school had been open barely

40

a year. The teacher, the only Christian there, took two days on foot to reach Kihurio across the mountains. His school band turned out to greet us, and so did the local elders, drunk to a man. I later learned that the best way to get to Mabilioni from Kihurio was from the station at Mkomasi, boarding a goods train going up to Same and Moshi. You had to know the right day, but the train would stop for you outside the school if you asked it — and if you had a white face.

Completing the journey to Mkomasi, Archdeacon Sydenham dropped me off at the church there, together with Vinsenti the houseboy and my bicycle. He himself went back to Korogwe. I slept in the picturesque oval church which Father Russell had built, and was nearly eaten by mosquitoes. The whole of the next day I spent traversing the desolate landscape on the bike in search of villages. Then I rode to Kihurio and back, to see Father Rafael. The distance was thirteen miles each way, but it felt like three hundred. The corrugations on the road were deeper and more rock-like than any I had seen, and they were covered with loose sand. I lost count of my falls, and the hills seemed to tower into the heavens. Vinsenti and I returned to Korogwe by rail from Mkomasi.

We both came back to Mkomasi on the train a week later, and after waiting three or four hours at the station caught a passenger-lorry to Kihurio. (It called itself a bus.) This was marginally more comfortable than the bike, though it jumped and bounced alarmingly. The *Mzungu* or European had, of course, the seat next to the driver. The latter stopped at the loneliest part of the road, far from human habitation and on the steepest hill he could find, to collect his fares. He knew that had he done otherwise many of his passengers would have nipped off without paying.

The archdeacon was in no hurry to move me up to Kihurio permanently, for neither he nor I underestimated the rigours of living alone in the tiny safari house there and being cooked for on three stones. Plainly, however, the job could not be done from Korogwe, and at the end of the month I piled my impedimenta into a hired lorry and went, arriving the day before the mission's feast of little St John Baptist.

41

Vinsenti cooked a passable supper on his three stones and I lit the pressure lamp. It hissed like a snake but produced the best light in Kihurio. The teachers came to pay their respects, and we talked late into the night. Mwalimu Leonard, the headmaster, said as they left: "We are glad you have come, and we will try to help. But this is not an easy mission." Next moment I was under my mosquito-net — another luxury the Africans did not enjoy. In a couple of days, when Father Rafael had gone, I would be left alone with my two legs and a bicycle to cope with a parish large enough to be a diocese.

The following morning we had two services for the festival, and during the first one the sound of the approaching school bands from the outstations was plainly audible. After church the crowds moved off to a bumpy rectangle of red earth which by courtesy was called the football pitch. The jollifications went on all day. There were songs of farewell by the school children for Father Rafael and his family, and songs of welcome for me. Then came the dramatic sketches, some of which reduced the populace to tears of laughter. One sketch contained a magnificently made-up medicine man whose antics brought the house down. It was good to see that people could laugh at what until recently would have been taken with deadly seriousness. At least that is what I thought until we reached the second part of the drama. This was about a modern European hospital, whose patients fared a great deal worse. The over-all message was not clear, especially since much of the sketch was in Pare, the local vernacular.

Next morning as I stood at the altar the wind moaned, the candles guttered and the sand flew in clouds through the church windows. The teachers and I prayed together for strength to do the job. Two matters demanded immediate attention. The first was the crowd of baptism candidates who were already assembling for their instructions. The other was the problem of my future house. It was a wreck, and had to be wholly rebuilt.

*   *   *   *

On the first score, the baptism candidates, I need have had

no fears, for the mission catechist, Mwalimu George Ngadala, took my place whenever I was occupied with builders. He taught far more effectively than I. Mwalimu George belonged to the Zigua tribe, and was one of the most remarkable men I have ever met. He was still quite young, and his devotion and enthusiasm shone out of him. He was a man of prayer, with a passionate love for his Saviour and for the people he had been sent to serve. Whenever it was practicable he joined me in church not only for the daily eucharist but for daily mattins and evensong as well. His humour and good nature were infectious, and in the direst crisis he was (unlike myself) unflappable. He — even more than Mwalimu Leonard, the head teacher — was to be my guide and friend.

Reconstructing the priest's house proved a mammoth task, and as the work proceeded during the following months (or stood still, or went backwards) I felt that never had so many done so little in so long. No action whatever could be secured without protracted negotiation. Broken stone had to be transported by lorry for the new floor: cement had to be fetched from the station and river-sand and timber and roofing grass from various remote locations. The Indian and Arab lorry-owners demanded exorbitant sums, and were beaten down only after long and sometimes acrimonious exchanges. When at last a contract was made it was no guarantee of action, and was in practice binding only on one side. Weeks would pass before the lorry actually showed up, and the excuses for delay were multifarious. "I had no time." Or: "I forgot." Or just: "There is no hurry."

The workmen were worse. When we first talked work they would usually refuse to mention any sum whatever, putting the onus on me. I had with great difficulty to find out from others what a fair price for their labours would be, and then to propose a half or a quarter of that amount. This was a necessary act of self-defence, giving me some bargaining power when they fiercely demanded three or four times their just due. "That is much too high," I would say with spirit. The negotiator would frequently agree, mentioning then a marginally less wicked figure. If after an hour or two no agreement had been reached one party might make a demarche,

I was well situated for this manoeuvre, having to retreat no further than my safari house. The problem was that one then had to start again from scratch or, if I wanted a particular man or he wanted the job, face-saving formulae had to be devised in order to make possible the re-opening of the discussion. This game could be played by any number of players. When work actually started the workmen showed a genius for getting in each other's way and destroying each other's meagre achievements. At times I suspected a conspiracy to provide each other with perpetual employment — or, at least, a perpetual income.

The biggest problem of all was getting water to the site. A gentleman called the *Mgawa wa Maji*, or Divider of the Waters, ostensibly controlled the flow of the various irrigation channels, and was known to be susceptible to bribes. In the end I learned that he had precious little authority, and that people stole the water from one another. This left me with no option but to employ a full-time man to direct the water to our work whenever we needed it. Unfortunately he seldom turned up until the workmen had gone home.

To add to my woes the builder refused resolutely to clear up the piles of rubbish he produced, arguing that he was a skilled workman and that *that* was a labourer's job. I sat him down on a chair, and said: "Fine, I will get you a labourer." Stripping off my cassock I went to work with a will until, horrified at the idea of a European actually soiling his hands, he pleaded with me to desist. In fact I did a great deal of manual work at Kihurio, including stone-breaking; but this was always to encourage voluntary labour on schools and churches.

In spite of these vicissitudes I was in my house after three months. It had a living room, a dining room and a bedroom, but it lacked inside doors and the front door would not lock. I was able to install some simple furniture and a mosquito-tent over my table and chair to make it possible to work at night. The house had a separate kitchen at the back, with a wood-stove and a long metal chimney through the thatched roof. This became the domain of Allen, my new and youthful Pare cook and houseboy, whose matrimonial and domestic

44

adventures would demand a chapter of their own. The African houseboy who introduced me to Allen summed up his culinary powers in the words: "His puddings are three."

The final touch of civilisation was the battery-operated "wireless" paid for by my family in England, which gave almost as much pleasure to my African visitors as to myself. Batteries were usually out of stock in Tanga when most needed, and in 1953 the coronation service of Queen Elizabeth II became fainter and fainter, to the chagrin of the African audience who crammed every room of the house.

*   *   *   *

No sooner was the priest's house habitable (I will not say finished) than we set to work on a house for the new deacon who was due to come in a few months. We were in fact building throughout my years at Kihurio.

The school and church at Ndungu, twelve miles further along the road, were at a distance from the centre of population and of a squalor, filth and decrepitude which it is difficult to describe. The church, where I slept from time to time, boasted a concentration of mosquitoes per cubic inch which was unrivalled in the parish. They seemed to howl rather than whine, and left one bruised, sleepless and fever-stricken. (I know the malaria-bearing anopheles is silent. His companions were not.) For half an hour after getting into bed one had to do battle with the insects which had got into the net: and if the food had been bad and one had to trail down the garden path in the middle of the night the penalty was high indeed.

I put it to the local people that it would be wise to re-build the whole outfit in a more salubrious vicinity and adjacent to the centre of population. The good sense of this was apparent to everyone, and in course of time bricks were burned, corrugated iron bought and the job done. Other schools followed suit — though in some places it still seemed beyond the capacity of the local folk to put up even a simple thatched shelter without arguing about it for a year.

The idea of voluntary labour caught on more quickly than I

had hoped, and within a year or two substantial financial giving had replaced the odd mealie cobs which were initially placed in the collection bags. With some help from the diocese we put down a cement floor in the parish church at Kihurio and added a corrugated aluminium roof. (Aluminium reflected the heat, while iron absorbed it.) As soon as the thatch was off the unexpected happened. It poured with rain!

Mwalimu George Ngadala, the catechist, and I — and later Bwana William, the deacon — spent most of our time on safari, and there was a rich reward in the form of serious Christian converts. We would always go in different directions. Both George and William had a deep concern for people and a genius for evangelistic work. We travelled on foot or by bike or on the "buses" which started in the still, small hours and often enough decided by popular vote which way to go. Inevitably, however, the administrative work and the growing building programme began to be left to me, while the Africans got on with the real missionary work.

At Kihurio itself the mission became so popular that there was talk of a new and bigger primary school and even of a middle school, the first step to a secondary school. The benefits of Christian education were plain for all to see, and even the Muslims sent their children to our school. I pointed out, of course, that a new school was impossible without a new site: and that meant land. Land was the most sensitive of all subjects, but the people made no difficulty about it at all.

The Chief, who had become a Christian, helped, but used no duress. The necessary land, well watered, was finally made over to us in the presence of the District Officer from Same, the original owners being well compensated with fertile land near their own homes. What we did not know was that there was a tiny group of hard-core Muslims who answered the muezzin's call to prayer at noon and who had different ideas about our future.

*   *   *   *

Soon after my arrival at Kihurio from Korogwe I set off for

46

Vunta, our main outstation up in the hills. The hill country, going up to five thousand feet, comprised the entire central area of the mission district, and was a world apart. I was told it would take me six hours to climb up to the little mission, but in fact I did the journey in four. The first hour and a half was through waterless scrub and thorn. You then clambered up the steep path for three hours before coming out into green downs and lush and fertile country. The sound of waterfalls and rushing streams was never far away. The cold could be bitter in winter and the grey, wet days were reminiscent of England.

The welcome, however, was warm enough. The teachers thoughtfully gave me an hour's rest before the school band put on its act. The school at Vunta was built of stone, and the church and the little safari house were of mud. They all leaked abominably, but there were no mosquitoes. I soon learned that the hill people could not sleep on the plains without contracting malaria, often the fatal cerebral type. All our main events — festivals, baptisms, confirmations — had to be duplicated aloft.

I was able to go out visiting with the teachers in my black English cassock. There were no villages, the round beehive huts being widely scattered. These had no windows, and were dark and smoky inside. The number of people who emerged when one called "Hodi!" was astonishing.

My experience at Kizara had taught me how to spend a tolerably comfortable night. This time I had a pile of blankets and a Tilley kerosene radiator, which soon became the envy of the teachers. The thing to do in the morning was to leap out of bed, unhampered by a mosquito-net, light the radiator with spirit and jump back into bed until the room was warm.

That first morning was both chilly and wet, and only a handful turned up at church, very late. When the catechumens were dismissed hardly anyone was left but the teachers. Over the years this situation improved dramatically. The church, re-built, became a real house of prayer, crowded by new Christians.

From Vunta I walked south for a further four hours to a new school where, in those early days, there were no Christians at

47

all apart from the teachers. On another occasion I walked six hours northward to an Anglican catechetical centre called Mtii. Here it had proved impossible to start a school since the area was worked by a Lutheran mission and the government, understandably, offered no grant. The group of Anglicans there was extraordinarily faithful, though they were visited by a priest only once or twice a year. Their leader was called Mzee Eliezar, *mzee* meaning old man. His ignorance of Christian doctrine was, through no fault of his own, as astonishing as his radiance and the depth of his Christian compassion.

After church at Mtii I raised the matter of Christian marriage. "What is that?" Eliezar asked, with real puzzlement. "You mean all these people who have received Communion in church this morning have never been married in church?" I asked. "We would not know about that," he replied.

Indeed, how could they? Yet in fact the Christians of Mtii were mostly living in faithful monogamous unions. As a young and enthusiastic priest I was inwardly horrified at the absence of church weddings, but I had enough sense to ask myself: What would Our Lord have done? Nothing, I suspected.

As I walked down the mountain into the heat I realised how much we depended on our schools. But we could not have schools everywhere, and God had His ways of looking after His faithful people without us. It was a long time before I was able to visit Mtii again; but when next I went I ministered the Sacrament to those who came forward for it without any questions asked.

Up in the hills the menfolk usually knew enough Swahili to make conversation possible. Most of the women spoke only Pare, which cut them off not only from the clergy but from most of the teachers too. I determined to learn this vernacular, and set about writing my own grammar-book and vocabulary. I could obtain only one book in Pare, an antiquated New Testament put out years ago by the Seventh Day Adventists. By 1954 I was able to preach simple sermons in Pare, and conduct elementary conversations. My efforts must have been grotesque, but people laughed with pleasure. And when I was called to minister the last rites to old people, or to hear confessions, the language had an immediately practical use.

*   *   *   *

Back at Kihurio trouble was brewing, and none of us could understand it. The people who had so willingly given their land for the new school started ploughing it up and planting it, pulling up the pegs and generally behaving with sullen resentment. Muslims were thought to be behind the trouble, and indeed they organised a school boycott — an unheard of thing in those days. An outhouse at the further edge of the mission burned down one night in mysterious circumstances.

I consulted the Chief, and we called a meeting. There was overwhelming support for the school, and the previous owners of our new land went along with the majority. No, they did not want their land back. I asked whether the people would like us to abandon the project, at least for the present, and was howled down. To make assurance doubly sure we asked the District Officer to come from Same and go into the whole matter again. The verdict was the same.

I put the matter out of mind, for I was almost continuously on safari and in any case I had a new toy. This was a BSA Bantam two-stroke motorcycle. Father Edward Lury had resigned from the Mission and was selling his *pikipiki* (that was the Swahili onomatopoeia) for twenty-five pounds. Gifts from friends and the proceeds of several articles in the *Tanganyika Standard* enabled me to accumulate that sum. I went down to Tanga by train to collect the machine and after a few lessons went for my driving test.

"Where will you be driving?" asked the inspector. "Upcountry," I answered. "You will hurt no one but yourself up there," he commented, and wrote out the licence.

I zoomed out of Tanga, where in 1953 the tarred road survived for only a mile or so beyond the town's edge. Then, in deep sand, the bike went one way and I another. I picked myself up and completed the sixty miles to Korogwe — and the next day the sixty miles to Kihurio — paddling whenever the sand became too deep. I suffered from sunburn and

49

windburn for a fortnight: it was almost as long before I could sit down with any comfort.

The motorbike was the source of much joy and much woe. It almost doubled the amount of work I could do, for journeys could now be completed in hours which previously had taken days. It reduced my dependence on porters, who were virtually unobtainable. But it took an appalling hammering on the potholes and corrugations of the Kihurio "main road" and cost me a small fortune in repairs. On occasions I would be stuck at the roadside for hours until a passing lorry from a sisal estate would rescue both me and my mount. Spares had to be sought as far afield as Nairobi and England, and took weeks or months to arrive.

The worst journey of all on the bike was a return trip from Korogwe in the middle of the rainy season. I made a quick getaway during a fine interval, hoping to reach the dry country before the next cloudburst. My luck was out, and the dry country was very wet indeed. For two hours I pressed on in the driving rain, there being nowhere to shelter in the open country. At last, as the downpour became heavier, I pulled up at a little tea-shelter where a handful of Africans were huddled. After an hour the rain slackened and I prepared to set off again. The bike, however, refused to start, and my minimal mechanical knowledge was of no avail. Fortunately there was an earth-moving company not far away, and a friendly European mechanic came to my rescue. When at last the machine fired the kick-starter had given up the unequal struggle and I was reduced to push-starts. Beyond Mkomasi gluey red mud built up on the tyres and the wheels would turn no more. Dusk had fallen before a lorry loomed up in the streaming rain: it transported me, soaked to the skin, the remaining dozen miles to Kihurio.

It was shortly after this, in April 1954, that the big blow struck at the mission, and I found myself with larger troubles to think about.

*　　*　　*　　*

Mwalimu George, the catechist, and I were in church on a

Monday morning, making preparations for Holy Week and Easter. Outside there was a shout: "Fire!" We rushed out, and saw that the thatched roof of my kitchen was ablaze. Teachers were already running from the school to help Allen, the cook, who was tearing off the burning thatch. The only water available was in a barrel, and this someone knocked over in the initial confusion. A crowd collected in minutes to watch, but no villagers offered to help apart from one or two Pare Christians.

A stiff high wind was blowing as usual, and though the kitchen was a dozen yards from the house it needed only a spark to set my own roof alight. The teachers and I battled with the flames, using sand instead of water and pulling off armfuls of thatch. It was of no avail, and within moments we faced a raging inferno.

Only then did I realise that the deacon's house was at risk. If it had been burned Bwana William's children would have been trapped, and the fire would have spread to the rest of the mission. "Leave me," I shouted to the teachers. "Go to Bwana William's." They obeyed without question, and saved both the deacon's house and their own school and homes.

Meanwhile I rushed back into my own house twice, to save what possessions I could, before being overcome by the heat and the smoke and finally staggering to a safe distance. Several valuables were retrieved, but most of my worldly goods were destroyed. The fire burned out in an hour or two, but continued to smoulder for the rest of the day and part of the night. I was able to wheel the motorbike to safety.

By this time a huge crowd of sightseers had collected, but few showed much concern or made any move to help. The explanation of this was to emerge later: it certainly was not characteristic of ordinary African people. One or two of the Muslims appeared not displeased.

By the afternoon the teachers were as tired as I, and the schoolchildren were sent home for the remainder of the day. Some of the men had burns, but their main concern seemed to be for myself. It was agreed that as soon as possible I must get to the telephone at the sisal plantation at Ndungu, and inform the police at Same. A day and night guard was to be

51

placed on the house to prevent looting — the obvious object of some of the spectators — and steps taken to ensure that Allen did not run away. In the event Allen (whose family were among the trouble-makers) was picked up by the police several days later and held for some time for questioning. No evidence was ever found against him or anyone else.

Before dusk I ran over to Ndungu, exhausted, on the motorbike, and the Europeans there were kindness itself. The manager, a Mr Taylor, put me up for the night and provided immediate necessities. The next day he drove me to Hegongo, over a hundred miles away, to see the bishop. By chance Archdeacon Stephens and Archdeacon Sydenham were both there. They had just concluded a dire financial conference.

The bishop and the archdeacon were sympathetic enough, but made it plain there was no money whatever except for the most vital necessities — and certainly none to replace my own property or to re-build the house. The diocese was four thousands pounds in debt.

"Would you like a move?" asked the bishop. "You have had a rough time." A move was the last thing that I wanted. To run away would have been cowardly, and calamitous in its consequences. Loss of home and possessions was a small thing compared with the shame and folly of abandoning one's work at the first serious setback. "No," I replied. "I will stay, house or no house."

This was apparently the wrong reply. I had been in UMCA long enough to notice that the standard answer to trouble on any mission was to move the priest-in-charge. There was an embarrassed silence. "We shall have to see," said the bishop. "As a matter of fact, I had been going to write to you about a transfer. We have a problem. Father Lury has withdrawn his resignation, and we have to find him somewhere to go. You will be due for leave soon, and at this stage we cannot send an African priest to Kihurio to hold the fort. Lury is the obvious man. A linguist, too," he added, with a touch of inspiration. "But Lury is too senior a priest to be asked just to fill in a furlough." It had all been worked out.

"I don't see," I replied, "how a priest can achieve anything if he is continually to be moved about and never to have the

52

chance to live with failures as well as successes." I bit my tongue to prevent myself saying: "Did Our Lord run away?" It became plain that the bishop was not to be diverted from his plan. There was nothing more to do except to ask him to give the matter more thought. He promised to do that, but had to go off to Zanzibar almost at once for his annual Easter visit.

I returned to Kihurio by train, to live in the little safari-house and have my meals cooked once more on three stones. Easter was upon us, and all the safaris the festival entailed. The mission staff were friendlier and more helpful than ever. Within a month the troubles were all over and the local people were falling over each other to help. The mere fact that their priest came back turned the tide.

Though no arsonist was ever identified — an accident could not be ruled out — the source of the unrest was quickly found. A tiny group of hostile Muslims, quite unrepresentative of the majority, had put it about that I had paid the Chief for the land that had been given to the mission, and that the Chief had put the money into his own pocket. Hence the popular resentment. Once this lie was disposed of the mission went from strength to strength. I did not see the new primary school or the middle school, but both were completed.

Bishop Baker was told the facts, but they made no difference. Representations by the churchwardens and the church elders were equally without effect. My faith in the bishop and the Mission was severely damaged, but I felt it would be unwise to make any irreversible decisions until I was in a calmer frame of mind. After all, Father Lury was a good and experienced priest. And I myself had made mistakes that no doubt he would be able to avoid.

What I was offered was a job at Zanzibar cathedral, looking after the few churches in the country districts of the island. And leave in the English summer first. There would be time to work out means of escaping the clutches of an unsatisfactory bishop and moving to some other part of the mission-field.

In July I returned to England for the first time by air. After buying what clothes I could in Tanga I flew in a little five-seater to Nairobi in Kenya, where I nearly froze and from where the journey to England would take three days, flying during the daytime only. At Nairobi the airline put us up for the night at the Norfolk Hotel, where, as I entered the dining room, I saw a large notice: "Gentlemen will wear white ties." I had no tie, white or otherwise.

I sat down at a table, and the head waiter pointed to another notice about white ties. No dinner came. "I don't have a tie," I said to the head waiter. "But I do want my dinner." He was unyielding, so I tried the management. There was no help there either.

Returning to my seat in the dining room I had an inspiration. I had noticed that all the waiters were Goanese, who would unquestionably be good Roman Catholics. I beckoned the head waiter again. "Waiter," I said, "I don't have a tie. I am a priest. We don't wear ties." "Yes, Father," beamed the waiter. "Certainly, Father. That makes all the difference, Father. What will you have, Father?"

In London I put it to the General Secretary of the Mission that I would like a transfer to another diocese. "I am afraid," he said, "that won't be easy. The bishops usually stand together, right or wrong, and back each other up." The sensible thing to do — indeed the only thing to do — was to bide one's time.

4. Isle of Cloves

ZANZIBAR Island was not new to me. I had spent a couple of holidays there and six weeks helping at the cathedral over Easter in 1951, before going to Kihurio. It was indeed a holiday paradise, a coral island clothed with dazzling green in the turquoise of the Indian Ocean. The clove trees and the coconut palms covered it like a carpet, and the scent of the spice, the main source of its wealth, was everywhere. Temperatures varied from about 70° to 95° Fahrenheit (20° to 35° Celsius), but there was often a breeze from the sea. Unlike most European residents, who were prostrated by the heat and the humidity, I enjoyed the climate hugely.

This Isle of Cloves, as it was often called, stood about twenty-five miles east of the Tanganyika coast and together with Pemba Island, another twenty-five miles to the north, formed the Arab sultanate of Zanzibar, under the protection of Great Britain. The monarch was His Highness Sultan Seyyid Khalifa bin Harub, while the power behind the throne was His Excellency the British Resident. They were known as H.H. and H.E. respectively. It was customary to sign the visitors' book of each of them, though, since the state was Islamic, ladies did not sign the Sultan's book.

Zanzibar city was the most southerly Arab population-centre in the world. For centuries Arab traders had come in their dhows on the North-East Monsoon in November, returning with the South-East Trade Wind in April. Many stayed, however, to build an advanced civilisation far from their homeland, though this civilisation was marred by the horrors of the slave trade till the coming of the British in the nineteenth century.

55

The approach to the island was breath-taking. On the water-front stood the spectacular Bet-el-Ajoib or House of Wonder, now housing the Secretariat. This was flanked by the Sultan's palace and an impressive eighteenth century Portuguese fort. Beyond the front was the old Stone City, whose big Arab houses boasted the magnificent brass-studded doors which were characteristic of Arab dwellings throughout the island. Behind the Stone City lay the narrow, winding bazaars, typical of the East. Here incense-sticks vied with less savoury odours. The clocks on both the Bet-al-Ajeib and the Anglican Cathedral showed Swahili or biblical time. At noon the hands stood at six, to the confusion of visitors.

By far the most noticeable feature of Zanzibar in the fifties, however, was its excellent race relations. There was no colour bar of any kind. The secret was that the races did not threaten one another. The Europeans (there were only a few hundred of them) did the administration, and held no property. The Indians were the shop-keepers. The Arabs owned the clove and copra plantations. And the Africans, largely from the mainland, did the manual work — until midday, after which they slept in the shade. Almost everyone was satisfied.

My own first visit to Zanzibar had been in 1949. At Mombasa in 1947, before I had set foot in Tanganyika, I chanced to meet Archdeacon Clarabut, then in charge of Zanzibar cathedral, who was there on leave. "Come and have a holiday at the mission," he said, and I thought he meant it. UMCA missionaries only had holidays on other missions, and we took with us a shilling a day for expenses. "Clara," as the archdeacon was known among his acquaintances, was an eccentric with a kind heart but a gruff manner. At the mission he welcomed me with: "Have you brought any money?" I replied: "The usual shilling a day."

"Not enough," was his response. "It is four shillings here."

"Then I will sing for my supper," I said. I did not know that I would have had to preach and help with the work anyway: but I was young and enthusiastic and felt that a change was as good as a rest.

After a couple of days Clara said: "You will be wanting to visit Sharpe at Pemba." This was true enough. Canon Sharpe was a saintly priest who suffered under a domineering nurse on the northern island. "I wouldn't be in a hurry to come back," said Clara. "Sharpe doesn't get a lot of visitors. You will enjoy Pemba and he will appreciate your help."

So off I went to Pemba in the steamer *Al Said*, which sailed every Friday for Wete, the capital, returning on the Monday. It made the voyage overnight. Either you did the round trip or you stayed over two week-ends. Only many years later was a daily air-service started.

In the early morning the ship stood off Wete harbour, since only the tiniest vessels could come alongside the wharf. Getting ashore was no easy task — there was a free-for-all to hire the small boats which swarmed round the ship — but Canon Sharpe was there waiting for me on the jetty. We made our way up the crowded single street to the mission. Even then it was not a little dilapidated, and there were very few Christians, all mainlanders.

Pemba proved a fascinating place, and I would gladly have stayed till the second week-end. But my time was limited. "You could get a dhow back any day," suggested the canon. "The journey only takes twelve hours." Dhows in the sunset in Zanzibar dhow-harbour, or on the open sea, looked picturesque and romantic. But I knew they stank to high heaven. However, I had long ago been told that the chief requisites of a missionary in Africa were a good sense of humour and a bad sense of smell, and by mid-week I had settled for a dhow. I took with me a rhorkee chair and some sandwiches and a vacuum flask.

The stench was far worse than I had anticipated, and the sanitary arrangements were over the side of the vessel and in full view. We left at seven in the evening, and I comforted myself with the thought that we would reach Mkokotoni in Zanzibar by seven the following morning.

A brisk breeze caught the sail and drove us southwards. The moonlight was bright, and the view of the Pemba archipelago unbelievably beautiful. On a myriad islets the palm-trees glittered, mirrored in the shining sea. The wind sang. For a few hours it was glorious. Then, before dawn, the breeze dropped, and we glided to a halt. This, I was told, was the will of Allah.

Allah took a long time to relent. How long we were becalmed I do not know. The sun rose, and there was no shelter from its pitiless rays. Hour after hour we rocked uneasily on the open sea, and the burning sun became a crescendo of torture. No land was in sight. No other vessel was to be seen. The dhow became an inferno in the middle of nothingness, its passengers reduced to a state of inert torpor. "Where are we?" I asked the *nahodha* or captain, my throat dry and lips cracking. It was a foolish question, and it received the predictable answer, "Allah knows." He had no compass — dhows did not carry such things — and would have been little wiser if he had had one.

At last there was a tiny puff of wind, and then a breeze which started uncertainly but shortly grew in strength. We were off again. Zanzibar island hove into sight, and by the late afternoon we reached Mkokotoni. No one apart from myself appeared much perturbed. The *mudir* or Arab administrative officer of the village had received a message and was looking out for me. He plied me with coffee, and before dusk I was on a crowded vehicle which called itself a bus, heading down the narrow tarmac road towards Zanzibar city.

The "bus" was hardly more attractive than the dhow, and swayed horribly. Its driver seemed quite unmoved when a similar vehicle hurtled towards us in the gathering gloom, its lights blazing and horn blaring. Someone had to yield, for there was no room for two vehicles to pass. At the last moment our man left the tar, swung round a palm-tree and regained the road, apparently without moving an eyelid. Clara gave me a delightful welcome and showed real concern.

I think it was the next morning that he announced: "I am selling the car." The archdeacon's car was famous throughout the island, and could only be induced to start after being pushed round and round the cathedral close. He had bought it years ago for forty pounds. Apparently an Indian purchaser had promised to buy it if it would go up a nearby incline. He didn't believe it would, but when it did he was as good as his word. "How much did you get for it?" I asked. "Forty pounds," was the reply. Only later did I hear that at the last moment Clara had said to the Indian: "Oh, I forgot to tell you. You had better ask the garage about the battery. They let me have it on loan."

* * * *

Clara had gone when I arrived to work in Zanzibar in Lent 1955, and had been replaced by another archdeacon. This was none other than Thomas Dix, whom I had first known at Msalabani. We both lived in the extraordinary mission-house at Mkunazini, adjacent to Bishop Steere's imposing Gothic cathedral. (Though basically Gothic, the cathedral made some concessions to the East.) The house was a two-storeyed affair with upstairs verandahs and stairways and a connecting out-door bridge. I was given what seemed to me a palatial suite of three upstairs rooms. There was electric light, and water came out of taps. The windows had no glass, but didn't need any: cold and theft were alike unknown. Arabic and Indian music from a thousand radios poured into my rooms day and night.

I quickly made friends. There was George Mbaruku, a delightful African teacher and dispenser who was an expert on the pure Swahili of the island. I knew him from earlier visits, and he was soon teaching me to write the language in the Arabic script. There was Philip Mgaya, the newly ordained and highly Europeanised deacon who lived with us in the mission-house. And there was Tom Laver, the white principal of Kiungani High School a few miles up the coast.

Tom rode a motorbike, but his sight was not too good and he had a habit of gesticulating with both hands while talking to his pillion passenger. He took me for some hair-raising rides. Shortly after my arrival he was driving a friend round the city in the early evening, when he completely failed to notice the Sultan's scarlet motor-car with its red flag flying in the breeze. It was customary for all vehicles to pull into the side and stop when the Sultan passed on his evening drive to his summer palace at Kiwani — or on any other occasion — and for foot passengers to stand still and wave. The courtesy

59

was always graciously acknowledged by the benign, white-bearded monarch. Tom sailed straight past. He received a tail note from the police the following morning.

I had returned from England by sea in order to bring with me a new motorbike which I had just acquired. But it had been left behind on the London docks, and arrived a couple of months later. Desperate to get on with my job in the scattered country churches I tried travelling by "bus" with my new Nyasa houseboy Samwil. This involved huge delays, and meant that occasionally I failed to turn up for services altogether. I then decided to hire a motorbike. However, this had to go to a garage for repairs and, in the hands of an incompetent mechanic, went up in flames. I was still battling with the insurance company when my own machine turned up. But the buses were not finished with me yet, and within a week one of them had hit me in the rear as I stopped at a halt sign. Both rider and mount survived, somewhat battered.

Keen as I was to do my new job (what little there was of it) I had another and urgent reason for spending as much of my time as possible in the country districts, away from the mission. Life at the mission was unbearable. Within a couple of days of my arrival I realised that something was very gravely wrong, though it was some time before I realised the full horror of the position. Archdeacon Dix went round like a bear with a sore head. At first I thought he was just in a bad temper, or suffering from depression. When he brightened up I put it all out of my mind. I realised I had lived alone for quite a time, and that probably I was far from easy to get on with myself.

But Father Dix's moroseness returned, and got much worse. He would fly into unprovoked rages about trifles. Then I realised he was doing very little work, and spent his days joy-riding in the mission car and his evenings at cinemas and parties. Finally I saw, what everyone else had seen long ago, that all this was done with a young married Arab lad called Ali. The thing was a public scandal. The mission was a hell to live in and the Church's work was being wrecked.

I suppose Dix must have been a homosexual: but I knew nothing about homosexuals in those days, and the idea of a homosexual priest was unthinkable anyway. What was I to do? Few of us found our bachelor lives easy, and temptations could be grave. I said what I could, with reasonable tact, but was brushed off. It was a difficult matter to take to the bishop, and I discovered soon enough that he knew all about it anyway. He simply had not the strength to deal with it.

On one occasion Bishop Baker was staying with us, and I asked him to visit our church at Dunga: I think it was to confirm some older people who could not get to the cathedral. To this he gladly consented. I myself was not allowed the use of the mission car, and could not drive it anyway. I had assumed that it would be available for the bishop, who (also unable to drive) would readily find a chauffeur. But not a bit of it. Father Dix was out in the car with Ali! The bishop accepted a lift on my pillion, but was saved from that embarrassment by a rain-storm. "I'll take a taxi," he said.

An occasional visitor to our mission was Dr Lyndon Harries, the writer and Islamic scholar. He saw the position for himself, and was horrified. "I have stayed at thirty mission-stations in East Africa," he said. "This is the worst." Dr Harries did what I could not do, and took news of the situation to the General Secretary of UMCA in London. Dr Broomfield was a diplomat. He could not interfere directly, nor could he go over the head of the bishop. But he took it upon himself to write to Father Dix. His letter was necessarily discreet, and in practice it did no good.

During the archdeacon's leave in England, however, we all enjoyed a respite. I could do less work at the country churches, since I was in charge of the cathedral and both the African and European congregations. (The latter included the British Resident, a regular churchgoer.) But I got hold of the car, a decrepit Ford Anglia, and found a friend to teach me to drive it. It was a joy to be able to keep going in the tropical rain-storms, which were no fun at all on a motorcycle.

Dix came back unchanged, and life at the mission became a deepening nightmare. I fled to the country churches. Samwil fell ill, and Simon, my houseboy at Kihurio, came over to help me out. He was a friend as well as a domestic. My little motorbike groaned as it carried both of us, two panniers, rucksack, camp-bed, etc. to the furthest churches. It could not, however, manage the cinóma, now a fully fledged film-strip projector. This was still a powerful instrument of evangelism, and had to be brought by bus. I would spend the afternoons visiting the villages among the coconut plantations, and at night would put up my screen and talk to the little crowds who came. Our Christian people were all mainlanders, but African Muslims would sometimes come to outdoor film shows at night.

As the months passed I was increasingly conscious of the absurdity of trying to teach Christianity in a Muslim state with only a marginal knowledge of Islam. I began to take an interest in the religion of the majority of the people. The majority of the Muslims were orthodox Sunnis, but the Indians mostly belonged to one of the minority Shiite sects. On Muhammad's birthday I went to the Sunni *maulidi*, when the city was lit in a blaze of fairy lights and Arabic poems were recited or chanted endlessly.

Ramadhan, the month of fasting, was a mixed blessing. The fast was complete during the daylight hours, but was compensated for by much riotous eating — often gorging — during the hours of darkness. People got little sleep, and made up for the lack of it during work the next day. At the end of Ramadhan came the great feast of Id-el-Fitr. The large green open space of Mnazi Mmoja became a huge fair-ground. There were Arab sword-dances, and the throbbing of African drums went on day and night. Everyone had a marvellous time, and there was not a drunk in sight. Alcohol was banned on the island, except for infidels who had to get a permit to buy it. What Christian country, I wondered, could celebrate a festival of this magnitude and stay sober?

At Id-el-Fitr the clergy were among those commanded to the reception at the Sultan's palace. There were speeches in the crowded throne-room. His Excellency the British Resident made a loyal address in English, which was then interpreted into Arabic and Swahili. His Highness the Sultan made a gracious reply in Arabic, which was translated into English and Swahili. He made a suitable reference to the British

62

Crown. When it was all over we streamed outside and drank sherbet.

In the garden I happened to bump into the Resident's *aide-de-camp*, whom I had known for some time. We paused to chat. "Excellent speeches," I commented. "Obviously," was the reply. "I wrote the lot."

The celebrations of the Indian Ithna'ashri Muslims were taken as seriously as those of the Sunni majority. I went to witness the annual commemoration of the martyrdom of Hussein, grandson of the Prophet and "saviour of mankind," which I learned took place on the tenth day of Mohurram in the year 61 AH (October 10th, AD 680). The occasion was one of public penance mixed with rejoicing. In 1955 it fell on August 29th, which was a public holiday throughout the island.

On the eve of the festival the Ithna'ashri mosque was draped with black flags and the adherents of the sect wore black garments which seemed to me like boiler-suits. Traditional processions issued from the mosque, the first including a splendid figure of a horse, for a horse was involved in the story of Hussein. (Until recently a real horse had been used, the only one on the island. It had no work except this annual procession, and had died a few years ago — whether of old age or boredom I do not know.) Another procession carried portable multi-coloured shrines, resembling domes and temples and minarets and decorated with tinsel and fairy-lights and artificial flowers. Still other processions were of children, with banners and vestments, or of people dancing and chanting.

The final processions consisted of flagellants and were the most gruesome. They were made up of men and boys stripped to the waist and wailing "Hussein! Hussein! O Hussein!" while flailing their breasts frantically with barbed chains. Blood splashed all over the place, and I was left in no doubt about the reality of this extraordinary penance. I was jammed in the crowd and could not move. My best white cassock was spattered with blood and had to go to the laundry the next day.

Though I made good Muslim friends in Zanzibar my knowledge of Islam was then, and remains today, superficial. I felt this disqualified me from doing serious missionary work in the sultanate. In any case it was abundantly obvious that direct evangelism would have been bitterly resented and quite ineffective. UMCA did not have any long-term thought-out policy for its missionary work in this part of its field.

The Mission had had a magnificent history in Zanzibar, since its inception in 1864 under Bishop Tozer. But its work had always in practice been confined to freed slaves and mainlanders. I learned something of this history from Father William Sudi, the African priest at the cathedral. Father Sudi was a good and conscientious priest who got on with his job unobtrusively. I remember his wry humour. In the cathedral vestry during Holy Week, when we were exhausted with preparations for the Easter ceremonies, he would murmur placidly: "Yatakwisha. It will all come to an end."

"If you want to know about the early days," he told me, "you must talk to my mother." So I went along with him to see old Agnes Sudi, who must have been in her nineties. Agnes had been born on the mainland near Masasi, and was sold into slavery as a child of about twelve. She was in one of the slave-dhows captured by the British, and was included in a batch of freed children who were handed over to the then bishop and educated by the Mission. She never heard of her home and family again, but she went to the mainland later with her husband, now dead, who was cook to the explorer Stanley. Unfortunately I took no notes of her recollections. At the settlement for freed slaves at Mbweni, whose tumbledown church was still in use, there were other elderly people who could have told me much of the old days if my heart had not been set on the future rather than the past.

But was there any future for Christianity in Zanzibar? Obviously UMCA on the island was spent as a missionary force, and was desperately in need of new management. But was there anything *anyone* could do to carry the Gospel further? Christians had not then invented the pejorative term "spiritual colonialism" to nullify Our Lord's command to preach the Gospel to all nations. Nothing much could be done immediately in the city or the plantations. I decided to explore the countryside beyond, which was little known. It was here that the early inhabitants of the island lived.

* * * *

As companions in this enterprise I inspanned George Mbaruku and Tom Laver, whenever the three of us had the spare time. We went to Kizimkazi at the south of the island, and found a twelfth-century mosque which was still in use. We went to a place called Bwejuu, where the children ran away at the sight of white faces. There were no Christians in the area at all, apart from the occasional policeman or official. The population consisted entirely of the Wahadimu, the indigenous black people of Zanzibar. The men were friendly enough and offered us coconut juice; but obviously they wondered why we had come. They were unaccustomed to visitors.

We found our way to Kawengwa beach, on the inaccessible east coast. There were miles and miles of empty palm-fringed beach running down to the dazzling sea. Far out the coral reef protected the shore from the breakers of the Indian Ocean and from the sharks, and the obvious (and only) thing to do was to swim. It was gorgeous. We had a picnic, and that gave us an idea.

It was well known that Europeans went out for picnics, and some people of other races followed their example. We would go for picnics in remote places, and use the opportunity to get to know people and talk to them and make friends. This became our plan, and I was always careful to explain who I was. Obviously I did not wear clerical clothes: an open-necked shirt and a pair of shorts and sandals were all any of us wore. A little cross indicated my job.

Nungwi, north of Mkokotoni at the extreme tip of the island, was another obvious place to explore. We discussed this with the Arab *mudir* or administrative officer at Mkokotoni, whom I already knew. "The road is appalling," he said, "but you can go. Your blood be upon your own heads. There is a telephone, and I will let the *sheha* know you are coming." The *sheha* was the local chief.

65

The road to Nungwi was a twelve-mile horror, and we came off our bikes on more occasions than one. But we got there in the end, in the blistering heat, and, after our picnic, explored the lighthouse. But first, of course, we greeted the *sheha* and his elders. I showed them my camera, and asked if I might take photographs. They agreed, and later I made another trip to give them the pictures. They were thrilled, and this was the beginning of long conversations which included religion, about which they spoke freely enough. The only school at Nungwi was the Koran school, and there was no dispensary. It did not seem to me beyond the bounds of possibility that sometime in the future they might consider the possibility of a mission school, but it would have been entirely premature to have raised the matter at this stage.

Across the sea to the north-west was the mysterious and remote island of Tumbatu, which was seldom visited by strangers. I asked about this, but was not encouraged. Slightly more accessible was the Michamvi peninsula, north of the little fishing town of Chwaka on the east coast. The two settlements on the peninsula could not be reached by road, but might be approached from the south on foot or across the bay by canoe. Tom Laver and I chose the latter mode of transport. Our canoe — like virtually all in Zanzibar — had outriggers, and this one had a sail which our paddler could not use because the wind was contrary. It took an hour and a half to cross the still, clear water, which was of an almost emerald green. After a journey enlivened by dolphins and flying fish, we landed on a white, nearly deserted beach in the heat of the day. Just a few fishermen were about, and women searching for sea-urchins on the shell-covered shore.

The boatman pointed out to us the path through the coconut-palms to the nearer of the two settlements. We arrived unannounced, and asked for the *sheha*. He received us with friendliness and courtesy, though he was plainly puzzled to know the purpose of our visit. After an hour or so we set out for the further village, but the afternoon was so hot and the coral path so rough that we abandoned the attempt or, rather, deferred it to a later occasion. The open country was a dazzling green, and all nature, apart from the brilliant songbirds, was taking a siesta. As we returned to the first village we noticed the enormous nests of the golden weaver-finches in the palm-trees. Apparently they were a pest, but they were very beautiful.

Our sheha was more than willing to sit in the shade and chat, and I told him frankly that I was new and just wanted to learn about the island and its people. He agreed that I should use my camera, though at the sight of it the women fled. As at Nungwi I returned with the photographs some time later, and he and the elders were delighted. Visits of this sort could have no immediate, practical result; but they made for friendship and understanding. At least I learned something of the native peoples of the island and the huge difficulties which would face any missionaries who might attempt to work among them in the future.

As the months passed I became more and more determined to visit the remotest place of all, the island of Tumbatu to the north-west. In the end I arranged a visit through the good offices of the mudir at Mkokotoni, and five of us, including Father William Sudi, set out accompanied by the mudir's young Arab deputy. We made the three-mile crossing in a dhow, notwithstanding the vow I had made to myself never to travel in one of these vessels again.

Tumbatu was to prove a fascinating place, which could have few modern parallels. I was told during the crossing that its population of several thousands consisted entirely of one tribe, the Watumbatu. Originally they were a mixture of Africans, Persians and Arabs: but for hundreds of years there had been no further intermarriage and they were now a tribe in their own right — aloof, and hostile to all change. They had been Muslims since at least the thirteenth century, and, with their Koran schools, were obviously civilised and were literate in Swahili in the Arabic script. The men were seamen and travelled great distances in their dhows: some of the women had never left their island home. I learned that these people would have nothing whatever to do with western civilisation. They would have no government school, no dispensary, no policeman, no outside official, no Indian shop-keeper. Nobody drank alcohol or made trouble — on pain of immediate and final deportation from the island.

It took us over an hour to get across, and we landed nearly a mile south of Tumbatu town. There was a good path, but the island had no roads. There were no cars, bicycles or ox-carts.

The mudir of Mkokotoni had built himself a little palm-thatched rest-house on the island, and it was to this that we were ushered. We were received by the senior *sheha* or chief, who proceeded to show us round and who never left us during the remainder of our visit. Women and children frequently ran away from us, but the menfolk were gracious and hospitable to a degree. The houses in the town were mostly wattle-and-daub and thatched with palm-leaves. They were so close to each other that their eaves touched. The streets were narrow and winding, like those of Old Mombasa or the bazaars in Zanzibar city: but they were destitute of all traffic but pedestrians. We counted five grave-yards, which gave some indication of the age of the settlement, and were shown three mosques, one of them very ancient. After taking off our shoes we were admitted to the newest of the mosques.

When our tour was complete we were escorted to a *hoteli* and given warm milk to drink. Here we met the chief imam or religious leader, who was quite delightful. Finally we were taken back to the rest-house to collect our small luggage, and were regaled with coconuts: after which, with the most wonderful courtesy, it was pointed out that the wind would soon shift and make our return journey long and difficult. I was told on the way back that though the Watumbatu were completely genuine in their welcome for strangers no one at all found it wise to stay for more than a few days. In a letter to England I wrote; "Missionary work on Mars would be more feasible than in Tumbatu."

Shortly after our outing to Tumbatu I explored the smaller island of Uzi off the east coast of Zanzibar, and this was altogether more encouraging. George Mbaruku accompanied me. At low tide it was actually possible to reach the island on foot, negotiating the intervening mangrove swamps with the help of a guide. This we did, completing the journey in about an hour. The welcome we received was startling and effusive, and owed something to the fact that George encountered patients whom he had treated at the mission clinic in the city.

In a very short time we were talking to both the sheha and the imam, the Muslim religious leader. We learned that there were about nine hundred indigenous Wahadimu on the island, and it became plain (though we were not told) that they sat rather more lightly to their Muslim faith than the Wahadimu we had already encountered. Within limits they were open to new ideas. There was an evident wish among them to widen their horizons by learning the Latin script in which Swahili is today commonly written. I promised to return with books and pictures. We left in the evening by canoe, having been showered with gifts. One of our best friends was the imam.

I kept my promise, and the response on our return was more than I expected. Within an hour of our arrival I was sitting under a tree and teaching a group of menfolk to read the Latin characters. We had friendly talks about religion too. It was not long before the sheha was sounding me out about the possibility of a mission school. I had to point out that even if this were practicable it would not be universally popular amongst his people, and much caution and discretion would be necessary. Nevertheless I could not but feel a certain elation. Everyone had told me that missionary work among the indigenous people of Zanzibar was out of the question. This was no longer certain, though precipitate action would have been dangerous.

During the bishop's next visit to Zanzibar I told him of my contacts with the people in the remoter areas, and on this occasion he listened carefully. At the time he was in practice more concerned with winding down the work of the Mission for financial reasons than with embarking on new projects. Several longstanding missionary enterprises were on his list for closure, including the mission school at Kiungani. Nevertheless he gave me a hearing and a reasoned reply. The Mission had no money for new catechists or teachers. And, even if it had money, any attempt to convert Muslims, even

among the Wahadimu, would arouse enormous political reper-
cussions and might provoke not only Islamic fury but government intervention.

I had to concede that on this question the bishop was
probably right. But what was the use of being a missionary if
one could not propagate the Gospel? Was I just wasting
precious time?

Meanwhile in early 1956 the situation at the mission-house
deteriorated as Father Dix became increasingly unbalanced. I
often did not react well, and felt that my own Christian life
was in shreds. Then one day Dix laid hands on me after
some comment which I had thought wholly innocuous. I
was mercifully able to restrain myself, but realised then that
patience was no longer a virtue. The rumour got around that
the clergy were fighting. Plainly it was beyond my power to
mend matters, and I must go.

No purpose would be served by approaching the bishop
again, so I took the course which was not allowed: I wrote
directly to the General Secretary in London asking for a
transfer to another Swahili-speaking diocese. This time, know-
ing the situation from Dr Harries, he at once approached
Bishop Leslie Stradling of the new diocese of South West
Tanganyika. I was offered the post of priest-in-charge of the
mission at Milo, high up in the chilly hills of Tanganyika's
Southern Highlands. Bishop Baker raised no objection, and
probably heaved a sigh of relief.

At Milo, I learned, they had wood-fires, and glass in the
windows! Swahili was spoken there, but only as a second
language. I spent my spare hours (there were quite a lot of
them) in my last months at Zanzibar studying yet another
vernacular with no written grammar. To the best of my
knowledge it was spoken by only two people on Zanzibar
island, but they both rallied round.

* * * *

I was happy at the prospect of going to Milo, but realised it
was time to start thinking about the long-term future — and
perhaps a more normal life. I did not have to think long. It

was not unusual for nurses from the mainland to come to Zanzibar on holiday and stay with the sisters across the road. We invited them to tea and addressed them as Miss So-and-So. We were proof against their charms. Or were we? When in late 1955 Miss Rhodes turned up from the mission at Minaki near Dar-es-Salaam I invited her to tea and suggested a ride on the motorbike. We ended up with a bathe at Mangapwani beach. That was all.

The following January, however, I had occasion to go to Minaki for the diocesan staff retreat. I think I kept my mind on the retreat as long as it lasted, but I had a few days' holiday afterwards and Miss Rhodes and I went for several discreet walks through the maize fields. By now she was Gladys. There was no doubt she was a dazzling girl as well as a devout and dedicated missionary. She had a mop of gorgeous red hair, winning freckles and a radiant smile. It was because I too tried to be a single-minded missionary that I had firmly put her out of my mind. I had no intention at all of getting married and returning to England, as many priests in the Mission had done.

I left Zanzibar in August 1956. In order to take the motorbike with me I made the crossing to Dar-es-Salaam in a schooner. The voyage was horrendous, and I was as sick as a dog. The plan was that I should have a fortnight's holiday at Minaki and then accompany Bishop Stradling in his truck up to Milo, a journey of nearly six hundred miles over very bad roads.

Gladys and I continued our walks through the maize fields when she was off duty: and she said "Yes." We agreed that somehow we would stay in Africa and continue our missionary work. We were too happy to worry much about the practical difficulties. Neither of us, however, was prepared to break our contract with the Mission, and we had a year and a half to go. This seemed a long time, but we determined to complete it before going home to England to marry. (England was still home then, not Africa.) God would plan the future.

When Bishop Leslie Stradling turned up at Minaki I realised he was a very different sort of bishop. He was easy to respect and easy to get on with, and a ready listener. Relaxed and patient, he nevertheless meant business and got things done.

His quiet humour was infectious and he had that most price-less of episcopal gifts, the ability, before getting his own way, to persuade you that he was right. I found he usually was. I thanked him for the job at Milo and told him about Gladys.

"Well," he said. "I am happy for you both. Milo is *not* a place for a married priest, but we have time to cross that bridge. It will all work out. I would be glad if you and Gladys would not publish any formal engagement just yet, so that the folk at Milo don't think of you merely as a bird-of-passage. It will do no harm to keep quiet for a bit." The bishop's truck was in dock at Dar-es-Salaam, and fortunately its malady proved to be far worse than had been anticipated. It was well into September before he could get away, and Gladys and I took advantage of the extra holiday to have more walks in the maize-fields.

We paid several visits on the bike to Dar-es-Salaam, fifteen miles from the mission. The gravel road down to the coast was badly corrugated and covered with loose sand, and we had one bad fall when a passing ox made a frontal attack on us. The motorbike went one way, I another and Gladys over my shoulder. The bike was bent and buckled, but there was no damage to ourselves which was not remedied by a swim in the sea. "About our engagement ring," I said, as we picnicked afterwards. "They don't sell them at Milo. If I send you the money, will you choose it and buy it?" Finding the money out of an annual allowance of £30 was not easy, but I did my best. It was many years later when Gladys admitted: "Well, as a matter of fact, it was not enough. But I made it up."

Then it was goodbye. The following year we had a holiday together on a farm half-way between Minaki and Milo. By this time Gladys had moved even further away, to the hospital at Korogwe. I did not see her again until, in 1958, I looked down from the promenade deck of the *Durban Castle* in Tanga harbour and saw her in a little boat coming across to the ship for England.

5. The Roadmaker

"I WISH you luck with the motorbike," said Father Christopher Woolley, the outgoing priest at Milo Mission, as he patted his horse. "There are practically no roads, and, well, look at the hills. I think you would do better with four legs. Or, like most people who have worked here, just two." Father Woolley had a point. Milo — a huddle of red-brick buildings which might have been in the middle of Europe — was built high on a ridge in the Southern Highlands of Tanganyika. Most of the mission-district was far below, a panorama of hills and valleys stretching as far as one could see and attainable only by a series of precipitous descents. The little red church on the hill-top was dedicated to the Transfiguration of Our Lord, an event which occurred on a mountain. There were times when, for hours or days on end, the mission would be blotted out by dank Scotch mists. Sometimes it was an island above a sea of clouds.

A week had passed since my arrival at the mission. The journey from the coast in Bishop Stradling's truck had taken three days, the bishop himself having gone ahead and left me to travel with his driver. Simon and his newly-married wife Margaret accompanied us. Simon had gladly agreed to come with me into this unknown land, being by this time more a friend than a "houseboy."

The first hundred miles or so, as far as Morogoro, were on a good metalled road. This did not last, and the subsequent "Great North Road" proved to be hideously corrugated. At Iringa, still four hundred miles from the mission, we left behind the last telephone. At Njombe we were among the high hills, and the cold was bitter. We looked in at the little post-office, which was eighty miles from the mission. It boasted a telegraph since the telephone system did not reach so far. Our post, I knew, was brought weekly by a runner who took six days to do the return journey. During those last eighty miles to Milo the earth road deteriorated rapidly as the mountain views became more spectacular. After a little village called Mlangali it became a bumpy nineteen-mile cart-track which spiralled its way up the mountain-side and through forests and swirling clouds to the mission.

We arrived on a Saturday afternoon, and on the Sunday morning I produced my first sermon in the Pangwa language, carefully written out and memorised during the previous weeks. The Pangwa tribe were a dour and backward people whom it was difficult at first to get to know. Those in church that Sunday gave not the slightest indication as to whether they understood what I was talking about. But, months later, one of the church elders gave me an intelligent assessment of that sermon. "You spoke the Pangwa of our grandparents fairly well," he said. "The older people understood you better than the younger." I had relied heavily on an old and disintegrating Pangwa New Testament, from which I had drawn up a vocabulary and worked out the grammar of the language. Meanwhile many of the old words had in practice been replaced by their Swahili equivalents.

There were half a dozen Europeans on the mission-station, and personal relations were good. There was no question of being isolated from one's own kind. The work would be like that at Kihurio, with the difference that it was long-established and there were large numbers of Christians. The married African priest who lived nearby, Father Joseph Mlele, was a delightful young man and a tower of strength. He was not a Pangwa — the first Pangwa priest was ordained a year or so later — but he was fluent in both Swahili and the local language.

The dominant character on the mission-station was the Mothers' Union worker, Miss Grace Nobbs, known affectionately by the Africans as *Mama Nobosi*. She was the kind of woman who could easily have been a dragon but had long decided not to be. She looked after the housekeeping and ran us all firmly, doling out three bottles of paraffin a week for our hurricane lanterns. At one stage she had been thrown from her horse and very seriously injured.

It was soon obvious that the real problem at Milo was going to be not personalities but penury. The mission had very little money indeed, for housekeeping or for anything else. Necessities which had been provided by Zanzibar diocese — bedding, towels, soap — here had to come out of our annual £30 allowance. I knew there would be no money for the motorbike. But the prospect of not being able to use my pressure-lamp at night was bleak: all my reading and writing depended on that. Sadly I packed away my paraffin radiator and lit the wood fire. The wood was wet and the flue an architectural disaster. Smoke billowed out into the room, percolating into every nook and cranny apart, possibly, from the chimney. I decided that it was better to be cold than to suffocate.

It was useless to complain, for the money was not there. I decided on a private fund-raising campaign. Fortunately I had a little cash saved up, enough to run the pressure-lamp for a time. That gave me five or six hours at my desk at night when not on safari. After writing my weekly letter to Gladys and my weekly letter home I wrote articles for the local newspapers in Dar-es-Salaam and even, occasionally, for English journals. Not all were published, but in time I was able to buy a few tins of paraffin and a drum of petrol and have them brought up by truck from Mlangali. Letters to friends and family in England brought in some welcome gifts — gifts made, I knew, at great personal sacrifice.

Shortly after my arrival Father Woolley said: "Come with me to Mavala. It will give you an idea of the work." Mavala was our nearest outstation, with a church and a school only three miles away along the "road." We started very early. I declined a lift on the horse, and went ahead on the bike. Father Woolley arrived a few minutes later and tethered his beast to a tree. We both began to hear confessions before the service, and the crowds seemed interminable.

Father Woolley's performance that morning (or, rather, that day) astounded me. He heard confessions for about three hours. Then there were a few baptisms and a couple of weddings. These preceded the Sung Eucharist and sermon, and after that followed the inevitable *mashauri* or matrimonial problems. I helped as best I could, but after the service crept away, exhausted, for a quick cup of coffee from a vacuum flask. When I got back Father Woolley was still at it. He never tired or showed the slightest haste. His mind was always on the people he was dealing with, to the exclusion of all else, and he seemed unwearied. He was obviously a source of strength to a lot of simple Christians, and they loved him for it. But how he got through so much work without stopping I never knew. I realised that if that was what was expected of me I would fail the test.

It was perhaps four in the afternoon when the last of the people had gone. Only then did a second vacuum flask appear. "Let's go," said Father Woolley, apparently a little tired at last. "How?" I asked, suddenly looking at the tree to which his horse had been tethered. The animal had tired more quickly than his master, and had untethered himself and gone quietly home. A slightly pained expression passed over Father Woolley's face. "Poor thing," he said. "I shall have to walk." Pointing to my pillion, I said, "Jump on." As we dismounted at Milo he said: "Maybe you've got a point about the bike after all. Thanks. I think I will see to the horse and go and have a nap."

Mavala was the only outstation which could be visited in a day. The normal practice of the clergy was to undertake foot-safaris of between one and two weeks, spending a single night at each station and then walking on to the next. I tackled my first such safari within a few weeks of my arrival at Milo, walking down into the heat of an area called the Luana valley with a team of five porters. The porters were necessary because the little wattle-and-daub safari-huts were destitute of any furniture whatever. One had to take everything: folding table and chair, bed and bedding, clothing, canvas bath, food and cooking utensils and the church box. The problem was that porters were becoming more difficult to get and increasingly expensive.

At the first station I arrived after midday and there was a

76

crowd waiting for confessions and interviews. Later on groups of "hearers" and catechumens turned up for instruction. Just before dusk we had an informal service of preparation for Holy Communion, in the vernacular, and it was only when this was over that I could sit down and talk to the catechist and his family. Simon cooked for me, and before going to bed I read Evensong alone by the light of a hurricane lamp. In the morning everyone came to the Swahili eucharist, after which the marriage-problems went on until the heat of the day. Not before then could I pack up, say goodbye to the catechist and walk on to the next station. There the programme was repeated.

It was seldom, in fact, that the progress from one station to another could be described as walking. It was more often a question of climbing. One would struggle up steep wooded ascents and then clamber down into a valley with a rushing stream which could be heard long before it could be seen. I was hopeless at the log-bridges which the Africans crossed with such ease, balancing loads on their heads. Usually it was easier to take off boots and stockings and wade through the torrent.

The biggest station in the Luana valley was at a place called Mawenge, where the church had fallen down and a new one was being built by voluntary labour at a leisurely pace. This was a centre at which Christians were accustomed to gather from the length and breadth of the valley, and sometimes there would be week-long instructions followed by an adult baptism. Occasionally the bishop himself would come, and there would be a confirmation.

It happened that my arrival at Mawenge coincided with a meeting of the church elders to talk about building. I pointed out that the safari-hut was open to the heavens, and would be uninhabitable during the wet weather. "That," said the chief spokesman, "needs money." He knew perfectly well that it was the job of the local Christians to keep the hut in repair, but felt it worthwhile to try his luck with the new priest. He was convinced, like his fellows, that the white people were awash with cash and that we were in this job for our own benefit.

"There is no money," I explained. "No money, no roof" was the substance of his reply. "No roof, no priest," I replied. "No priest, no mission." I refrained from adding "And no school either," since I needed a reserve of ammunition. The spokesman looked as if he had not heard aright. "Can the shepherd desert his flock?" he asked plaintively. "Can our father abandon his children?" I decided to be tough, and said: "Of course he can. If they leave him to be leaked on." There was much shaking of grey heads, but the hut was repaired before the rains came. Not, however, before an outraged Providence had visited condign punishment on my hard-heartedness.

The following day, while I was packing up, I momentarily put my sun-hat down on the ground. Then, replacing it on my head, I felt a sudden jab of fearsome pain. The agony was so acute that I briefly lost consciousness — but only briefly. The pain was with me day and night, and it was impossible either to work or sleep. Simon explained to me that I had been stung by a scorpion which had found its way into my hat. Nothing that anyone did gave any relief from the pain, and I have no recollection of how, three days later, I at last reached Milo.

My next trip was into another valley, this time that of the Lugalawa river. We had a church and school some twenty miles away, on the other side of the stream. I enquired about the terrain and determined on an experiment. I believed I could get part of the way on the bike. There was a firebreak which led on to a footpath, which in turn led to a rough motorcycle track made for the Roman Catholic fathers who had a big new mission in the area, and big new motorbikes. I sent a message, asking that I be met at the furthest point the bike would reach.

There was no one there, for a very good reason. A completely new motorcycle track had been made by the local Anglican Christians as far as the river and beyond it to the church and school. The river itself was spanned by a new bamboo bridge. I dared not ride over this swaying structure, but successfully paddled the bike over it, in bottom gear, with my feet. There was applause and singing as I roared up to the church door. The porters turned up with my luggage hours later, by which time I had visited the Christians in the nearby villages with the teacher. I stayed at Lugalawa a week, teaching and baptising, and then continued on foot to the more distant outstations.

On the way back I called on the Roman Catholic fathers at their impressive new mission. They were delightful people, and their hospitality was lavish. No mention was made of the fact that their converts had largely been made from among our Anglicans, and that there had been liberal distributions of blankets and salt. Those were un-ecumenical days! It was at a later date that one of the fathers acknowledged to me that in spite of their superior buildings (and 500 c.c. motor-cycles) they rather envied us. At least the Anglicans built their own churches and regularly paid their church dues.

The motorbike-track idea caught on. Within a month an eight-mile track had been made from Milo down to a teaching centre at a place called Luvungu. It had a rough surface and a horrendous gradient, and my front brake-cable snapped on my first attempt to get down it. The only problem about getting back was that one had to go hell-for-leather to maintain one's momentum up the hill. Simon manufactured a new brake-cable out of an old clutch-cable, and the bike was roadworthy again.

The journey to Luvungu, which I made frequently, took me not the usual three hours, but a mere forty minutes. I would arrive there full of energy and spend an afternoon visiting the Christians in their villages before returning to Milo for the night. In the morning I could return and take a service, spend an hour or two with the people, and get back to the mission for lunch. Shortly I was taking two services at different stations on the same day, without haste. This was considered almost miraculous. The bike seemed to be an idea with a future.

*   *   *   *

In November we were all expected to go to the diocesan conference and synod at Lidull, on the shores of Lake Nyasa

79

(now Lake Malawi). Members of the diocese were a widely scattered team, doing similar Christian work but often without contact with each other or opportunity of consultation except during this one week a year. The gathering and the prayer together were important. So was the diocesan finance committee, which met before the conference. This was devoted to "bridging the gap." Every mission-district had submitted detailed estimates of its minimum financial requirements, in excess of local revenue, for the coming year. The bishop would explain how much money was actually available, almost all of it deriving from the Mission's supporters in Britain. There was, of course, never enough. The gap had to be bridged by patient negotiation among the mission staff and the African clergy.

Getting to Liuli was not easy. Milo was a hundred miles from Lake Nyasa, and Liuli was a long way down the lake. The first step was to get to our mission at Manda, on the lakeshore. There was a road of sorts from Mlangali, and we attempted the journey in a hired five-ton truck. A teacher who accompanied us to move house found that his furniture disintegrated en route.

The road resembled a dried-up river-bed, and the bamboo bridges groaned and crackled as we inched our way cautiously over them. One bridge was at an angle at the bottom of a gully. Two were broken down completely, leaving the driver to manoeuvre his way through the river itself. The first of these manoeuvres took nearly two hours, and involved unloading the entire truck. Even then we would not have got across had we not been carrying some spare planks which we fitted under the wheels. The second crossing took a mere half-hour. But this was not the end of our woes, for after dark we got stuck in the sand for an hour. Later still we were baulked by a sandy hill on which the wheels spun helplessly. This cost us a further hour and a half, the whole journey taking fourteen hours. Mercifully everyone entered into the spirit of the occasion, and there was no ill-humour.

It was very hot at Manda. Most of us tumbled into bed after a quick meal, but some hardy creatures went bathing in the lake. The following day we completed the trip to Liuli with an uneventful seven hours in a motor-boat. It was all worth it, for the bishop inspired us with new enthusiasm for our work.

We needed it, for the return journey was another marathon. The motor-boat sank, fortunately before we had got on it, and there were problems in getting another. At Manda, where we arrived on a Wednesday, we had ordered four Landrovers to get us all back to Milo. We waited for them two days in vain, finally deciding that we must do what our predecessors had done: walk. It would take three days. In the middle of the Friday night, however, a police vehicle got through and the officer told us that two Landrovers were on their way, having been held up by torrential rain. They arrived a few hours later and we set off, after mechanical repairs, at ten o'clock on the Saturday morning.

It was long after dark when we turned up the Milo road, but we were hopeful of reaching home by half past nine and getting a good night's sleep before the labours of Sunday. But it was not to be. One of the Landrovers finally abandoned the unequal struggle, and everyone somehow had to squeeze into the other. This coped manfully, grinding up the hills in four-wheel-drive and bottom gear. But several miles before we reached Milo our fuel ran out.

An archdeacon who was coming to Milo for a holiday accompanied me to the mission on foot. We left the remainder of the party with the vehicle and, after a short rest, I returned to the Landrover on the motorbike with a gallon of petrol. I had never previously risked going out at night on the bike, especially on a muddy road, but all was well. We got to bed sometime in the small hours, but were in church not much after six the same morning.

(The following year we all went to Liuli again. This time there was no motor-boat, and we had to make shift with canoes, waiting a night for the paddlers to sober up. A troublesome hippo performed submarine antics beneath us, and we formed a canoe-convoy lest any of us should be upset. Happily the hippo went away. We were a day late in reaching Liuli and missed the finance committee: but the others had combined to give us a fair deal. On the way back I was

81

awakened, while sleeping at Manda, with the biggest invasion of biting ants I had yet encountered. One could only flee. All the sleeping accommodation was occupied and the priest-in-charge consulted his wife, who ran the little hospital. "You will have to make do with the labour-ward," she said. "There is no one there.")

*   *   *   *

Back at Milo there was an influx of baptism candidates and a pile of bills and correspondence, not to mention a set of account-books which would not balance. I off-loaded much of the teaching on to Father Joseph Mlele, who did it much better than I, and worked far into the night at my desk.

Before Christmas the two of us tried to cover as much of the district as we could to prepare the people for the festival. (By this time Father Woolley had gone to England on leave.) The weather deteriorated rapidly, and Milo was enveloped in a thick mist. A fine, cold rain fell through the mist. It looked as though the festival would be washed out.

In the event the church was packed to the doors on Christmas Eve, and there were people who could not get in. I conducted a Pangwa carol-service before celebrating the midnight mass. The plan was that I should leave the services on Christmas morning to Father Mlele and go down to Luvungu on the bike. Whether this would be practicable now seemed doubtful.

At first light on Christmas Day the clouds lowered but the morning was fine. I prayed that the rain might not fall until I was back at Milo, for though getting down the hill on the bike might not be difficult the return journey was likely to prove impossible in the rain. In spite of the early hour the people turned up in throngs, delighted to have a service in their own church on the festival instead of having to wait, as in the past, for their turn in one of the priest's foot-safaris afterwards. The rain held off, and everyone understood my desire to flee when the service was over. I arrived back at Milo in the middle of the main service of the day, and was able to help Father Mlele to give Holy Communion to the

82

crowds inside the church and outside it. There was dancing in the open air afterwards, though I could not but feel it lacked the exuberance which one found among the lowland folk. Perhaps people were dancing to keep warm!

During the wet months which followed there was no alternative but to go to most of the outstations on foot, when it was possible to go at all. One usually used the direct paths made by the Africans, scaling gradients that nothing on wheels could ever tackle. Occasionally a safari-hut would be totally uninhabitable, almost roofless and with a floor like a midden. After a word of reproof to the local elders, who would take belated action, one would walk on to the next station, perhaps two or three hours away.

At a village called Ludende I was too exhausted to walk further, and the roof of the hut looked as if it might be good in parts. Simon placed my bed, table and chair strategically, hoping they might avoid the worst leaks. As an extra precaution I slung a waterproof groundsheet from the rafters over the bed so that that at least might be dry. Rain-soaked beds were the ultimate misery.

It was after dark (and fortunately after supper) that I discovered this roof was one of those through which the rain just rains unimpeded. I leapt into bed, and was snug enough. The problem was that next morning it was still raining, and a couple of hours passed before I could get up. Dressing was a muddy business, but the sun came out and the people came to church as usual and everyone was happy.

We finally reached the little mountain village of Ivonya, where we had our furthest outpost. This was the end of my safari, and when I had finished my work nothing remained but to get back to Milo as quickly as possible. On a previous occasion I had done this journey (or, at least, most of it) on the bike, with Simon on the pillion. It had meant a fifty-mile detour, but we were home before dusk. Now I faced a three-day walk. After only an hour the buildings of Milo appeared in the hills across the valley, seemingly quite close. In the afternoon they were visible again, apparently neither nearer nor further. Next day we walked for six hours without seeing them at all. On the third day we reached them after a steep climb of two-and-a-half hours. There was plenty of time to think as one walked.

One of the things I thought about was the future. How much longer could this sort of trekking go on? It was already very difficult to obtain porters, and, not unreasonably, they demanded more money than we could pay them. In any case, how long would priests be available, white or black, to do this kind of work?

At Milo a medical crisis awaited me. The English nurse came in great distress saying she had a patient in need of a caesarean section, whose life she was powerless to save. The visiting doctor had left some days ago. Could I possibly get hold of a Landrover at Mlangali to take the woman to Njombe hospital? She knew — we all knew — that once upon a time a UMCA nurse had saved lives by doing a caesarean section herself, following the book step by step. I had every sympathy with our nurse when she said: "I simply dare not try."

It would, I knew, probably be impossible to get the motor-bike to Mlangali through the forest, with its slippery hills and long stretches of deep mud. Only a four-wheel-drive vehicle could be depended on. Nevertheless a life was at stake, or rather two lives, and Simon volunteered, unasked, to make the attempt. Within minutes, tired as he was, he had jumped on the bike and was away in search of a Landrover.

Some hours later, during the afternoon, the nurse came to see me again. She had, almost miraculously, succeeded in delivering the baby without a "caesar." Both mother and child were safe. The medical crisis was over, but the danger to Simon was not. It would soon be dusk, and there was no sign either of a Landrover or of him. We organised a search-party, and set out on foot. I took it for granted that the father of the girl who had been saved would be glad to help, being thankful to have a daughter and a grandchild alive. But not a bit of it. It required some tough talking to persuade him to join us — we really needed his help — but he slipped off at the earliest opportunity to a nearby beer-drink. No word of gratitude was ever spoken by anyone in his family, and we were left with a substantial bill for the Landrover.

We met Simon foot-slogging, exhausted, up one of the hills

a few miles away from the mission. He had come off the bike, which was damaged and was now in the Landrover. This was bogged down somewhere in the forest and could not be rescued until the following day. It was only a month or two later that we were faced with a similar medical emergency, and I rode down to Mlangali myself to hire a truck. Both the truck and I got back to the mission without incident, only to find that the mission doctor had just turned up and the emergency was over.

It was episodes such as this which convinced me of the necessity of doing something to improve our appalling communications. Telecommunications were impracticable, but we *could* improve the existing roads and make new ones. We could make a new, wider and better-drained track through the forest, avoiding the quagmires and the more precipitous hills. And we could drive a motorable road, in the opposite direction, through the mission-district itself to our big out-station at Ketawaka, seventeen miles away. This would begin to open up the whole district. Road-making was hardly a priest's job, but I had less than a year to go at Milo, and maybe this was a permanent contribution I could make. Father Mlele's pastoral work was more effective than mine: but how would he and his successors be able to carry on in future years if they had no means of getting about apart from their own feet?

I discussed this with Father Joseph himself, and with almost every group of elders in the district. The idea caught on, and people began to dream of having bicycles. The District Officer at Njombe was keen, and wanted to open markets as well. Both from the point of view of the Church and of the local population something had to be done to bring the Milo area into the mid-twentieth-century.

A start was made on the Ketawaka road on the Friday fast-days in Lent. We began with the eucharist in church and went off with our hoes to the top of the slope at the end of the existing track. Work stopped at midday for prayers at the roadside, and we returned to church for a little service when it finished at three o'clock. I had then (and still have) not the slightest notion of how to survey a road, and of course

85

we had no instruments. We just looked at the hills and tried to visualise zig-zags which would cut down the gradients, and looked for propitious points for making bamboo bridges. There were places where it was necessary to dig into the hill-side — avoiding rocky bits, of course — and we aimed at a width which would take one car. It was not anticipated that vehicles would meet. When really steep gradients were inescapable we resorted to "corduroying," making a surface of tied bamboo-poles on which wheels could take a grip.

There was much rejoicing when we got as far as the church at the little village of Ludende, and of course I used the road for the motorbike — though we were looking to a future with a truck. It was about this time that I discovered the secret of getting the bike up the more difficult hills, which previously I had negotiated by pushing it with the engine running in bottom gear. (It was only a little 150 cc machine.) A visitor to the mission said: "Why on earth don't you take the silencer off? No one will mind here, and the thing will go up the side of a house." The racket was horrific, and people in all directions knew I was coming. I soon discovered that early in the morning it sufficed to collect a congregation for church even if my message had not got through. "The UMCA *pikipiki* (motorcycle)," people said unchristianly, "is better than any Roman Catholic *pikipiki*. It makes more noise."

We worked on the road throughout the southern winter, work becoming slower as more and more trees had to be felled in the lower, hotter regions. The bishop, who was coming for a confirmation, promised to arrive at the further end of the district, beyond Ketawaka, on foot, and to walk to the end of the road. There we were to meet him with a hired Landrover.

The road, even in its incomplete state, greatly facilitated my regular visits to a number of the churches. I got through to the end of it at Ketawaka, asking folk to help me carry the bike when I reached insurmountable obstacles, and after taking the usual service drove to and fro supervising the work along that stretch. Then back to the next church for another service and more supervising.

Bishop Stradling was taken ill before he came to Milo at the

86

end of September, and he sent a message to say he would have to change his plans and come to the mission on the old road in his own truck. I confess to keeping very quiet about this until the last moment, for if the news had spread work would certainly have flagged. However, the job was completed on time. And no one was disappointed, for the bishop agreed to tour the length of the road in a hired Landrover, visiting all the churches. He met scenes of huge enthusiasm, and the journey almost resembled a royal progress. He collected a small mountain of gifts, and on his way back had, smilingly, to turn down several dozen people trying to thumb lifts.

Before he left the bishop told me he had another English priest to take my place next year, Father John Robinson. He was the owner of a Landrover, and would be willing to bring it to Milo.

* * * *

In July Gladys and I had our long-awaited holiday at a farm above Iringa, and we began to plan our marriage and our future. But the holiday was in doubt until almost the last moment: there was no nurse to take Gladys' place at Korogwe, and she was asked to call it off. However, the diocesan doctor, Dr Lesley Sitwell, learned of our problem and offered to go to Korogwe for a fortnight to take over. The situation was saved. The motorbike broke down on the way to Njombe; but, poor mechanic though I was, I had it going again in less than an hour.

"I am planning two children," said Gladys, her hair golden now in the sunshine. But we had to admit we had left it rather late: we would both be thirty-seven when we married next year. Gladys had news of a possible job in Southern Rhodesia. A friend of hers was also a friend of Canon Pat Mason, priest-in-charge of St David's Mission, Bonda, in the diocese of Mashonaland in that country. Pat Mason wanted to leave in order to found the new mission of St Peter, Mandea, in the Honde Valley. I would shortly be receiving a letter from him, asking me to go to Bonda. It seemed a very good offer. Gladys said simply that she would go anywhere provided only it would be possible to bring up and educate our children. She was very sure about those.

Our two weeks seemed to last two days. Back at Milo I received Pat Mason's offer, and accepted it. Then I received a letter from the new bishop of Mashonaland, Cecil Alderson, which in practice countermanded Pat's invitation. His advisers, he said, told him that St Faith's Mission, Rusape, was in more urgent need of an experienced mission-priest, and it was this that he was offering me.

I had serious doubts about St Faith's, though I knew it to be one of the oldest and most famous missions in Rhodesia. The bishop himself told me about St Faith's Mission Farm, a co-operative venture on the mission land run with the Africans by Mr Guy Clutton-Brock. The latter's excellent qualities did not include being a churchman. In various letters he was described as "Number One," and it seemed to me that the position of the new priest-in-charge might, whatever the goodwill, be an awkward one. Obviously, however, I had to accept the job if I wanted to go to Rhodesia at all.

Father John Robinson arrived with his Landrover shortly before Christmas. The festival was as wet as it had been last year, but he was undeterred. His vehicle had a winch at the front, and all you had to do if you were in trouble was to tie a rope round a tree and winch yourself out.

One Saturday, however, he failed to turn up at the mission after a trip to Njombe, leaving me, on the Sunday morning, to cope with services in two widely distant areas of the district. "Sorry," he said when he arrived back at lunch-time. "There was nothing wrong with the winch, but there was no tree."

By this time I had got a push-bike for Father Joseph Mlele, and the plan was that he should inherit the motorbike when I left. The delightful new Pangwa priest, Father Mtweve, was the only one of us who still had no means of getting about but his own feet — until he inherited the bicycle after my departure. He too arrived before Christmas. He was the first of his tribe to be ordained.

Meanwhile, the Ketawaka road had already revolutionised transport in the whole district. The lorries of African and

Indian businessmen would roar up to the mission, and their owners, after they had greeted us, would drive on to the remoter areas to open up their work. Soon the greetings were skipped, and the lorries and cars sped past us. Among other things the businessmen sold bicycles which were snapped up by those local people who could afford them, and were then seen being pushed up (and sometimes down) the daunting hills.

After Christmas, when the clergy were working in different parts of the district, Father Robinson drove us all down into the Luana valley in his Landrover. We dropped Father Mtweve at Mawenge, where he set out on a foot-safari, and the rest of us went on to visit the string of churches in the area so that the people might meet their new priest-in-charge. On our way home Father Robinson said: "Let's try some of the *pikipiki* tracks."

The truck made remarkably good progress along these narrow paths, the main problem being the bridges, which were too narrow and too weak for the vehicle. At one point we asked some of the local men to cut some poles and help us widen the bridge on the spot. Further on we twice had to take the car through the shallow streams, winching our way out when we got stuck.

The next week we set out for Lugalawa, where the local Christian people had made ready for us. Several miles before the church and school we ran into a new, wide road which they had made specially for us. The *pikipiki* bridge had been rebuilt over the Lugalawa river, having been washed away in the rains. But the stream was broad and a bridge for the heavier vehicle was impracticable. The folk had contented themselves with making a clearing at the roadside and erecting a notice in English: "Car Park."

My last job at Milo, apart from attending several farewell parties organised by the Africans, was the production of a new edition of the Pangwa hymn book. The old printed books had almost all disintegrated, and the hymns were falling out of use. It took me several months, working at night whenever I was at the mission, to re-type, cyclostyle and bind them.

On a Sunday morning in mid February we sang the old

hymns from the new books, and after church Simon and his wife and I jumped into a hired truck and were off. I said good-bye to Simon and Margaret at Morogoro, and took the train to Dar-es-Salaam and the *Durban Castle*.

The Universities' Mission to Central Africa eventually considered proposals for mending its authoritarian ways — I was not the only one who had been pleading for change in letters to London — but what happened to them I do not know. Later, in 1965, the Mission was absorbed into the older and more amorphous Society for the Propagation of the Gospel, and lost its identity altogether.

Gladys and I never returned to Tanganyika, today's Tanzania. We knew a little about Mwalimu Julius Nyerere, the teacher who had left Pugu Roman Catholic school owing to his political involvement and who became the country's first President. We heard distantly of independence in 1961 for Tanganyika and in 1963 for Zanzibar. We heard of the unspeakable horrors which followed the communist invasion of Zanzibar in 1964, and of the uprising, put down by the British, in Tanzania the same year. We read, too, of the millions of Tanzanians who were forcibly removed into collective villages, and the vast misery to which this led. It was plain that none of these things derived from the ordinary peace-loving Africans among whom we had lived, but we learned nothing of the driving forces behind these revolutions. Our minds were set on another country and on other work.

Gladys lost both her parents in the months preceding our leave in England, and this cast a shadow over our homecoming. But nothing spoiled our wedding, on April 26th 1958, in Gladys's village church at Flockton in Yorkshire. Nor could anything destroy our happiness during that English summer. In the English autumn we returned to Africa confident that we were obeying God's call. We had no inkling of the baptism of fire which awaited us at St Faith's Mission, Rusape.

90

6. Rhodesia

IT was breath-taking: a garden-city in the brown endlessness of Africa. The jacaranda trees, which lined the streets and avenues, were springing into purple blossom in the sunlight. Spathodeas and bauhineas were everywhere, while walls and hedges were ablaze with hibiscus and bougainvillaea.

We were in Salisbury, Southern Rhodesia, and it was September 9th 1958. Old-style colonial buildings with wide verandahs still predominated over the skyscrapers which came with the prosperity brought by the new Central African Federation. "One of the most beautiful small cities in the world," someone had called it. Moreover, it seemed astonishingly efficient. The tropical sun beat down pitilessly, and fans whirred drowsily in spacious offices. But everything worked, including the people. It was not the Africa we had known.

Southern Rhodesia dated back to the arrival of Cecil John Rhodes' Pioneer Column in 1890, which occupied Mashonaland without a shot being fired. Rhodes' purpose, through his British South Africa Company, was commercial and imperial: but in establishing peace and western civilisation he saved the Shona people from total extermination by the Matabele, the warlike offspring of the Zulus. Matabeleland, too, was incorporated into the new country a few years later. In 1923 the territory was formally annexed to the British Crown and became a self-governing colony with a technically non-racial franchise. By the end of the 'fifties it had enjoyed half a century of peace and outstanding material progress. Race relations were less strained than in South Africa, its southern neighbour.

For my wife and me the transition from England to Salisbury

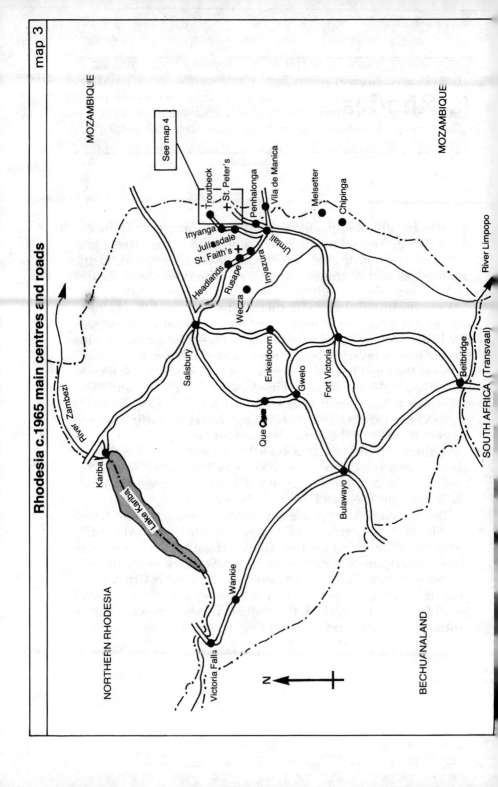

map 3

Rhodesia c.1965 main centres and roads

was abrupt. Gone were the days of leisurely sea voyages. Air travel was normal even for missionaries now, and our Viscount accomplished the journey in three days. We looked in at Rome, Benghazi and Entebbe, and were deposited on the tarmac of Salisbury airport, tired, shaken and exhilarated. We were shaken in more ways than one. Conversation on the 'plane with Rhodesian passengers had been disturbing. "St Faith's Mission?" one of them had said. "A hot potato. Drop it before it burns you."

St Faith's was obviously the eye of a whirlpool of controversy. It had recently provided a home for an African who had married a European wife, something which was simply not done in Rhodesia. (White people were always called Europeans.) Gladys and I, who thought marriage across the colour-line unwise, could not see what the uproar was about. But uproar there had been. Bishop Cecil Alderson, Bishop of Mashonaland, had told us all about it when we had met him in England. He had told us, too, more about St Faith's.

"The mission has huge lands," he had said. "It ran to ruin because the menfolk were away, working in the towns. Father Stowell (your predecessor, who left two years ago) was a practical priest, but was swamped with work. With the previous bishop's blessing he invited Guy Clutton-Brock to take over the farm and get the men back to work on it. C.B. has formed a flourishing co-operative, bringing in helpers and finance from England. The farm today is a model of inter-racial co-operation and an example to the whole country. I back it whole-heartedly, and want you to do the same."

Stocky, greying and with a twinkle in his eye, Bishop Alderson — himself a newcomer to Rhodesia — was a man accustomed to rule. He had brushed aside the difficulty that most of the farm's white workers were not Anglicans and that they seldom or never entered the church. He brushed aside, too, my plea that I was a missionary who knew nothing about farms and that I wanted to go to a straightforward mission. It was St Faith's or nothing.

I told this to my companion on the 'plane. "Drop it," he repeated. "We Europeans are not all die-hards. We know there are things that must be changed as fast as possible,

93

but not faster. But your Clutton-Brock has alienated almost the entire white population, not just the reactionaries. He is an extreme liberal, and extremists don't help us. They hold things back." Then he added: "I am sure you know the last white priest at St Faith's collapsed with a nervous breakdown, and had to leave the country in a hurry. It has taken two years to find a sucker to replace him."

* * * *

Archdeacon Wood met us at the airport and after a couple of days in Salisbury drove us the 116 miles to St Faith's Mission. "Leave the farm to C.B.," he said in the car. "You have an enormous mission-district to look after. Actually there are *three* mission-districts in three native reserves, and only three African priests to help you with the whole area."

The road to the little settlement of Rusape was tarmac all the way, though in parts the tar was still narrow: when cars met they had to pull over, raising clouds of red dust. For the nine miles beyond Rusape the tracks were of earth or gravel, and dust-devils whirled ahead of us and sometimes swallowed us up. The countryside was bare and undulating, with clumps of trees surrounding the scattered European farms. For the first time we saw the spectacular rock-formations and granite domes or *kopjes* which were characteristic of Rhodesia.

Then, suddenly, we were passing the buildings of the mission-farm, crossing a stream — "Jordan," because in the old days it was used for baptisms — and driving through a magnificent avenue of eucalyptus trees. The archdeacon pulled up outside the priest's house, a long, sprawling bungalow with a tin roof and a verandah. The garden was rather wild, dominated by a magnificent flowering syringa tree and dotted, unexpectedly, with Cape oaks. Multi-coloured bee-eaters twittered from the branches. Not far away was the historic thatched mission-church, built by the hands of priest and people together in 1909. The mission itself, I learned, dated back to 1896.

People soon began to collect to welcome us, and we found ourselves shaking hands with the local African priest, with the sisters of the Community of the Resurrection, with Guy Clutton-Brock and John Mutasa, the farm-manager, and his staff: then with the churchwardens and schools-superintendent, the village headmen and their people and, most conspicuous of all, the women of the Mothers' Union in their white, blue and black uniforms. There was much singing, with the magnificent harmonies of Africa, and the welcome on the faces of my new parishioners was unaffected and sincere. I knew, of course, that Africans always welcome newcomers, and watch them like hawks afterwards!

There were speeches outside the church, all in English or interpreted into English from Shona, the vernacular. The most memorable was by C.B., tall, fair-haired and sun-burned, who spoke with moving sincerity and a ready smile. John Mutasa had just a hint that the missionary paternalism of East Africa was not for St Faith's. Every speaker had a welcome for *Mai* (Mother) Lewis. I had a surprise up my sleeve for all of them. Shona was a much more difficult language than Swahili; but having started to study it at Milo I now had my two-minute reply ready in Shona, or at any rate Shona of a sort. The women were ululating with joy as we went into church. I had not realised, however, that to the white people present the vernacular was a closed book.

The church was old-fashioned Anglo-Catholic, much Africanised. Candles on the altar blazed through the gloom, but in the nave banners hung with family totems, lion, elephant and baboon. The rood-screen was of crossed assegais, and an old spirit-drum stood by the lectern with a single candle to light the reader. The "pews" were reed mats, with a few stools and benches as a concession to the Europeans. The service was conducted by the archdeacon, whose sermon was a weary business since it had to be interpreted sentence by sentence from English. By the Sunday I had contrived a rudimentary sermon in Shona. The people laughed at the right places, but (as in East Africa) assumed poker faces when I perpetrated my more egregious linguistic howlers.

A month later Bishop Alderson came for my formal induction to St Faith's. A woman on the farm staff, Patricia Chater, wrote afterwards: "As on all Anglican missions, Father Lewis, as priest-in-charge, was made responsible to the Bishop for St Faith's lands, schools, clinics and people (which included, of course, 'our' co-operative, the community centre, the store, the mill, the butchery, the Scott Bader tractor and all). The words sounded out of touch with reality." I don't think the writer ever realised that my thoughts were much the same as hers.

The day after our arrival C.B. and John Mutasa, the farm-manager, showed me round the farm. It was certainly an impressive achievement, though heavily dependent on over-seas funding. Agriculture, however, was only a part of its purpose. There was a political motive too, on which Christians might well hold more than one view. C.B. was an idealist. Listening to his almost lyrical description of what the farm was trying to do I could not but admire his sincerity and dedication, and determined to give him all the support I could.

John Mutasa was almost as genial as C.B. himself, and I was not to know that his geniality cost him a great deal. Only years later did I learn of the clash he had had with the Diocese of Mashonaland. Following a suggestion of Father Stowell he had formed a "Makoni church council" in the local Makoni African reserve, and by prodigious efforts had raised a sub-stantial sum of money for the church. The church even opened a bank account in Rusape, and posted a cheque for £150 to the diocesan office in Salisbury. A diocesan bureaucrat returned the cheque, pointing out that the account had been opened without diocesan authority! After that John had turned to African politics.

Having been introduced to the farm I called, with Gladys, on the sisters in their little convent of thatched rondavels (round huts) which, with their conical roofs, looked like something out of "Snow White and the Seven Dwarfs." They gave us a delightful welcome. Sister Esther, their superior, had been on the mission for thirty years. Their world was far removed from that of the farm and their lives were dedicated to the work of the Church and the service of the local people. They were not blind to the good work of the farm, but felt that it overshadowed the mission and its primary task of preaching the Gospel. During the following weeks I got the message that they looked to me to bring the church back into the centre of things.

This was more easily said than done. The land had originally been given to the mission in order that, in a pagan society, Christians might gather round the church and resist the pagan pressures. The families living on the mission now, however, were second and third generation Christians, and both they and the land were controlled by C.B.'s farm.

* * * *

Relations between the mission and the farm were not the only problem, as Father Martin Musengezi soon made plain. He was the local priest, a fine pastor, and it was he, perhaps, who was happiest of all at the arrival of the new priest-in-charge. As acting priest-in-charge he had had a grim two years. We planned the future together in the thatched mission office where he told me about our seventy churches and forty schools. When I asked him what was the biggest problem he answered simply: "Money! There is just no money."

"The diocese pays the stipends of the clergy," he explained, "but we can hardly live on them. Church collections amount to a few shillings. For the rest we depend on the schools, on the government grants and the fees paid by the parents. And we have to send an assessment of £112 a month to the diocese. It is going up by £30."

I soon discovered that a heavy price was paid for the government grants for the schools, which came from the taxes of the Europeans. The mission's schools-superintendent did a fine job — Father Stowell had had to do the work himself — but he needed the help of all three African priests as schools-inspectors. Had this not been given the schools would have been closed by the Native Education Department, and the enraged populace would have turned against the Church.

"No," Father had said, when I questioned him further. "We do not visit people in their homes. We haven't time.

And dozens of Christians are living without Christian marriage because we can't get to their churches to marry them."

It was during one of these sessions with Father Musengezi that a delegation of men arrived from one of the outstations. It proceeded with much ceremony, and since Father was addressed as the intermediary (as custom dictated) the flood of words was beyond my understanding. I gathered, however, that the purpose of the visit was something more than to greet the new priest-in-charge. Father put it all in a nutshell, in English. "It boils down to this," he said. "They are asking whether you are going to leave them to die unbaptised." I gave them the best assurances I could. Then, when they had made their departure, I turned to the pile of correspondence on my desk. I pushed a bill over to Father Musengezi.

"What on earth is this?"

"It is a bill from the diocese."

"I can see that. But what for?"

He shook his head. "They come regularly."

I soon discovered that the mission was alleged to owe the diocese several thousand pounds. The origin of the debts was shrouded in the mists of history. In his letters to me the diocesan secretary, a retired brigadier, had an irritating habit of referring to them as "your debts," as if I were personally responsible for them.

I sat at the ancient typewriter and composed a concise letter to the brigadier, explaining that I had no debts at all and that the diocese could whistle for its money. On reflection I tore that letter up and typed another, saying the same thing with circumlocution and impeccable courtesy. I heard later that howls of anguish went up in the diocesan office nevertheless.

"Father," I said, pushing the typewriter aside, "what do we do? Where do we get the money?"

"Not from the pockets of our people," he replied. "They are poor, and crippled by the diocesan assessment and the school fees. We priests are already regarded as tax-collectors."

"The teachers are quite well paid."

"They just won't give. They think the mission is wealthy. It will take time to teach them to give."

"We haven't got time," I said. "For a start we must raise

money in England. After all, we are a *mission*, not yet a self-supporting parish." I dismissed the idea of trying to raise funds from the local whites. The farm had put paid to that.

"Appeals," Father explained patiently, "need the permission of the diocese and the Society for the Propagation of the Gospel in London. They won't allow one mission to go it alone."

"That's too bad. Why shouldn't we start some Friends of St Faith's in England while we are negotiating with them?"

"Because," said Father Musengezi, still patient, "the Friends of St Faith's have been going for years. All the money is used by the farm."

I was deflated, and thought long.

"Well," I suggested at length. "No one can stop me begging from my own friends in England." And that is what I did, with some success.

"In the meantime," I added to Father Musengezi, "my own first job is to visit some of the outstations and get to know the people."

"You can't," he responded unhappily. "The Chev. is not ready."

In the terms of service I had signed I had been promised a vehicle, provided not by the diocese but by the "parishioners." This turned out to be an aged Chevrolet truck, disinclined to further movement of any kind. We went to see the farm engineer, who had promised to look at it.

"I have met my match," he said, dejection written all over his face. "Honestly, I would sell it for scrap."

"Would you do that for me?" was all I trusted myself to reply.

*　　*　　*　　*

"So it is check, but not mate," I told Gladys that evening. She had been busy unpacking and making a home in unpromising surroundings. "Our feet have taken us round all three villages on the mission," she said. "Maybe they will take us further."

Foot-safaris (or, rather, treks, as they were called here) had been abandoned years ago. Indeed St Faith's was not without

99

cars. The farm had several, the education-department had one for its superintendent and some of the teachers had vehicles of their own. But there were none for the clergy. We would make a start by walking. Porters were totally unobtainable, but a number of the school-children had bicycles with carriers, and we would pay them out of our own pockets. This scheme actually worked,

The nearest outstation was Epiphany mission, older even than St Faith's and only four miles away. We scrambled along the rocky path and over the river, chattering with the schoolboys. These practised their English, and we our Shona. The people we met greeted us as friends, and we felt we were back in the Africa we knew.

The church at Epiphany, old and tumbledown, was made picturesque by the flowering shrubs which clung to its walls. The message we had sent ahead had not arrived, but old Canon Muhlanga was overjoyed at our coming. He was the first African to be ordained as an Anglican priest in Southern Rhodesia. As he was telling us about the old times, local Christians who had heard of our arrival began to drift in from nearby villages to welcome us. We were soon being instructed in the ceremonial greetings.

"How are you?" one would start.

"I am well if you are well." The qualification was essential.

"Have you had a good day?"

"I have had a good day if you have had a good day."

Or, in the morning: "Have you slept?" To which the answer was (even if you had not had a wink): "I have slept if you have slept."

The hand-clapping which accompanied the greetings (and expressions of thanks) baffled us at first. Finally we deduced that it was performed finger-tip to finger-tip by the men and with crossed palms by the women. Since, however, we were instructed by both men and women there was much confusion, accompanied by shrieks of laughter.

After the service next morning we found ourselves inundated with gifts, chiefly chickens and fruit. Before moving off to the next out-station, at a place called Madziwa, we off-loaded these on to an understanding and grateful Canon

Muhlanga. The journey through the heat of the day to Madziwa left us weary and footsore, but we were welcomed by the teachers who had received our message and were awaiting us. Later we went out with the head teacher, in the cool of the evening, to visit the local Christians as they returned from their fields. Some of the women were already at home, pounding maize-meal.

My sermon next morning was supposed to be extempore, but broke down through lack of vocabulary. It ended up with a spontaneous pantomime which provoked uproarious mirth but which must have been of doubtful spiritual value. The conclusion was inescapable: I *had* to find time for language-study. No other out-station was within walking distance, so Gladys and I turned our steps back to the mission. The journey was a fifteen-mile slog in the blazing sun.

We had made our gesture, but it could be no more than that. C.B. appreciated it, for he himself both practised and preached the simple life. But the fact remained that Gladys and I were no nearer to being able to reach any of the distant out-stations. Gladys came up with the immediate answer. She had a little money, having resigned from her superannuation scheme in England. "Let's buy a motorbike," she said. We did: and it took us, in spite of appalling roads, to all the stations in the nearby Makoni African reserve and to a few more distant centres which did not require overnight baggage.

Father Musengezi advised me to pay my respects ceremonially to the local chief, Chief Makoni, and his elders. Properly speaking I should have offered a goat, but a goat was not easily obtainable and in any case could not be accommodated on the bike. However, my information was that cash would be equally acceptable, so the appropriate amount was packed up in a large envelope. I made a speech to the Chief's intermediary and the elders, explaining that my "goat" seemed a small one but was, in fact, as big as the next man's — and I trusted it would serve as well. Though my speech was in Shona, the intermediary turned to the Chief and repeated it all with much embellishment. The Chief expressed satisfaction that the proper procedures had been followed, thanked me through his intermediary for the goat and welcomed me to his fiefdom.

Soon the motorbike was taking Gladys and me to Rusape, Umtali and Salisbury. And it enabled us to make a start on visiting the local European farmers whose lands surrounded the mission. They received us with every courtesy, while making no secret of their suspicions of St Faith's. "It is a hotbed of the African National Congress," they said.

This I frankly disbelieved, for the African National Congress was overtly political and anti-government. It was not long, however, before I discovered for myself that the leaders of the farm, including C.B., were indeed members of the ANC, and that anti-government political documents were being produced on the mission. This was, to say the least, an embarrassment, for it was assumed that I, as priest-in-charge, went along with the activities of the ANC. The fact was that the ANC was a legal organisation, and members of the mission were entitled to belong to it if they wished. But I myself had no intention of getting involved in Rhodesian politics.

One day a note was slipped under my door which stated: "Mr Joshua Nkomo will be speaking in the Community Centre this afternoon." Joshua Nkomo was, of course, the black nationalist leader. I had given no consent to this visit, and indeed had not been consulted about it. But news of it spread throughout the district, and I soon had some awkward questions to answer.

It was already clear that the farm ruled the roost and the priest-in-charge was not in charge at all: indeed he had little say. But this had long been the case, and it would presumably take time to get across the message that co-operation, so loudly preached, must now become a reality. I told the farm folk bluntly that I was no dictator but expected to be consulted.

A few nights later a group of Africans came to see me in our home after dark. They said they appreciated the efforts I was making to learn their language, and they spoke in Shona most of the time. Indeed they were not able to do anything else. The assertion frequently made by the farm staff that "nearly everyone speaks English" simply was not true.

The plea of my visitors was a simple and moving one. "We

want our mission back," was the substance of what they said. "We are grateful for the jobs provided by the farm, but that does not mean that we want to be ruled by the farm staff. Why is everything in the village committee done in English? Why cannot we speak our own language — and say what we really think? Why does the church have no say?" I explained that I had clear instructions from the bishop to back the farm. "Well, please tell the bishop that we want big changes. We cannot speak for ourselves for fear of losing our jobs." I said I would give the matter thought, but asked my visitors to remember that I was still very new.

After that several more groups came, always after dark, always speaking for the most part in Shona and always with the same message. I discussed the matter with Sister Esther and the other sisters, and asked their advice. "But that is how the people feel," they said. "And that is how we feel. We are all looking to you to give a lead."

"But the bishop . . ." I began.

"The bishop," said Sister Esther firmly, "must surely listen if you speak to him. It is up to you. We have tried to talk to him, but he brushes us off."

I put the position to the farm staff, who were frankly incredulous. They were busy planning an inter-racial conference on "Central Africa Past and Present" which would obviously have to be in English and which would bring people to St Faith's from all over the country. This, surely, could only be good. Next I wrote a careful letter to the bishop, describing the representations made to me by my African visitors and the sisters. His answer was terse: "People will always complain."

My own feeling was that probably no one had a monopoly of right in this matter, which needed time and prayer rather than precipitate action. Meanwhile I must get on with my priestly job. This was difficult, for the amount of administrative work was crippling. One morning, in a pile of correspondence and forms, I found five letters from Bishop Alderson — not all sent on the same day, but all requiring immediate replies. (There were letters from the diocesan secretary too.) The mission office and the mission secretary, one of the sisters, had been entirely taken over by the educational work, into whose vortex I would have been sucked myself had I not put up a frontal resistance. My answer to the problem of "admin" was to open a new mission office and to accept the unpaid secretarial services of Mrs Hilary Broderick, widow of one of the pioneer missionaries of the diocese.

Mrs Broderick was a wonder. Not only was she a highly competent shorthand-typist, but she could make up courteous and effective letters at a mere hint. When the bishop wrote to say that during the absence of leave of the schools-super-intendent I must take over his job I only had to say: "Tell him I am a priest and have no time." The letter she produced for my signature was sweetness itself, and did not at all represent my true feelings. She could, too, be quite ruthless with my own letters. When I got worked up about something she would say. "Purple passage. Cut." And cut it she did. She was always right.

It was probably due to the reason and moderation of Mrs Broderick's letters, and her experience of the psychology of bishops and diocesan officials, that the diocesan secretary wrote to me in December to say that the diocese was about to buy a four-wheel drive vehicle for the use of the clergy of St Faith's. This was an answer to prayer and meant that we could begin to tackle the real work.

Before Christmas Gladys and I toured the Chiduku African reserve, beyond Rusape, in the new vehicle. So atrocious were the roads that the twenty-mile journey from the town to our Holy Name Mission at Matsika took us well over an hour. Father Cyprian Tambo, who was waiting to greet us, was, technically, my assistant. In practice, he just got on with the job, consulting me at our occasional clergy meetings at St Faith's. (Father Demadema, in charge of the even more distant St Anne's Mission in the Wedza reserve, sensibly did the same.) Father Tambo was responsible for 43 schools as well as Holy Name Mission, and he did his job on a battered bicycle. He had learned his enthusiasm from the renowned poet-priest and ascetic, Arthur Shearley Cripps.

The church at Matsika was an enormous affair of brick and corrugated iron, which was packed to the doors for the Sung

104

Eucharist on Sunday. Then Gladys and I set off in the truck to visit some of the outstations in the reserve — places rejoicing in names such as Bvekerwa, Mutangavura, Tandi, Chitsva and Gundu — and stayed a night at each. We slept in trek-huts with scant thatch, and got thoroughly soaked.

On our way back to St Faith's we paid a short visit to the Makoni reserve which abutted on the mission lands. At most centres we received an enthusiastic welcome, but at a couple of stations agitators had been at work telling the elders that school fees must not be passed on to the central mission. In the circumstances it was a financial impossibility to keep the schools open, and the bishop had told me to close them. After fruitless meetings with the people I had done this, reaping much unpopularity as a result. One head teacher spat in my face! Now we walked into the middle of a church and schools boycott which took months to resolve.

Shortly after Christmas (which was celebrated with much fervour in all our churches) Guy Clutton-Brock left St Faith's, with his wife Molly. He had wanted to move on more than a year ago, feeling that he had established the work of the farm and could safely leave it to others. But he had been persuaded to stay until the new priest-in-charge came. He was respected even by those who disagreed with his policies, while Molly had done magnificent work in her Mukuwapasi Clinic for crippled children. She had trained an African nurse to follow her. The young white farm bursar took over as spokesman of the farm. He was a non-practising Baptist who openly scoffed at the Church.

*　　*　　*　　*

Meanwhile I had come to the conclusion that the best service I could render the mission was to grow out of my pidgin Shona and make some real progress in the language. I determined to abandon everything and spend a month at Nyakatsapa language school north of Umtali. Gladys came with me. But we were not there long.

At midnight on February 25th 1959 the Southern Rhodesian government declared a state of emergency, and within a few

105

hours the authorities had rounded up almost five hundred of the most active members of the African National Congress. These included John Mutasa and several other St Faith's people. (C.B. was arrested in Bulawayo a day later, the only European victim of the crackdown.) I could not believe my ears when the message reached me over the telephone. We got back to the mission as quickly as we could, though I decided to delay just long enough to prepare a talk to help reduce the tension.

After the return of Dr Hastings Banda in 1958 to neighbouring Nyasaland (later to become Malawi under his presidency) a huge agitation had begun in that country against the Central African Federation. Riots had broken out, police had been stoned and missions attacked. Apparently the African National Congress lay behind the trouble. The action of the Southern Rhodesian government was a pre-emptive move to prevent similar outbreaks within its territory. It ignored the fact that the ANC had not been banned in Southern Rhodesia, and that many of its members were moderate men.

At the mission the armed territorials had left by the time we arrived, but the place still swarmed with police. However, my speech pleading for calm was not necessary. There was much distress, but no trouble of any kind. My first job was to visit the families of those who had been arrested. The schools and the farm were already planning to carry on in spite of the loss of their leaders. The next day I went to Rusape to see the Native Commissioner and the police, who were apologetic about the whole thing but acting under orders. They readily agreed to keep off the mission unless and until I invited them in.

There followed days of letter-writing, public and private, and a visit to the detainees in Chikurubi gaol in Salisbury as soon as this was allowed. I saw everyone in Salisbury who I thought could help, though I had to be content to approach the Prime Minister, Sir Edgar Whitehead, by letter. I was not able to visit John Mutasa, who was detained at Bulawayo at the other end of the country. Needless to say, Bishop Alderson was loud in his protests, and much more influential.

The detainees were in fact released after a few weeks, in

106

response to a public outcry both in Rhodesia and Britain. But some of the protesters were more an embarrassment than a help, and put me in an acutely difficult position. The young farm bursar was in England during the troubles, and claimed that the government was trying to close St Faith's down — St Faith's being an inter-racial "co-operative farm and industrial community." "Europeans," he claimed, "have smashed the Africans' traditional way of life and given them nothing in its place." An organisation called the Africa Bureau held a public meeting in London, at which the bursar spoke. It issued a statement accusing the Rhodesian government of making "a frontal attack on one of the few places in the territory which is practising a real partnership between the races."

These statements were irresponsible and untrue: and though I had been consulted about none of them I was, as priest-in-charge of St Faith's, held accountable for them. I decided to react. In both the British and the Rhodesian press I made it abundantly plain that I deplored the action of the Southern Rhodesian government. St Faith's was *not* "a co-operative farm and industrial community," it was one of the oldest missions in the country, well able to speak for itself. The Europeans in Rhodesia were *not* smashing the Africans' way of life: they were specifically preserving it while also offering them both Christianity and a modern western lifestyle. St Faith's was *not* almost alone in practising racial partnership: other missions were doing that too. Our position was merely weakened by the laying of false charges against the government. It seemed to me that, however much one might support the inter-racial ideals of St Faith's mission farm, some curbs must be placed on its evident determination not only to speak and act for the mission but actually to take over its leadership.

Events denied me time to plan any strategy. By now Holy Week and Easter were upon us, and I was off to Matsika to help Father Tambo, leaving Father Musengezi and a new deacon to minister at St Faith's. At Matsika an enormous concourse of Christians camped round the mission from Good Friday till Easter Monday, and Father Tambo and I were busy not only with the services and the preaching but with many hours in the confessional. Even at St Faith's there were 400 communicants on Easter Day, and throughout the district it was apparent that the renewed efforts of the clergy were meeting with a growing response from the people. I needed all my time for my own job. At one outstation I discovered that the Christians had not been visited by a priest for three years.

After Easter the diocesan synod took place in Salisbury. At this the Dean of Salisbury, the Very Reverend Gonville ffrench-Beytagh, moved a resolution deploring the new repressive legislation being introduced by the Southern Rhodesian government. I seconded his resolution, and we were supported by a Queen's Counsel. But most of the Europeans present could not stomach overt opposition to the government, and the synod voted to "proceed to the next business." The debates were entirely in English, and some of the Africans had very little idea of what was going on.

Father ffrench-Beytagh, who was anything but a conservative, had earlier written in the English *Church Times* pointing out, in fairness, the difficulties the government faced. His words, and his resolution in the synod in spite of them, showed the immense difficulties facing Christians who tried to be just to both sides. "The vast majority of the population of the Federation, black and white," he wrote, "believes that the government acted rightly in proclaiming the state of emergency." "The relief of many Africans at the proclamation has been very evident." "It is the moderate African who has been threatened with injury to property and to person and with death because of his desire to co-operate with the Europeans, and it is for his benefit that many of the present regulations are designed." "The African National Congress has lost its high ideals and its leadership has become virulent and corrupt."

During my absence in Salisbury at the synod C.B. visited St Faith's without my knowledge, and this time his influence was not a moderating one. Before leaving for Salisbury I had sensed a softening on the part of the farm staff, giving hope of more co-operation in the future. On my return it seemed to me there was a perceptible hardening of attitudes, a yearning for the good old days when the church could safely be ignored.

I spent hours in discussions with the farm staff. No one was more reasonable than Patricia Chater, the farm-secretary, who was herself an Anglican. She did not budge, however, from her often stated position that much of the support in England for St Faith's "comes from people who are little interested in religion." "The continuance of this support depends on conformity with the African Development Trust's non-denominational policy. There can be no question as to the lines on which St Faith's must be developed."

The African Development Trust was the main source of the farm's finance. And its policies were not merely non-denominational: they had a strong political content. The real snag, however, was that word "must." St Faith's Mission and its priest-in-charge *must* conform. Final control was vested in an organisation outside the country which was little concerned with the furtherance of Christianity. This was the crux of the struggle which soon developed.

It did not take me long to discover that the African Development Trust had "invested" over £40,000 in the farm, which it could call back at any time. The diocese of Mashonaland was responsible for the whole sum, which could have bankrupted it. Even the bishop had little freedom of manoeuvre. His admiration for C.B. was unquestioned and sincere. But C.B. had in any case the whip hand.

From the farm bursar who was still in England I had already received a letter attacking my handling of St Faith's and indicating the line I must adopt. "The set-up in Rhodesia," he wrote, "is nearly 100% anti-christian and immoral . . . There can be no sitting on the fence for the Church in Rhodesia: it is either for the status quo or against."

It was this over-simplification that was the nub of the problem: the assumption that the farm people had a monopoly of truth and were entitled to control and speak for the rest of us. It seemed to me that most of the contending forces on the mission and in Rhodesia were represented by Christians of one sort or another. I was determined not to be committed politically till I had been in the country long enough to

109

understand the issues — though my hand had been forced on the state of emergency — and in this sense I could *not* support the farm any longer. I was prepared and anxious for give-and-take, but there had to be give as well as take.

Meanwhile, the sisters and a few other responsible members of the mission staff, white and black, had written independently to the bishop suggesting that it would be wise if the bursar did not return to St Faith's. How could you have a white missionary who openly derided the Church? Sparks were bound to fly, and it would be better to give the new priest-in-charge a chance to work for the unification of the whole mission.

The bishop saw the force of this argument, and was very nearly persuaded by it. He had not been at all happy to have his own position usurped by the bursar on the matter of detainees. In the event, however, he was talked over by C.B. and asked the young man to come back.

Sister Esther and her community, who were by far the most self-sacrificing Christians at St Faith's, were nearly in despair at what they saw as "a mission in chains." They felt their new priest had lost his opportunity and was bending over backwards, at the bishop's behest, to appease people who had scant concern for the Church. Many of the Africans felt the same way, and were preparing to adapt themselves to the restoration of the *ancien régime.* The new priest had, in their view, proved a broken reed.

Perhaps they were right. I had simply not realised how much hurt I had been inflicting on the sisters and the church-going Africans by what I thought was simple loyalty to a superior I had promised to obey — and an attempt to be reasonable with the representatives of "liberal" opinion.

The fact was that no one on the ecclesiastical mission at St Faith's had the slightest wish to control the farm and its farming operations. But we were all weary of being spoken for and dictated to by the farm-staff, whose primary interests appeared to be neither religious nor agricultural but political. Whether their politics were right or wrong was not the point. The fundamental issue was whether a Christian mission, which existed to spread the Gospel, was to be run by practising churchpeople or by men and women with very different concerns.

At the end of May I made up my mind, after much prayer, that the time for compromise was past. Either I should do my job and run St Faith's or I should get out. The question was: Ought I to resign and go back to England, or to take off the gloves and fight back? Gladys was pregnant, and I was unwilling to subject her to the unpleasantness from the farm which any stand for the Church would make inevitable.

"What do you want to do?" she asked.

"If I were alone I would see it through," I admitted.

Gladys paused only a moment before she said: "Fine. We'll stay."

We had not reckoned on the almost total commitment of Bishop Alderson to the other side.

7. The Struggle for St Faith's

IT WAS the farm side which opened the hostilities. One morning the bursar, back from England, walked into my office in a rage and poured out a flood of accusations about my alleged mishandling of St Faith's, and the people I was supposed to be persecuting. "You must go," he said, "before you can do any more harm." He went on for some time. The young man was determined to drive me out and leave the farm staff in total control.

Early in his outburst one of the teaching sisters walked in, having made an appointment to talk to me about schools. Seeing what was going on, she sat down and made notes! I could hardly imagine that they would be needed, so wild were the charges. Indeed the bursar admitted later that they were made simply to get rid of me. He ran out of steam in the end. I myself said nothing at all until he was quite finished. Then, after a long silence, I asked: "Will you go to Salisbury and tell all that to the bishop?" It seemed the most sensible way to dispose of a ludicrous incident. Nevertheless it was a mistake.

Shortly after my arrival at St Faith's folk from the farm had twice gone up to Salisbury to complain to Bishop Alderson about some arrangement or other that I had made, without first discussing the matter with me. On both occasions they had returned with a letter giving me instructions, my own side of the story having gone unheard. The letters were marked "Private and Confidential."

On the episode of the bursar it would obviously be impossible for the bishop to act in this way. There were dozens of witnesses of my every action at St Faith's, and indeed the

113

bishop himself had just visited the mission. It is true that after the Confirmation (there were 188 candidates) he had spent almost all his time with the farm staff, and neither the churchwardens nor the sisters had had any discussion with him. But he accompanied me to our big mission centres at Goto and Matsika, confirming 377 youngsters and adults at the first and 422 at the second. At Matsika over a thousand people crammed into the church or stood outside. It must have been apparent to him that the clergy were doing their job and were getting a response.

However, the young bursar duly went to Salisbury, and his return was followed within a day by a letter from the bishop. I could not believe my eyes as I read it. He had swallowed the lot! "You are mishandling St Faith's in every department of personal relations, African and European alike, so badly that they are getting worse day by day."

I was offered the choice of resigning immediately or being given till Easter to clear up the mess. The letter was marked, inside and out, "Personal and Confidential." When I had recovered from my anger (which was only after a visit to church) I tried to make a plan. I wrote a conciliatory letter to the bishop, asking him to reconsider what he had written and suggesting that he might have been misled. This produced a furious response. It began: "The increasing complacency of your communications . . . " Plainly the clergy did not usually stand up to him, even politely!

It seemed to me that this nonsense must somehow be stopped. Over the months I had repeatedly queried with the bishop his demands for confidentiality, pointing out that "the truth will stand the light." I had never actually said: "I have nothing to hide. Have you?" But he must have known that that was my feeling. Now I decided to ignore the demand for confidentiality. I took the letter proposing my resignation along to the churchwardens (one was black and the other white) and to Sister Esther.

The result was immediate and electric, and never had I seen such anger amongst the churchpeople. A delegation went up to Salisbury the following weekend consisting of the other clergy and the wardens, three of the sisters and almost the entire mission staff. It protested to the bishop in the strongest terms, and was given a far-from-friendly reception. It then demanded the dismissal of the bursar without delay, and, when the bishop demurred, threatened the resignation of all the Europeans serving the church and schools — apart from the sisters, who were under religious obedience to their Superior. Finally the bishop, a very unhappy man, capitulated, obviously unconvinced. The bursar disappeared from the scene, with much consequent distress among the farm's staff and overseas supporters.

*　*　*　*

John Mutasa took over as spokesman for the farm as well as its leader, and it was not long before his first salvo was fired across the bows of the mission. Father Musengezi was moving to Chiduku to take over from Father Tambo, and the church council was organising a farewell party for this much-loved priest. A boycott was proclaimed in the three villages on the mission. However, a larger-than-expected crowd turned up on the day, and the party was an uproarious success.

Meanwhile my refusal to resign had provoked furious thought among the leading figures of the diocese in Salisbury. For a long time there had been plans to make the farm into an independent co-operative or company, and none of us had any objection to these provided they left the ecclesiastical mission free to do its work. The practical difficulties, however, were considerable. I was not invited to take part in the discussions in Salisbury.

Bishop Alderson paid another visit to St Faith's towards the end of September, specifically to sort out the future of the farm. This time the churchpeople were determined to be heard, and the African clergy together with the wardens and the sisters organised a day and night prayer vigil in church to this end. Its results were not immediately evident, for the bishop, as on previous occasions, spent almost all his time with the farm staff. On this occasion he had, of course, the justification that he had come to deal with the farm and not the mission. The churchpeople had, however, kept their

115

powder dry. They had drawn up a petition to the bishop asking him to give them a hearing.

It was, I think, on a Monday evening that the worst happened. The bishop called an unscheduled meeting of everyone at St Faith's. He began it by publicly tearing up the churchpeople's petition, unread. It then went on, hour after hour, till nearly midnight, with the farm people being given unfettered freedom to attack. The tirades came tumbling over one another from all sides. A small, well-organised and vociferous band had demanded and planned the meeting, and were baying for blood. They almost chanted: "Father must go." Both the African churchpeople and the European made efforts to intervene, but were silenced. I was thankful that Mrs Broderick, realising what was going to happen, had insisted that Gladys stay at home.

Only after a sleepless night did I hear the reactions of the horrified churchpeople. "A wolf-pack," said some. "They wanted a crucifixion," commented another. News of the meeting spread like wildfire throughout the countryside and even among the local Europeans. Only one thing was obvious. This was the end. The bishop wanted me out, and I would have to go. Apart from anything else, Gladys was nearing her time. She needed peace. We decided to stay till the St Faith's Day festival, in a week or so's time. Meanwhile the bishop realised he had gone too far, and that he was likely to face a backlash both white and black. He wrote me a private apology, which was without effect simply because it was private.

Both the bishop and John Mutasa and his friends had, in fact, overreached themselves. And the ordinary African Christians throughout the district took advantage of the St Faith's Day festival to show their feelings and demonstrate their confidence in the mission. They would have come to the festival from the outstations in bus-loads anyway. But this year they came in dozens of bus-loads, and the hymn-singing and the school-bands and the popular rejoicings were on a greater scale than ever. The crowds were so great that the Solemn Eucharist had to be held out of doors, and for the first time we imported loudspeakers to reach the outer fringes

116

of the congregation. Canon Chipunza, an old and much respected priest from Umtali, was the preacher. In an astonishing feat of spontaneous oratory, which obviously came from his heart, he threw down the gauntlet to the bishop and challenged the people to come out into the open and support the church, the mission and their priest. He was fêted afterwards.

"I don't think we can leave after that," said Gladys. "Bishop or no bishop, we can't let all those people down."

On November 23rd 1959 our daughter was born. A smiling fair-haired child, she gave us much joy during a time which otherwise was far from pleasant. We called her Margaret Faith, and she was baptised by Father Musengezi.

Some sort of balance was now restored between the mission and the farm, though the struggle was not over. By this time, however, the diocese had made the fateful decision to re-establish its control over the farm, which was running at a serious financial loss. The decision of the Diocesan Standing Committee, including its African members, was unanimous.

It was before the end of November that Willie van Zyl arrived to take over the management of the farm from John Mutasa. Willie, an Afrikaner, had been a member of the Dutch Reformed Church and a farmer in South Africa. He felt so strongly against *apartheid*, and was so keen to win a fair deal for the Africans, that he had abandoned his own Church and become an Anglican. He was about to train for the Anglican priesthood, but had meantime offered his agricultural services to the diocese of Mashonaland. The hope was that he would be able to make the farm economically viable and would help to heal the breach between church and farm. However, the remaining white members of the farm staff put in their resignations.

For a time there was sullen resentment amongst some of the Africans on the farm, but there was evident satisfaction amongst others. The latter seemed to be the majority, for after Christmas crowds of villagers, finding that the restraints of the past had disappeared, got up a big freedom procession and went round the villages singing hymns and freedom songs.

*   *   *   *

When the news broke of the diocesan take-over of the farm
the expected hubbub broke out in the newspapers in England
and in Rhodesia. "The End of Multiracial Experiment,"
screamed one headline. "Multi-Race Farm Abolished,"
shouted another. "Vow Broken" and "Partnership Smashed." There was much more in the same vein. I wrote as
prolifically in reply as the farm folks wrote in protest, forgetting that these newspaper storms blow over very quickly.

In any case the Africans had by now made the wordy battle
their own. Six of them got together, taking no advice from
any European, and wrote to the English *Church Times* a letter
which was published in January 1960 under the heading:
"Africans Now Speak for Themselves." Their English was
imperfect, and in criticising Guy Clutton-Brock and John
Mutasa they did not use the restraint which courtesy might
have suggested. "The people of St Faith's," they wrote, "are
now the happiest people in Southern Rhodesia, since Mr
Clutton-Brock and Mr Mutasa left. When they say St Faith's
Farm is now dominated by whites, it is untrue. It is *vice-versa*.
There were six Europeans on the Farm side, while to-day
there is only one. All five Europeans are replaced by Africans
. . . Partnership has been practised since the foundation of
the Mission in 1896." The six signatories included Job Kekana
the well-known sculptor, a headman, a churchwarden who
had lived at St Faith's since its beginning and some ordinary
workpeople. (Job Kekana was by now the chief spokesman
of the African churchpeople.) All these had a hard time when
their letter was seen by the farm people, and Bishop Alderson
wrote to the *Church Times* dissociating himself from their
views.

C.B. joined the battle but was despatched pithily in the
English *Observer* by Mr Gibson Mandaza. "Sir," (wrote the
latter) "You report Mr Guy Clutton-Brock as saying that the
Agricultural Committee of Mashonaland Diocese, which has
taken over St Faith's Mission Farm, is 'composed entirely of
Europeans.' I am a member of this committee, and an
African." On the other side a certain S.J. Khamba, writing

118

from St Faith's in the *Church Times*, attacked the six and extolled the farm as it had been run in the past. "Dictatorship has now in fact come to St Faith's. The Africans at St Faith's are now the unhappiest in the colony." The writer's excellent English suggested that he had had European help, and we were all baffled to know who S.J. Khamba was. Ultimately we discovered he was a school-boy of indifferent English who stayed at St Faith's during the holidays.

Meanwhile a concerted counter-attack from the farm was being mounted. It was directed initially against old Benjamin Mutseriwa, the saintly African churchwarden who had lived his whole life on the mission and who had signed the first *Church Times* letter. With the encouragement of the clergy he had applied to become a sub-deacon, in order to administer Holy Communion. Following Church of England custom, however, a formal *Si quis* had to be read out in church, giving anyone who objected the opportunity to allege an impediment. John Mutasa and his two friends, James Makoni and Nathan Machiha, did exactly that. What they wrote to the bishop I do not know, for it would have been impossible to find a more innocent old man than Benjamin. But the bishop ruled that he must wait six months before becoming a sub-deacon. He put up with the delay very humbly. However, the ultimate object of the new campaign was, of course, myself.

As the church had continued to lose its grip on the mission in 1959, sexual immorality in the mission villages had assumed new and alarming proportions. One father had beaten his wayward daughter, assuming it was a waste of time to bring her to the obviously helpless clergy. And a young man called Thomas deflowered the daughter of one of the priests. Thomas was to become a prominent parliamentarian of the future Zimbabwe, but we could not know that. I learned locally that he was a trouble-maker and had been dismissed from St Faith's by the former bursar. Since he was neither a tenant nor an employee he had no title to live on the mission.

Thomas wanted to marry the girl, and this seemed right. However, she was a trained nurse and a brilliant member of a brilliant family. Her father was totally opposed to the marriage, and according to the African custom of those days the father had the last word. But Thomas had no intention of submitting to African custom. He went up to Salisbury to appeal to the bishop, and came back with a very reasonable letter suggesting that neither the father nor I had any right to stand in the way of the marriage. Since the young people were of age the bishop was plainly right. Both the girl's father and I accepted this, though the former reluctantly.

Thomas seemed to think he had won some kind of victory over the clergy, and was now entitled to live on the mission and to have direct access to the bishop at will. He returned to St Faith's early in the new year, and made so much trouble that Willie van Zyl and I asked him to leave within six months at the latest. I checked this action with the archdeacon first, and informed the bishop. Thomas, however, immediately went off to Salisbury to appeal to the latter, and was at once received.

The following morning Gladys and I had planned a day-off in Umtali to celebrate Gladys's birthday. As we were about to leave the telephone rang, and it was the bishop in a high temper. He reeled off a series of charges brought by Thomas, starting with the supposed dimissal of a tenant and continuing with the allegation that I had sent Thomas away with a day's notice. I felt it was pointless to state the facts of the case, which everybody knew. The episode spoiled Gladys's birthday outing, and when we got back Thomas was waiting with the expected letter ruling that he should not be removed from the mission without episcopal consent.

A few days later I myself was due to have an interview with the bishop for which, unlike Thomas, I had had to wait a couple of months. Gladys and I went to the capital on the motorbike.

This time I was determined to speak privately but firmly about conduct which I believed was palpably unjust, unworthy of a bishop and calculated to make the work of any priest-in-charge impossible. However, I was forestalled. The bishop motioned me to a chair, and handed me a letter. It was a demand for my resignation, stating simply that the job was too much for me.

120

I had long ago lost my sense of humour, but was in no mood for capitulation. I said "No," adding however that I would welcome a public dismissal. Before returning to the mission Gladys and I went to see the Dean, who shared our astonishment. In the end he said: "Forget it. The old man has had a black-out. I will talk to him."

By this time I knew that support for the line I had taken at St Faith's was not confined to the mission: it was countrywide. The bishop would not dare to sack me. But, as my old mother used to say: "There are more ways of killing a cat than choking it with cream." And the Mutasa band did not give up easily. The sequel to this encounter was so bizarre that I would not dare to commit it to paper if detailed records from the time did not still survive. I have them before me as I write.

On March 4th 1960, Bishop Alderson of Mashonaland (who had also lost his sense of humour) wrote:

My dear Lewis,

I have received a formal complaint from some of your congregation at St Faith's, which says: —

'On Sunday, February 14th 1960 during Mass at St Faith's Church the Revd A.R. Lewis, giving the sermon to the congregation, said that there were three devils at St Faith's who were doing Satan's work and working against the Church.

'Soon after Mass Fr Lewis told James Makoni, in front of some of the men, that he was one of the devils referred to during his sermon, and that the other two were John Mutasa and Nathan Machiha.'

The bishop wrote that he was not anxious to hold a public inquiry, but that I should interview the persons concerned in the presence of the churchwardens who should then submit a report to him!

My reply was succinct: "I did not make any reference to three devils in my sermon on February 14th. At the time I did not even know the Shona word for devils." Since I was accustomed to preach only from notes I could not reproduce the precise words I had used on the work of Satan: but there was a churchful of Africans who could witness to what I had *not* said.

Unhappily the bishop was determined to pursue the matter, so I contacted the Dean and Canon Pat Mason of Mandea Mission, both of whom were on the cathedral chapter. The chapter was the only body constitutionally able to tender advice to the bishop unasked. My belief was that it might use a little ridicule.

But I was trapped again. Early in April the bishop paid a visit to the mission to meet with the tenants and describe the diocese's plans for the future of the farm. When he had completed his business he suddenly announced an inquiry into the question of the three devils, to be preceded by prayer! The complainants were called, together with the African clergy, the churchwardens and, it seemed, Uncle Tom Cobleigh and all. What followed was a re-run of the meeting last year at which a handful of malcontents were given free rein. The main accusation, about my sermon, was discredited immediately, owing to the testimony of all the witnesses in church. But the complainants were allowed to shift their ground to events outside the church, where I had no witnesses. After some hours the "inquiry" was left in the air without any finding.

This time neither Gladys nor I had any thought of giving up. We would stay put, come what may, till the mission could be a real mission and the church could do its job freely. The bishop was not God. The cathedral chapter took no formal action, but its members made their feelings so abundantly clear to the bishop privately that there was no further episcopal harassment.

By this time Holy Week and Easter were upon us again, and I threw myself into a two-week trek, preaching the gospel of the Cross. (Gladys could not come, of course, but she was surrounded by friends.) This made our problems seem rather trivial. Everywhere there were crowds who wanted to hear the Easter message. And when I got back to St Faith's it was plain that there had been a reaction to the recent inquisition. The churchpeople were weary of agitators and the mission

122

was back in business in a big way — in the business of bringing men and women to God.

The three devils were finally laid to rest after an active life of over two months. "My dear Lewis," the bishop wrote at the end of April. "I accept your assurance that you did not use the words 'Three Devils' in February and there is no reliable evidence that you did." There was no apology. I think it was Mrs Broderick — or it may have been Sister Esther — who said: "I wonder if the angels are laughing or crying?"

Shortly after all this a general consensus was reached that the peace of St Faith's would best be achieved by having a village committee which genuinely and indisputably spoke for the African people who lived on the mission. If the stranglehold of the farm had gone, we certainly had no wish to restore the rule of the clergy. An election was held — for the first time by secret ballot — and Job Kekana came out on top and became the first chairman of the committee. Four of the six signatories of the *Church Times* letter were elected, but none of the Mutasa group. It was a convincing demonstration of the real feelings of the ordinary people. Almost the first decision of the new committee was to conduct its business in Shona, not English.

*   *   *   *

It was at about this time that, in the course of my treks, I discovered two people who turned back the pages of history and told of how the mission had started and what it was for. One of these was old Lilian Changadzo, widow of the African martyr Bernard Mizeki. I had visited Bernard's shrine near Marandellas, where to this day huge crowds gather annually to pay tribute to the first Christian in Mashonaland to give his life for Christ. He died in 1896, murdered on his own tiny mission because he stayed at his post and refused to flee to safety during a rebellion. It was his witness, surviving and growing after his death, that made possible the foundation of St Faith's and the heroic missionary years that followed. The second voice from the past was that of John Kapuya, still a sprightly old man with many a story to tell. He had been

Bernard Mizeki's earliest Christian convert, the first of the many thousands who crowded our churches today. I learned that as early as 1920 2,000 Christians had gathered at the mission for the St Faith's Day festival.

Somehow, in the more than sixty years of the mission's history, things had gone wrong. The vision had been lost. Success and numbers were part of the problem, as was our heavy responsibility for education. Guy Clutton-Brock's experiment was another part. As C.B. and his friends strove to build the paradigm of a better Rhodesia, they had no direct intention to destroy the old mission and its faith. But, because their ideological commitment was primary, this was one of the practical effects. Could we, even at this late hour, get it right? Could we find a way of keeping what was good in the farm, while leaving the church and mission free to carry on the work of Bernard Mizeki and John Kapuya?

The answer was "No." And that was the tragedy of St Faith's. We never found the *modus vivendi* which would have enabled both parties to give of their best. In what finally happened at St Faith's I had no part at all, not having been included in the discussions at diocesan level. The lands were sold to the government, on the strict understanding that the Africans living on them were to enjoy them in perpetuity. The overseas investors were paid off. Part of the land became a "Native Purchase Area," where the tenants could run their own small farms — forming a co-operative or not as they wished — and part became ordinary tribal land. No one had to leave, and the African people were free of any domination by either the mission or the farm. On the part of most of them there was relief or outright delight, for, at last, people were at liberty to live their own lives. And the churchpeople and the mission staff were as happy as everyone else. The central mission-station — the church and convent and schools and hospital — was retained for St Faith's Mission under the authority of the diocese. It occupied an area of a hundred acres, out of the original twelve thousand, but this land was all we needed for our missionary job. It was my own wish to remain at St Faith's to help heal the wounds and build the future. But this was not to be.

My friend Canon Pat Mason, priest-in-charge of the fledgling Mandea Mission in the Honde Valley, had come to my aid in the corridors of diocesan power more than once during the struggle for St Faith's. Now he had been made archdeacon of a new area of which St Faith's was the effective centre. The job could not be done from the remote Honde Valley, and he proposed an exchange. My heart sank at the prospect of yet another move after only two years — how on earth could a mission-priest do his job if never allowed to stay put? — but he had won the bishop's backing. That was the end of the matter. In any case, after my initial taste of the methods of African nationalism, nothing could have suited me more than the last of the big old-style rural missions of Mashonaland. There, at least, a mission-priest could do his work without having to battle with politicians and look over his shoulder to a monarchical prelate in Salisbury.

Gladys and I left St Faith's at the end of June, when the mission had settled down to its new life and no one could say we were being pushed out. The Archbishop of Central Africa paid a very splendid visit to the mission, setting the seal of the Church's approval on the new dispensation. A small group of women came to our home with presents a few days before we left, and knelt as was the custom of the Mashona on such occasions. Their leader said simply: "Thank you, Father. We are glad C. B. brought our menfolk back. But we did not want to lose our mission. Now we are very happy."

The church was crowded for our farewell service, and afterwards we were overwhelmed with thanks and gifts. As we were getting into the car the crowd began to re-assemble on the lawn, singing hymns. Our last recollections of St Faith's were the strains of "Onward Christian Soldiers" in Shona and the pungent scent of the eucalyptus trees as we crossed the Jordan on a chilly winter's day.

*   *   *   *

For Gladys and me that was not the end of the story of St Faith's. It was Bishop Alderson's custom to do his correspondence by dictating into a dictaphone. (His secretary once typed a letter about "the sauce of temptation," instead of "the source of temptation".) Sometimes he would talk into his machine late into the night. On one occasion he had burst out, in the middle of a letter: "My dear Lewis, you may be right about the whole thing. But I don't think you are."

Of course, none of us had always been right about the whole thing. However, for me the principle was fundamental that a Christian mission should be run by Christians whose first concern was the furtherance of Christianity. In later years the bishop's attitude, happily, underwent a total change. Like us, he had to learn from experience in a new country. He learned that Rhodesia was not the South Africa where he had previously served. Freed from the enormous pressures to which he had been subjected, which at one stage brought him to the verge of a nervous breakdown, he saw very clearly what the churchpeople at St Faith's had been fighting for, and he respected us for standing up to him. Indeed respect on both sides led to understanding and something akin to friendship. The past was buried. The bishop destroyed the whole correspondence of the years of controversy which I, perhaps perversely, pushed into an old tin trunk which survived our many travels. On our visits to Salisbury Gladys and I (and Margaret Faith) frequently stayed with him at Bishop's Mount outside the city. In 1966 he made me Archdeacon of Inyanga. It was the first and only occasion I have ascended the ecclesiastical ladder!

At the beginning of 1968 it happened that Gladys and I were in Salisbury, lying low for a few days. The bishop discovered our whereabouts and called me to see him. His face was white. "What are we to do?" he said, and poured out the story of one misfortune after another on the African missions. He had had, at last, to face the fact that his policy of over-rapid Africanisation throughout the diocese had been a failure. Men were cracking under the strain of enormous responsibilities. Unaccustomed as he was to seeking counsel from any but his official advisers, who were scant help in a matter such as this, he nevertheless asked me what I thought should be done.

126

I had enough experience of African mission-work to be able to make a realistic and practical suggestion, and he listened intently. "Surely," I said, "there is still room for a white Director of Missions? But now perhaps it should be someone without authority: someone to whom priests can go privately for help and advice, but who cannot sack them or move them — and who will not talk about them even to you." He thought long. At last he said: "You are right. I will see what can be done." We shook hands as I left. "Yes, he said, "I believe you are right."

The next week he flew to Johannesburg with a health problem of which few of us had known. A few days later he died suddenly, at the age of 68, of a heart-attack. We had lost a friend. May God rest his soul.

8. Adventures in the Honde Valley

THE tropical downpours which for weeks had blotted out the country round Mandea slackened before Christmas 1960, and Christmas Day broke dry and cloudless. By early afternoon, the last of my three services over, Petronella and I were bouncing and lurching along the rocky track back to St Peter's Mission. Petronella, christened by Father Pat Mason, was the mission Landrover, and an archetypal boneshaker.

St Peter's was silent now, after the crowds of the morning. Tired, I looked forward to a quiet evening with Gladys and baby Margaret and to a traditional Christmas dinner. After a couple of mince-pies, my first food that day, I prepared to light the lamps before dusk. It was then that we heard the chug-chug. The sound got louder: chug-chug-chug. Puzzled, we went to the door to look. It was a tractor and trailer, and it did not stop until it had reached our bamboo gate.

The woman it brought was a hideous sight: fat and fleshy, but with her flesh torn to ribbons. "What . . . ?" I began, forgetting the usual greetings. "It was a crocodile," the people with her explained. "She was wading the Honde River." I shuddered, for I had done that myself in the course of my job.

Within moments Gladys was at work. She cleaned and treated the wounds, injected morphia and swathed the woman in bandages. But Mandea had no hospital, and the victim had scant hope of survival without a doctor. That meant Doctor Denys Taylor at Bonda Mission, forty-five miles away up in the hills.

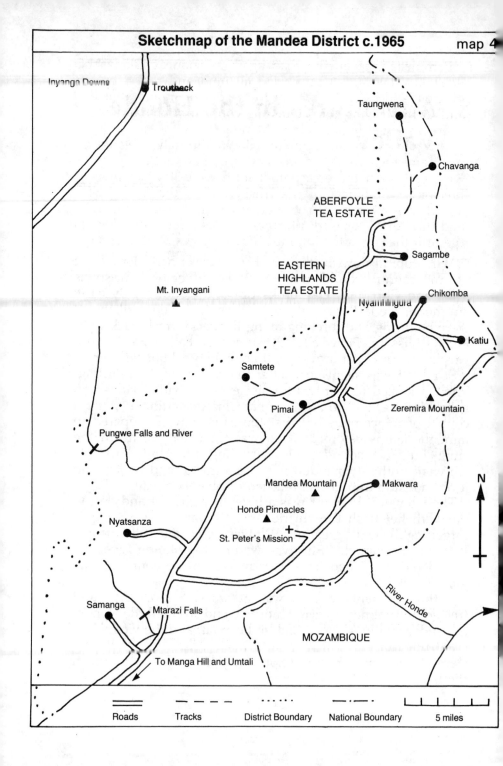

map 4

Sketchmap of the Mandea District c.1965

Inyanga Downs

Troutback

Taungwena

Chavanga

ABERFOYLE
TEA ESTATE

Sagambe

EASTERN
HIGHLANDS
TEA ESTATE

Chikomba

Mt. Inyangani

Nyamhingura

Katiu

Samtete

Pimai

Zeremira Mountain

Pungwe Falls and River

Mandea Mountain

Makwara

Honde Pinnacles

N

Nyatsanza

St. Peter's Mission

Samanga

Mtarazi Falls

River Honde

MOZAMBIQUE

To Manga Hill and Umtali

| Roads | Tracks | District Boundary | National Boundary | 5 miles |

Petronella was on the road again as soon as Gladys had finished. The earth tracks were all mud and rocks, but the menfolk and I got the patient to the doctor, hours after dark and in the driving rain. Our one concern after handing her over was to get back safely to Mandea.

The rain was now tumbling down through a blanket of mist, and the "roads" were more treacherous than ever. As we crept down the escarpment into our valley, an invisible precipice within feet of the truck, one of the men walked ahead with a torch. At the bottom the road was a quagmire, and the "drift" or ford a torrent. It was a few miles beyond the drift that my attention must have wandered momentarily. I was exhausted. The truck slid gently over into the ditch.

How many hours we laboured to get it out I do not know. The men were as unhurried as they were indefatigable, but they succeeded at last. We were back at the mission by one o'clock in the morning of Boxing Day. Gladys, of course, had waited up, and Margaret was asleep in her cot.

Neither of us had any thought of Christmas dinner now: only a cup of tea and bed. But hardly a quarter of an hour later there was a hammering at the door and the Shona cry for admission: "Go-go-go." It was a woman who had been bitten by a snake, and Gladys dared not leave her till dawn. Shortly after that the first of the day's patients began to arrive, though everyone knew that Boxing Day was a holiday and our little clinic was supposed to be closed.

The crocodile victim survived, thanks to a dedicated mission-doctor who worked through much of Christmas night. We never heard from her again, and I do not know her name. But word got round that Christianity is about helping people in trouble.

*　　*　　*　　*

We had arrived at Mandea in September 1960, Gladys and I and Margaret Faith. Shortly after we had left St Faith's Mission our truck ground to a halt with a screech and a groan. The rear axle of the four-wheel-drive vehicle had broken, and we had to limp back to St Faith's to hire another truck and a driver. This meant, however, that as we descended into the Honde Valley I had a much better view than I could have had behind the wheel, my eyes glued to the deteriorating roads.

Even in the blazing sunlight the "road" down the escarpment, cut out of the mountain-side, was so rough and narrow as to be barely practicable. Fortunately we met no other vehicle. Hair-pin bend followed hair-pin bend, and, half way down, one of our wheels slipped over the edge of the escarpment. The mishap was not serious, and the driver was able to reverse to safety. We descended nearly four thousand feet, from the cool high-veld into a shimmering furnace.

The panorama was spectacular, and beautiful beyond description. To the north the Mtarazi Falls tumbled 2,500 feet from the blue Inyanga Mountains to the floor of the valley. Eastwards the Honde River wound glinting like a snake through the rain-forest. In the middle view, towering above the gorge, was a giant rock-formation known as the Honde Pinnacles or the Virgin Rocks. The furthest of these had an uncanny likeness to the Virgin and Child: it seemed to claim the valley for Christ long before any church was built beneath it. St Peter's Mission lay between the pinnacles and the river — the latter being the eastern boundary of the country, beyond which lay Mozambique and the Indian Ocean.

At the bottom of the hill we left the "main road" leading to the tea estates for a loop which proved the merest track: the Mandea road. There were little thatched villages deep in the forest and among the clumps of bamboo, and from these the children ran out laughing and waving to us. "A good omen," said our driver.

The mission lay between two gullies on the rocky lower slopes of Mandea Mountain, above a group of tin-roofed stores and a primitive village. There were a couple of thatched classrooms, some new school buildings going up and a shelter of poles and grass which served as a church. Our future home was the mission-house, a white rectangular bungalow built by Father Pat Mason on the hillside below a forest of loquat trees. The garden was ablaze with white lilies, agapanthus and multi-coloured bougainvillaea. Father Pat and his wife

Estelle had moved into this house two years ago before the doors were on, and had been visited by a lion — the last to be seen in the valley. We saw its paw-marks in the cement floor. Pat had earned himself immortality by shooting it.

The school was on holiday when we arrived, and there was only one teacher and a few elders to greet us. But on Sunday morning it was a different story. The teacher and I shovelled out the cow-pats from under the grass shelter and carried in a school table for use as an altar. We had scarcely finished when the Christians from the whole countryside began to stream up the road to the "church." After the service the singing and dancing to welcome us went on for much of the day.

Gladys and I and Margaret were the only white people in the area, and the mission was twelve miles from the nearest telephone. But we never experienced any fear. We soon got used again to tropical conditions, to the whine of mosquitoes in the evening, to the shrilling of cicadas in the trees, to the clatter of bush-babies on the roof. Hyenas howled mournfully in the forest at night. When the rain came roaring through the valley the thunder was like the crack of doom. And there were flying ants and flying beetles and hornets and green (but innocent) praying mantises. One day a snake got into baby Margaret's nursery, and was quickly despatched. Shortly afterwards Margaret was stung by a scorpion, the most painful and dangerous of the insects. Gladys was there and sucked out the poison, and she came to no harm. Throughout our years at Mandea we had no doubt at all that we were looked after. Gladys was often left alone for days on end as I trekked to the furthest corners of the district.

Trekking, on foot or in the Landrover, was almost my whole work, for the scattered churches needed services and the schools in the bush had to be supervised. The outstations varied from a couple founded years ago by the Fathers at Penhalonga Mission — well established with their crowded little churches and schools — to isolated spots where a priest had occasionally taken a service for a handful of Christians.

Pimai was one of the latter. Father Mason had been accustomed to celebrate the eucharist there out of doors under the

133

shadow of a big rock near the Pungwe River: you could hear the roar of the torrent. I determined to do the same and sent a message to the local Christian elder suggesting a date and time. Edgar, the mission clerk, accompanied me, and I set up my altar, a folding card-table, and unpacked the church box. No one came. After waiting an hour or two I said to Edgar: "We'll carry on. At least we can pray for the people who haven't come."

Two mournful cows turned up in the course of the service. Three donkeys joined them at the end. The elder arrived when it was all over, apparently just to say "hello." We agreed to try again next week, and in the meantime he was to spread the word among the few Christians in the area. He didn't, and the turn-out was much the same, with the addition of a solitary woman. Again the elder appeared at the end, with the excuse, this time, that there was a funeral. It took me a year to collect a congregation of a dozen at Pimai — by then all human!

Near to the big rock was a crossing-place where people waded the Pungwe, a bigger river even than the Honde. Beyond this, I learned, was our "school" at Samtete, a mere shelter where nothing any longer happened. The crossing-place looked terrifying, but if Father Mason could manage it so could I. A few days later I sent a message to the elder at Samtete asking for carriers, and a helper from Mandea and I were there at one o'clock, the appointed time. No one appeared.

At three o'clock a man arrived from the opposite direction, on his way up to Samtete. "The children came down this morning with Satea," he said. Satea was the Samtete church elder. "It was about ten o'clock. But you weren't here, and they went back." This was beyond belief. No African in this part of the world was ever early. It was equally unthinkable that people should refuse to wait if the priest were held up — which in this case had not happened. I asked the man to take a message up to the elder, saying we were waiting at the crossing.

It was dusk when Satea turned up with a group of children as carriers. I was helped through the flood, and dried off as best I could in the gathering chill. "What happened?" I asked. The elder hesitated, but a whiff of his breath told me the story. He had come down early in order to hasten back to a beer-drink, and temptation had prevailed. However, with the aid of hurricane lamps and grass flares, and lusty singing by the children to drive away the animals, we stumbled our way through the forest and up the mountain. We reached the thatched "school" within an hour.

It had no doors and the windows, of course, had no glass. And it was cold. But there was nowhere else for me to put up my camp-bed. In the morning they told me that there had been a leopard about in the night, but by that time the matter was of merely academic interest. After I had celebrated the eucharist for the few Christians who appeared the elder accompanied me up and down the hill paths to the villages of the others. Many of them had lapsed into polygamy.

Satea's was a simple story. It really was not practicable to spread Christianity without a school. People longed for a school, and looked to the mission to make one possible. It was the key to a better future for the children. The parents were not, most of them, going to abandon the ancient ways, but they knew that a new world was opening up for the young — at least for those who could get into it. But the Samtete children couldn't. Year after year the Native Education Department had rejected our application for a school, and it might be a decade or more before so remote a place, inaccessible by road, came up for approval. The people were disappointed, angry and embittered. And they blamed our mission.

The Native Education Department's regulations prohibited all but officially approved government-aided schools, and its considerable efforts to approve new schools were strangled by a financial strait-jacket. In practice this meant that in all the primitive area north of the Pungwe River (which was quite different from most of the country) no child could set foot on even the lowest rung of the educational ladder. Worse, it meant that the Department had in practice a near-total stranglehold on the evangelisation of the area.

This, to my mind, would not do. I paid several visits to

135

Umtali, seventy miles away, and consulted officials of the Education Department. Their reply was always the same. Every application was considered annually, and if there were a strong case would be successful in due course. The officials were bound by the rules, and no one could jump the queue. No, we could not attempt an unofficial school of our own. Experience had shown that we would never have enough money, and sooner rather than later the problem would land up on the Department's door-step, demanding cash which it hadn't got.

The logic of all this was unquestionable. But so was my responsibility to get Christian work going amongst the people of Samtete. The Department's inspectors were Christian men themselves and were not unsympathetic: but they felt they could not budge.

I saw no alternative to writing to the press and getting a public debate going on government control of Christian missionary work. The inspectors in Umtali did not like it, nor did their superiors in Salisbury. And the diocesan authorities were annoyed because I had by-passed their bureaucracy. But the headquarters of the Native Education Department in Salisbury, while not yielding an inch, got the message that here was a huge backward area where the provision of schools was hopelessly inadequate. The possibility that the country north of the Pungwe might be given special consideration was put on the agenda.

In this lonely area Samtete was not the only place where urgent action was needed if Christianity were to gain a foot-hold. There was Katiu, and there was Chavanga. If I had not believed in God's guidance I would have thought that I stumbled on Katiu almost by accident. One of our two tiny official schools north of the Pungwe was at a place called Chikomba, deep in the forest. The teachers did what church work was practicable, with only occasional visits from the priest.

The nearest way to Chikomba from St Peter's was to cross the Pungwe several miles downstream in a dug-out canoe and complete the journey on foot. Kenneth Ndhlovu, the head teacher, met me, and the following morning, before

136

Salisbury, Rhodesia — renamed Harare, in the country now known as Zimbabwe

St Peter's Mission, Mandea, Inyanga,
celebrating its 10th anniversary on
September 28th 1968

Mr Clifford Dupont attended the Holy
Communion Service conducted by
Archdeacon Arthur Lewis

*In my usual attire
for the African scene*

Gladys at work in 1964

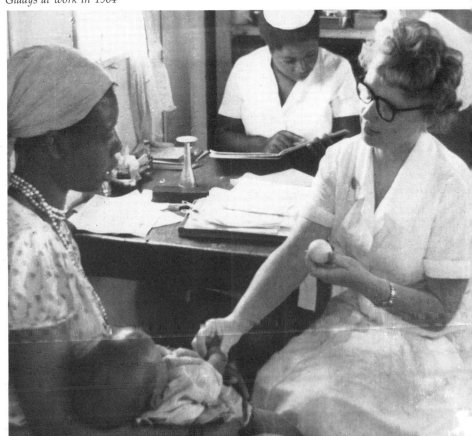

The joyous African look at Mandea in 1964, before the reign of terror

Priest's house at Kihurio in 1953

Bishop Alderson's visit to Mandea for the dedication of the new church on May 30th 1966

The Service with music at St Peter's Mission on September 28th 1968

The mission office, which served as a clinic in the early years

A festival at St Peter's Mission, Mandea, Inyanga, July 7th 1966

*The church at Msalabani
(Magila) in 1948*

Motorcycling in the bush in 1957

*After the terror: the priest of Mandea
Mission surveys his home*

The Honde massacre December 19th 1976 — a widow and her small child walk past the horrific scene.   Among the dead was the man who a few hours earlier was both husband and father

spending the day in the villages, I held a little service and inspected the school. Ndhlovu had a staff of one. The school-house had fallen down, and the children were gathered in the shade of the trees. At dusk the teachers and I chatted.

Kenneth Ndhlovu was a good teacher and a dedicated Christian. He had done some exploration with a view to expanding the mission's work, and mentioned Katiu only in passing.

"What is there at Katiu?" I asked.

"Nothing," he replied, "except the villages and lots of people."

"How many Christians are there?"

"None at all, as far as I know. No priest has ever been there. The occasional agricultural officer has camped there for a night or two. Apart from a few young men who go away to work the folk have seen no other white man."

"Let's go," I said.

We went the following day. It was several hours' walk, and the rushing Nyankombe stream was an alarming obstacle. The "bridge" consisted of two fallen trees, and, with help, it took me twenty minutes to negotiate it. There was, of course, no one to greet us or show us round. There was no church elder, and we had no idea where the headman lived. The women ran away at the sight of a white face, and the children howled. The men were civil, but puzzled. Our visit could only be a preliminary reconnaissance. We had been on our feet ten hours when, exhausted, we got back to Chikomba at dark.

Chavanga, far up in the northern hills, offered a different challenge. Forty years ago there had been a magnificent missionary effort from Bonda, but the mission there was over-stretched and Chavanga had had to be abandoned. The school was closed and the Christian converts left unattended. They never forgave the Church for first raising and then dashing their hopes. Nothing was left but a ruined church and a lapsed elder, Henry Mushaya.

I attempted to get to Chavanga at the beginning of November, and sent a message to Henry asking to be met at the usual crossing-place on the Chipote River. It was possible to drive the Landrover down a spiral track through the forest to within about fifty yards of the stream. A little clearing marked the place where Father Mason used to leave the truck, and here I waited with Canaan the cook. It was still early. The water tumbled and sparkled on the rocks: brilliantly coloured tropical birds darted among the trees, and there were huge butterflies of purple and gold and red. But of humanity there was no sign at all.

Perhaps an hour later a surly group of men with spears came silently down the track, waded the river and disappeared in the forest up the steep pathway towards Chavanga. They barely acknowledged our greetings. Shortly afterwards they were followed by a few women, who shrieked and fled.

"What shall we do?" I asked Canaan.

"I will make tea," he said, and got out the primus stove.

A little later he added: "I will cook lunch."

It was then that another group of men came down the track. They were taken aback by our presence, but were not discourteous. Did they, I asked, know Henry Mushaya? Yes, they did. Would they take another message to him, telling him we were waiting at the river? They supposed they would. We settled down to wait again. At four o'clock Canaan, efficient when sober, made more tea. "I don't think they are coming," he said. The same idea had occurred to me.

For a moment I considered the possibility of going on alone, but immediately dismissed the idea. Neither of us had been to Chavanga, or knew the paths through the forest or in the open grasslands above the tree-line. One might walk many miles without meeting a soul, and we could not carry even the essential minimum of food and bedding. Worse, at the end of the journey, if we ever arrived, there would be no mission and no one to receive us. To go on alone might mean to die of exposure.

The sun disappeared quickly behind the mountains and a chill set in with the dusk. Among the sounds of the oncoming night there was no human voice. At last I said: "We must give up." We had waited seven hours. Ignominiously we re-packed the Landrover and headed through the dark for Mandea. No further attempt to reach Chavanga could be made

138

until the following year, after the long summer rains. But I was determined to return.

Back at Mandea the mission flourished. Gladys was using the little mission-office, near our kitchen, as her clinic. Few patients came who had not been to the witch-doctor first, but the queues got longer every day. People had great faith in injections as the remedy for all ills. One day, after Gladys had announced whooping-cough inoculations for babies, a line of over a hundred mothers with children appeared, and most of the ordinary patients had to be told to come back another time.

The most serious medical difficulty was the absence of a ward where patients could be kept overnight. We had all the tropical diseases. On one occasion a girl unconscious with cerebral malaria was allowed to stay the night on the couch in the "clinic," but in the morning her relatives had to take her home in order that other patients might be treated. She survived.

Educationally, too, we were forging ahead. There was much joy in the district because, owing to the efforts of Father Mason, St Peter's school was to have the higher standards in 1961. This meant that ultimately children from Mandea would qualify for admission to secondary boarding schools and so might climb the ladder to white-collar jobs. Mr Edward Mangwanda, the head teacher, would have to make way for a man with higher qualifications, and his successor had already been appointed before my arrival.

Then, suddenly, the whole situation turned sour overnight. Mangwanda was a local man, and it fell to me to discuss his future with him. I offered him a choice of several jobs, including a headship not far away.

To my amazement he said bluntly: "I'm not moving."

"Well," I replied, "if you wish to stay at Mandea, I can offer you the job of an assistant teacher."

"That is out of the question," he answered. "I am staying in my present position."

Patiently I explained that the Education Department would not allow that.

Mangwanda was unmoved. He felt he had a trump card

up his sleeve of which I knew nothing. "I am staying put," he said, and walked out.

Meanwhile our church shelter had blown down in a storm and we were using a recently completed classroom and its verandah as a church. After the service on the last Sunday of term Mangwanda got to his feet, ostensibly to say farewell. He delivered himself of a long and vitriolic attack on the new priest-in-charge for turning him out of his job, and called for a church boycott until I backed down.

Mangwanda had been well enough liked, so the effect of this harangue was electric. I was faced with instant hostility on all sides. Privately I explained the facts to the other teachers and the churchwardens, pointing out that their children's future depended on our co-operation with the Native Education Department. Personally they were satisfied, but they were entirely unable to control the agitation which followed. A deputation of men — not churchpeople — told me I must yield at once or face an indefinite church boycott with pickets at the end of the road. If that did not work, teachers would be murdered.

What I had not realised was that Joshua Nkomo's newly-formed National Democratic Party, successor of the banned African National Congress, was already widely active, and there had been sporadic incidents of intimidation and violence in various parts of the country. (I seldom saw newspapers or had time for radio news broadcasts.) The idea of boycotts was in the air.

Other malcontents jumped on the bandwagon. Father Mason had warned me that there was a hard core of primitive people who hated the mission for intruding on their ancestral ways. There were, too, the former occupants of the mission site. These had conceded the poverty-stricken land (for which they had been compensated) only because they wanted a school. They, too, were glad of the opportunity to make trouble.

Soon the whole countryside seemed to be up in arms, though those actively involved were in fact only a small minority. The ordinary Christian people were terrified of the pickets and intimidators, and only a few dared to brave them. But we carried on as if nothing had happened. At the beginning of the holidays most of the teachers went away and forgot about the problem. Gladys's clinic was unaffected, and indeed increasingly popular. There was no danger in that quarter, so on weekdays I went off on trek and left Mandea to its own devices. This was not the last boycott we were to experience, and it taught me how to react. The secret was to go away and work in other areas where there was no trouble. Meanwhile I informed the inspectors in Umtali of the head teacher's attitude, and they responded at once. "Move," they told Mangwanda, "or face expulsion from the teaching service." He moved. Then some of the pickets and intimidators fell sick, and appeared in Gladys's queues. That was the beginning of the end.

Many of the mission's followers at Mandea were sincere and devout Christians, and once the initial shock of the boycott was over they were in no mood to tolerate the loss of their church or their school. The facts of the case became widely known, and people began to trickle back to church. At Christmas the trickle became a flood, and by the new year the boycott had been forgotten. The new head teacher, Mr Gervase Chidawanyika, was welcomed with song and dance, and was immediately and deservedly popular.

However, some of the locals in the immediate vicinity of the mission still did not like us. They took their revenge by grazing their cattle on the mission gardens, protecting their own with fences. One day I returned from trek after dark to find a bamboo barricade blocking the entrance of the mission. It was not the first, and its predecessors I had merely charged with the Landrover. This one, however, was of sturdier build, and I had to get out and dismantle it pole by pole. I was struck by a paroxysm of pain as a scorpion stabbed, and was off duty for several days. There was glee amongst our foes.

*   *   *   *

Our next boycott was not at Mandea at all. We had undertaken the supervision of the school at the Eastern Highlands Tea Estate, an arrangement which benefited both the company and our own work. In April of the following year, 1961, the management was plagued by a series of mechanical break-downs in its factory, and the rumour got around that the Europeans were intent on offering a human sacrifice to the spirits to lift the hoodoo. Three of our teachers, members of minority tribes, were said to be looking for a school-child for the sacrifice. The alien teachers had ultimately to be replaced by members of the local Manyika tribe, and even then it took us several months to get the children back into school. Meanwhile the feeling was such that a man was killed in an inter-tribal fight, and two Europeans barely escaped with their lives as they tried to separate the warring factions.

* * * *

In the early sixties Mandea mission began to be known as something of a success-story. This was due to two factors. The first was the personality of Gervase Chidawanyika, the new head teacher. He had an astounding ability to understand both his own people and the ways and thinking of Europeans, and to help us to understand each other.

The second factor, improbably, was shortage of cash. The financial position we inherited was grim. The Diocese of Mashonaland was supposed to be self-supporting, and there was little money for missions apart from school fees and local collections. When I argued that it was absurd to expect the heathen to pay for their own conversion the reply was that a proposal was being considered to abolish mission-districts altogether. The Church must stand on its own feet.

However, there were still people who remembered Our Lord's words: "Go ye into all the world, and preach the Gospel to every creature." I myself knew a number of such people — and churches — both in England and Rhodesia. I wrote to as many as I could, and started a newsletter about Mandea. This soon began to feature in local and overseas parish magazines, and in the press too. Prayer-groups were formed, with results that sometimes seemed miraculous. And money began to come in.

By this time nothing was plainer than the need for African

help with the directly spiritual and religious work. Sidney Manyau, our first catechist, turned up just when the money had arrived for his small stipend. He was a charismatic old man, a tireless walker and an eloquent teacher. In an interval in the rains I sent him off to the lonely places north of the Pungwe, where he performed wonders.

Sidney, of course, could not do the work of an African priest, and such a priest was our most urgent need. We were required by the diocese to build a permanent brick house, and actually raised the money for it. But the regulations demanded that the plans be passed by the diocesan building committee in Salisbury. By the time this body was satisfied the materials were rotting in the rain and transport from Umtali was no longer possible. The carpenter who was to make the roof-trusses took the plans home to study them. His home, unfortunately, was on the other side of the Honde River, in Mozambique. The river was in spate and he had to swim for it, the plans clenched between his teeth. He escaped with his life in the flash-flood which bore down on him, but the plans disappeared in the direction of the Indian Ocean. Meanwhile the African priest planned for Mandea was appointed elsewhere.

As the rainy season began to abate I headed again for our fledgling centres north of the Pungwe: Samtete, Katiu and Chavanga. At Samtete I was the bearer of good news. We had asked our friends to pray for a school there, and I suspect the inspectors in Umtali were among our friends. At any rate permission was granted, against all expectations, for a school next year. When I arrived Sidney Manyau had gathered a hundred children to greet me, a new wattle-and-daub school-house was complete and funds were being raised for a permanent building.

My next visit to Samtete, a few months later, was less successful. Hardly any of the menfolk were there. I was told they had all gone to an NDP meeting at the Pungwe bridge. The NDP was Joshua Nkomo's new National Democratic Party, and later the men were entirely honest about their reason for going. "We don't want our huts burned down at night with our families in them," they said. Well-dressed

143

agitators had visited the valley in brand-new Landrovers painted with slogans in English. They themselves did not leave the roads, but their message penetrated the furthest corners of the district. However when I visited Samtete yet again before the onset of the rains the menfolk turned out in force. With me I brought a builder who taught them to construct a brick-kiln and make bricks for their new school.

Katiu needed a different strategy, for the people there were not ready for a school. Sidney Manyau and I went the long way round, on foot. This avoided the hair-raising crossing in a coracle, and enabled me to take my film-strip projector. A clearing had been made for us in the forest, and the framework of a shelter put up. It had not been thatched, so I was thankful for the new tent I had just been given by friends. After the film-show Sidney Manyau and Canaan the cook declined the hospitality of the insalubrious villages, which were at a little distance. Looking at the sky they said: "It won't rain tonight. We will sleep out." In the small hours the rain came with a whoosh and a roar, and I squeezed them into the tent. In the morning we held an open-air mission-service, during which Sidney showed great eloquence and persuasiveness. Then he taught the children and I discussed the future with the men.

I had given much thought to the ban on unapproved schools. My idea for Katiu was a "catechetical centre," which, being entirely religious, could not be subject to any government restrictions. It was obvious to me that such a centre would have to teach reading, for how else could the pupils learn to read the Bible? Numbers were necessary too, for ultimately we should have hymn books. Christianity would be taught anyway — that was the acknowledged object of such centres — and I reckoned we could manage for a year or two without a school and could create the conditions for formal education. The people accepted this plan and agreed to put up the necessary temporary buildings and to find part of the catechist's salary. We had lots of ups and downs in the following years, but that is how things ultimately worked out.

Leaving Katiu we walked back to the truck and drove to the "drift" we had crossed so easily a few days ago. The previous night, however, the heavens had opened, and the stream was now a boiling torrent. There would be no hope of crossing it for a day or two, and yet it was the only way back to civilisation. There was nothing this side of the river but primitive villages, the border with Mozambique and then empty country.

Fortunately I had the tent and food, and Sidney and Canaan found hospitality in the neighbouring villages. It was hardly possible to sleep because of the raging of the flood. In the morning the water had dropped a little, and a messenger struggled through the stream and found an engineer-friend of mine at the nearer of the tea estates. He looked at the water, shook his head and gesticulated to show that he would return. Hours later he waded to us and offered to try driving the Landrover across, accepting no responsibility. It bucked and dived, and finally roared up the muddy slope at the other side. The rest of us waded after it with our gear, and we were away.

Ultimately the Aberfoyle Tea Estate constructed a "road" in the direction of the Mozambique border to transport labour, and I, of course, made use of it. The bamboo bridges were signed "Maximum load ¾ ton," adding, rather obviously, "Vehicles cross at own risk." On one occasion when the bridges were my only way back I looked in the mirror and saw that I was followed by four five-ton trucks.

Chavanga, which I had failed to reach last year, I finally reached in June in the middle of the cold weather. After the forest and the open rolling grasslands, the journey ended with a steep climb up a path we called the goat track. The ruined church was there amid the hill-tops, but no Christians survived apart from Henry Mushaya, the elder. (Even he had lapsed into polygamy.) We put up the tent, and a group of children collected and camped in the bitter cold for the length of our stay. The next day Sidney Manyau taught and I visited the scattered headmen with Henry. The isolated villages were the most primitive I had seen. Some of the adults still wore skins. The younger children were naked, grey with dirt and scrabbling among the goats and chickens under the eaves of the smoky huts. Drums throbbed night and day, and most of the people were stupefied with drink. For the first time I encountered a pagan community seemingly quite uninterested in the education of its children. I tried to organise a meeting about this for my last day, but no one came. As we left, however, the children who had camped with us sang us all the way down to the Chipote River.

Some months passed before I could return to Chavanga. As we climbed the goat track we saw a group of men sitting on the hillside near the church. "They are the headmen," said Sidney. We went through the ritual greetings, prolonging them to the best of our ability. Then silence fell. No one had anything to say, though obviously this was something more than a welcoming party. At last I broke the ice myself. "It is good to see you," I began. "You must have something to talk about." There were looks of considerable surprise. "You called a meeting," replied the spokesman. "This is it." In future years we had a long, uphill struggle to get the mission's work going at Chavanga, but after that meeting we never really looked back.

In the middle of 1961 I returned to Mandea from my treks for a large concourse of confirmation candidates from all over the mission-district. At nights I had a little time for newspapers and the radio, and I soon realised that something was happening in Rhodesia which gave great hope for the future.

In 1960 Britain had organised a constitutional conference on Rhodesia in Salisbury, and this had agreed on a new constitution which admitted Africans to Parliament — in increasing numbers until they would become a majority in perhaps fifteen years. Almost all the politicians agreed on this, including Joshua Nkomo and the African nationalists. On July 26th 1961 the new constitution was put to the white electorate in a referendum, and accepted by a convincing majority. Supporters of Sir Edgar Whitehead's liberal government (including ourselves) heaved a sigh of relief.

An indifferent world entirely failed to notice that something had happened which had never previously occurred anywhere. A ruling minority had willingly agreed to cede power to an untutored majority, subject only to a minimal transitional period to prevent the country collapsing into chaos. Unhappily this hopeful situation was quickly wrecked. Joshua Nkomo reneged on the agreement under pressure from his overseas supporters: already the demand was for immediate black power. Britain backed the nationalists. The Rhodesian whites, however, kept faith, and the constitution was duly enacted and brought into force. But both they and the peaceful black moderates — in those days the huge majority — were nearly in despair. The appalling catastrophe of the Congo, where the Belgians had capitulated to the black nationalists in 1960, was fresh in the minds of everyone.

Violence, rioting and arson broke out in various parts of Rhodesia during the latter part of 1961, and the NDP organised an intimidation drive in the African townships to compel the support of the black people. This time Sir Edgar Whitehead had no choice but to ban the organisation which incited the trouble. He acted on December 9th. On December 19th the NDP's successor was formed: the Zimbabwe African People's Union or ZAPU. But ordinary folk were beginning to get tired of what was thought to be the liberal government's pussyfooting with terrorists and extremists. Banned movements merely re-emerged with a new name!

*　　*　　*　　*

Mandea, mercifully, was far away from the trouble and July 1961 brought good news for Gladys and me. Neither of us was a youngster any more, but Gladys was pregnant with our second child. The problem was: Who was to run the clinic while she was off work? We made enormous efforts to secure another nurse, but not one, white or black, was prepared to work in so lonely and backward a place.

For myself the mission's success had brought new difficulties. My desk was piled high with forms from the Education Department. The job of managing the schools was crippling my primary religious work. Letters from supporters poured in, and they needed answers. Our urgent requirement was a mission secretary who could double up as a schools supervisor. I wrote to our friends and told them we still needed money; but even more we needed their prayers for a nurse and for a secretary.

I myself was much too faithless. In April I had preached at Hatfield church in Salisbury, and after the service a certain Mrs Ray Jackman had come to me and said: "Does the mission need a secretary?" I said it certainly did. But Mrs Jackman's family situation was such that quite obviously she could not come. I had thanked her for her inquiry, and said I could not think of making her already difficult circumstances harder. Yet she was a devout Christian and would have been the ideal person for the job.

What I did not know was that Ray, a methodical person, had set about tackling her problems one by one with a view to overcoming them. After a few months she wrote to say she had organised everything and would be free to come later in the year. She would accept the £30 a month I had offered. This was to have been covered by a grant promised by the Education Department, but to my dismay there had been a muddle and the offer was withdrawn. I cabled this news to Ray, who cabled back: "Will accept £20." I responded: "Our friends will find that" — and they did. Ray paid a short visit to St Peter's, loved it and moved in at the beginning of November. She proved an unforgettable character: a formidably efficient secretary who waded rivers, climbed mountains, slept in lonely places and was loved by everyone.

The problem of a nurse to take over from Gladys remained unsolved in spite of all our prayers. To the dismay of the whole district we announced that the clinic would be closed in October. In September I was interviewing prospective teachers for 1962. Among the candidates was a large and jovial man called Beaven Jari. He was entitled to a headship, and I offered him Chikomba which was to fall vacant since Kenneth Ndhlovu, the present headmaster, was to open the new school at Samtete.

"Fine," said Beaven Jari. "But I wonder if you could possibly find a job there for my wife too?"

"Is she a trained teacher?" I asked, since the Department had decreed that untrained staff were to be dismissed at the end of the year.

148

"No, but she has plenty of experience. Actually she is a trained nurse . . ."

"A WHAT?" I cried.

"A nurse, but she couldn't get a nursing job."

"Mr Jari," I said. "May we start again? Would you take a place on the staff of St Peter's so that your wife could run the clinic? I would promise you a headship as soon as it is practicable."

"Of course," Beaven replied. "I am sure Lydia will agree."

Mai (Mrs) Jari came to look at the job and took it over temporarily in October. She was as big, burly and jolly as her husband, and they stayed at Mandea as long as we did.

The time came when a cyclone cut off our valley from the outside world. The local witchdoctor's wife was ready to be delivered and things went badly wrong. It was well known that midwifery cases had to go to Bonda: had we weakened on this point the volume of work would have been totally crippling. But no one could get to Bonda now.

Ray Jackman drove Mai Jari to the village long after dark and they worked all night with a hurricane lamp in the stifling hut. Ray had no knowledge of obstetrics. Nurse Jari had the knowledge, but not the confidence. Lydia would say: "Should I . . .?" and Ray would urge her on: "Yes, do. Get on with it." That night's work went down into Mandea history, and in the morning both Lydia and Ray were exhausted and could hardly perspire any more. They left a happy mother, a howling baby and a delighted witchdoctor.

9. Rumblings of Revolution

ANTHONY, our second child, was born in Umtali on January 17th 1962. I drove him and Gladys down to Mandea before the cyclone broke and our valley was cut off from the world. Arriving at the mission I found Ray Jackman under siege in the office. The account-books were spread over her desk and a queue outside stretched down to the gate. "Help!" she called. Standing before her was a grim-faced man proclaiming his intention to murder one of the mission staff. She had persuaded him to postpone action until the priest-in-charge returned, and I had no choice but to take him aside and listen to his woes. Solomon would have had his work cut out, but as dusk fell the man went quietly away.

Gladys was on her feet again quickly, and soon I was trekking once more whenever there was a pause in the seasonal downpours. In addition to the strictly religious work there were interminable meetings about churches and schools, and as soon as the dry winter weather set in there was a fever of activity as new buildings began to spring up on all our outstations. However, the price of progress throughout the district was trouble at the central mission.

Every Sunday morning I spent several hours at Mandea, celebrating the eucharist, preaching and baptising. Then I was off to one or other of the bigger outstations to start again. Meetings of the church council at Mandea unavoidably took place on a Sunday when the menfolk were free, so I could seldom attend them. This did not matter since Gervase Chidawanyika, the new headmaster, was a brilliant chairman and could deal even with the handful of locals who had made so much trouble about his own appointment. These latter seldom came to church but had their fingers on the political pulse of the time and upset the work when they could

However church law dictated that the annual church meeting to choose the churchwardens and councillors, must be chaired by the priest-in-charge, so on that day I planned to stay at Mandea. Gervase Chidawanyika, as deputy chairman, could be depended upon for guidance if any really tricky problem arose or if the torrent of Shona eloquence left me baffled. Unfortunately Chidawanyika was delayed by a mechanical breakdown, and I had to cope alone.

After church I opened the meeting with prayer and tried to get down to business. The trouble-makers immediately pointed out the absence of Chidawanyika and stated that the meeting could not proceed without him. I replied that the rules required only a simple quorum, and that was obviously present. "You must postpone the meeting till another Sunday," one of the men argued truculently. I was not conscious that I had ever seen him before, but anyone on the communicants' roll was entitled to be present. Patiently I explained that I had no other free Sunday.

"Well, you haven't got your quorum," retorted the truculent one. He got up to leave, and most of the men followed him. Soon afterwards some of the women, frightened, left too. There was nothing to do but to abandon the meeting, leaving the mission-district without elected wardens and councillors. A few weeks later the ringleaders went up to the diocesan office in Salisbury to complain that I had refused to hold the legally required election! I asked Chidawanyika what had gone wrong. "Nothing," he said. "There is no grievance to put right. They are just anti-white."

The immediate result was that the volunteers who had been making bricks to build a little clinic abandoned the job. And without the bricks there could be no clinic apart from the office Gladys was already using. Ultimately I got round the church council problem by organising a committee to represent the whole mission-district, elected by the adult communicants of the outstations as well as the central mission and meeting at various centres in turn. Over the years this proved a great success.

Gladys and I soon found that our main problem was not the trouble-makers but sheer physical exhaustion. Night after night I was called out to minister to sick and dying Christians; and night after night I would bring them in to the mission for Gladys to help. Occasionally half the hours of darkness would be spent taking a patient to Bonda hospital. But we were in our chapel for mattins and communion at first light.

The last straw, however, was the witch cow. One bright moonlit night we woke to a new sound: munch, munch, munch. The cow was in the garden under our bedroom window, consuming the precious vegetables on which we depended. It had made short work of our bamboo fence. Almost drugged with sleep I drove it away and went back to bed. But it came back the next night, ravaging the teachers' gardens as well as our own. And it came back every month at the full moon.

I had difficulty in persuading our overseas supporters that the propagation of the Gospel in the Honde Valley demanded a five-strand barbed wire fence round our hundred-acre mission. But at least our continued sanity demanded no less, the money was found and the fence erected in a remarkably short space of time.

Our dismay was beyond bounds when, at the time of the full moon, we were awakened by the now familiar munch, munch, munch. It was, sure enough, the witch cow, consuming the remains of our garden. A standard fence, cattle-proof everywhere else in Rhodesia, had deterred it not a whit. Whether it got through it or over it we never knew. But with my own eyes I saw the beast approach the mission, make a dash for the fence and appear nonchalantly on our land leaving the wire intact. By this time we were desperate.

"Ray," I said one night, "what about your gun?" Ray's gun was a small pistol which she kept for self-defence. She was loth to use it, but agreed it would make a bang. It really only made a pop. The cow looked at us reproachfully, and continued munching. A conclave of the mission staff, called specially to discuss the witch cow, produced a bright idea by one of the teachers. "What about a lasso?" he suggested. The animal was ultimately cornered and surrounded by the teachers, one of them lasso in hand. At last it was still. "Now," I shouted. Suddenly the creature urinated copiously, and the teacher hesitated. Within moments it was through the fence, ready to fight another day. We thought we heard it laugh: but cows don't laugh, and that must have been our over-wrought imaginations.

By this time we had discovered the animal's owner, one Karimunenga, an old enemy of ours who lived at the village at the bottom of the mission road. He was enjoying himself hugely, and was wholly deaf to our entreaties. In despair I approached the District Commissioner at Inyanga, sixty miles away. "The legal remedy," he explained, his face deadpan, "is in your own hands. You catch the beast and walk it up to Inyanga. We will impound it, and it will not be returned to the owner until he has paid a fine." He added, in response to my query· "No, we keep the fine, not you." The ultimate solution was altogether more realistic. It was the formation of a consortium to buy the animal from Karimunenga at an exorbitant price. We turned the witch cow into very tough beef, ate it and enjoyed peace (at least from that quarter) ever after.

It was in the middle of the witch cow crisis that both Gladys and Ray Jackman, on separate occasions, were stung by scorpions. Both were inoculated with the normal antidote. Gladys, however, proved allergic to it, and a few days later was suddenly struck unconscious. She had just time to whisper one word before she fainted: "Adrenalin." She had made a split-second diagnosis. Nurse Jari rushed to the clinic, injected her and accompanied us as we made the fastest journey ever to Umtali hospital — just under two hours,.

Thanks to her own presence of mind Gladys recovered quickly. Without that presence of mind, however, tragedy could have overtaken us. We were learning that living in the Honde Valley was a dangerous business. In addition to the victims of scorpion-stings, patients were coming to Gladys in increasing numbers bitten by almost all the more deadly snakes: cobras, puff-adders, green and black mambas and gaboon vipers. If they got to her alive she always pulled them through.

The building of a clinic was an urgent necessity, but it was held up by the refusal of the men — who dominated all the meetings — to co-operate. "Why should Anglicans do the work," they demanded, "when the clinic is for everybody, and we get no preferential treatment?"

Gladys and I had long realised that it was possible to be an Anglican at Mandea without being a Christian. We had concluded, too, that in the vast majority of cases the women were far superior to the men. Most of them had real qualities of faithfulness and kindness and endurance, and they wanted a better future for their children. Too often the men were obstructive drunken sots. Polio was on the increase throughout the district; but it was the men who declared a boycott of the free inoculations for the children which the government enabled us to offer.

At this stage Gladys and I made a prayerful decision. For the sake of the women and children we would press ahead with the building of a temporary in-patient clinic, asking the help of our white Christian friends in Rhodesia and overseas. And as a matter of policy we would neither ask nor accept help from any local committee or council.

The tarred road from Umtali to Inyanga had recently been completed, and the contractors were selling off the pre-fabricated asbestos huts in which their men had been living. We purchased one of these triangular structures and had it re-erected on the mission. It leaked abominably and was stiflingly hot; but it provided a little consulting room, a treatment room, a covered verandah and a ward with space for four beds and (in practice) a dozen in-patients. One of the first patients was Lazarus who, like the witchdoctor's wife, became a Mandea legend.

It was evening when I was called to baptise the dying baby in a nearby village. His mother asked me to choose a Christian name, and — appropriately, I hoped — I chose Lazarus. After we had all prayed I said: "Bring him to the clinic. Perhaps God will give him back to you." Outside the hut I whispered to the mother: "We won't charge you anything at all." Great discretion had to be used in waiving our small medical charges, for what cost nothing was often thought to be worth nothing.

To our surprise Lazarus was at the clinic next morning, barely alive. In the daylight he was an appalling sight. His whole body was covered with suppurating blisters and sores, his eyes dripped with pus and his hair was the bright red of the malnutrition or kwashiorkor victim. The problem was not lack of food, but the mother's ignorance of food-values. The boy whined faintly. He was eighteen months old, and had been a toddler. He toddled no more.

Gladys set to work with a will. She put Lazarus on penicillin and vitamin B injections, fed him vitamin syrup and skim milk and treated his sores locally. We all prayed for his recovery.

A week later Gladys could detect an improvement, but no one else could see it. An uncle came to take the child and his mother away, saying the baby would die anyway. (He really meant to take him to the witchdoctor.) Only after long persuasion did he relent. After another week the improvement was dramatic, and at the end of the month Lazarus was walking and ready to go home. His story spread far and wide, and there is no doubt it did more for the Christian cause than any sermon of mine.

By the following year much of my own work, as well as our unofficial ambulance service, was being wrecked by Petronella the Landrover. On one occasion she had to be taken up to Umtali on a five-ton truck. On another she stopped twenty times on the way back from Umtali, finally coming to rest in the middle of the Ruda drift — the ford a few miles from the mission. On yet another, approaching Bonda Mission, she leaked and boiled so spectacularly that we resorted to the last expedient of the desperate, putting mealie-meal (maize meal) in the radiator to block the leak. Even this was not the sum of our woes, for when we finally halted at Bonda a heavy goods truck reversed into us and nearly put us all out of our misery.

Gladys and I and the children were due to go to England on furlough in the middle of 1963, and we could not possibly leave Ray and my African replacement with this wreck of a vehicle. My plea to the diocesan authorities was heard, and we were given a new Landrover. What was even more important, my appeal to Voluntary Service Overseas in England was also heard, and Sister Terré Mayman, a State Registered Nurse, was assigned to us for nearly a year.

It was with light hearts that Gladys and I crept and creaked our way up to Umtali at the beginning of April on Petronella's last journey. Sister Terré was there, and so was the new truck. We returned in even higher spirits with both. Sister Terré was a delightful person and was immediately and universally popular at Mandea. But the new truck received a welcome too. The women lined up and performed the ritual hand-clapping customary at the birth of a new baby.

Two nights later I was called to administer the last rites to Mai Janet Refu, a faithful old Christian who seldom missed Sunday church. I stayed some time praying with her and then hastened back to the mission (it was a Saturday night) to get some sleep before Sunday. This was a special day, Palm Sunday, and I remember it well. There were big crowds at the outdoor eucharist, which was preceded by the traditional procession of palms. The singing was accompanied by a big drum to keep the time, and everything proceeded with relative dignity till the cantor, who was leading the singing, noticed there was a disturbance among part of the crowd. A particularly large snake had taken its place in the procession! The cantor dropped his book, abandoned the hymn, seized a stick and annihilated the intruder. Then, unruffled, he began again: "All glory, laud and honour."

After the service I was off to our outstation at Samanga for a repeat of the whole thing, except the snake. It was mid-afternoon when I got back to Gladys and Margaret and Anthony. And it was only then that I thought again of old Janet Refu. Did she have to die? "Gladys," I said, "would you go and look at her?" Gladys had deliberately refused to learn to drive until Margaret and Anthony were older: she would have been roped in for perpetual ambulance-work and would have had no time at all for the children. But Sister Terré was an experienced driver. She was game, and the two followed the rough tracks until they were as near the village as the vehicle would go. After that they scrambled up the rocky footpaths until they reached the hut.

It was dark and windowless, and crowded with sympathisers consuming the precious oxygen which old Janet needed. Gladys tactfully got them all out and examined her, huddled unconscious on a mat beyond the smoky fire. She was alive, but might not last the night. It was almost certainly a case of cerebral malaria. Probably it would respond to treatment, but the treatment was chloroquine by injection. Gladys had no syringe with her, and the tablets in her bag were useless for an unconscious patient.

Gladys explained to the men outside the hut that there was hope, but that Janet would have to go to the clinic. The mission would undertake transport and expenses. The debate which followed went on for over an hour, at the end of which the spokesman delivered the common verdict. "Thank you, sister. But *Mbuya* (grandmother) is going to die. Let her die at home. Think of all the expense of bringing her body back from the clinic to the village."

In most cases Gladys would have let the matter rest. Cures can never be guaranteed, and in any case the outlook of a people cannot be changed overnight. But Janet was someone special, and Gladys made a last effort. "Just let us try," she said quietly. "Maybe God will help us." There was something about her manner which carried weight. More debate followed, but Gladys and Terré finally returned to the clinic after dark with Janet and some helpers. Both of them worked on her, and finally Gladys left instructions that if there was even the slightest deterioration during the night she was to be called. She was not called. In the morning she whispered to Janet: "*Mangwanani, Mbuya*" ("Good morning"). The reply was almost inaudible, but a reply there was. "*Mangwanani.*"

The battle which followed was not straightforward, and there were times when it seemed to be lost. But in the end Terré drove Janet back to her village, and even the menfolk were impressed. For years afterwards Janet walked the five miles to church most Sundays, and she always referred to Gladys as "*Mwokozi wangu*" (the one who saved me). Occasionally she would perform the little solitary dance with

158

which, in those days, Shona women would express extremes of joy.

Sister Terré took over the clinic while Gladys and I were in England, and achieved wonders. She wrote light-heartedly to the mission's friends about her experiences. "The patients lie mostly on mats on the floor. A ward round is highly unconventional, much of the time being spent on my knees. However, it has been suggested that this is how it should be on a mission." Her one mistake was when a baby had to be got to the doctor quickly, and a bus was about to leave from a nearby store. She gave the mother thirty shillings for fare and fees, and the mother promptly took the money to a local witchdoctor. The baby died.

Terré's biggest achievement at Mandea was the conquest of a measles epidemic — measles being a killer disease in Africa. With Nurse Jari she worked night and day, and at one stage she had thirty-seven patients squeezed into every corner of the clinic and the mission house. They all recovered.

*   *   *   *

Meanwhile politics, black and white, were obtruding increasingly on our lives. The year before we went on leave Gladys and I had had a short holiday at Beira in Mozambique. We stayed a night *en route* at the interracial club in Umtali, having dinner with a cultured African acquaintance who had not the remotest propensity to violence. He told us he was seriously thinking of taking out a ZAPU card to save his family from being molested and his car from being stoned. Returning a week later we drove straight up to St Christopher's church cottage in the Vumba mountains, south of Umtali, to complete our holiday. We discovered that an attempt had been made the previous night to burn down the cottage and its adjoining chapel, but that both had been saved by the combined efforts of the local people. However, the Africans in the hill country were no longer going down into the town, fearing violence if they could not produce a party card. Shortly afterwards we learned that ZAPU had been banned by the government.

The multiracial elections under the new 1961 constitution

had taken place just before Christmas 1962. A number of African candidates stood, but some of them — and their supporters — were petrol-bombed. Gladys and I had not the slightest doubt about the party we ourselves should vote for, though we very seldom talked politics either at home or among the Africans we served. We believed Sir Edgar Whitehead's United Federal Party was liberal in the best sense of the word, and was dedicated to a fair deal for both the black people and the white — and to African advancement at the fastest practicable rate. We were dismayed at the landslide victory of the new right-wing Rhodesian Front.

As I was trekking at one of the mission's outstations in the hills north of the Pungwe river a young teacher asked me wistfully: "What is going to happen to Rhodesia?" I hesitated, determined to steer clear of political issues. At last I said: "I suppose it depends on you. You have a vote. Use it."

"But, Father," he said, "I have a wife and children. The other day I received an anonymous letter threatening to burn down my house if I voted."

I began to wonder whether, in this situation, a Christian priest could or should keep silent about politics any longer.

*　　*　　*　　*

Ray Jackman had warned us that for family reasons she would have to leave the mission at the end of 1963. Her abilities and adaptability were such that she would clearly be irreplaceable. We needed a miracle.

On our way to England in the middle of the year Gladys and I and the children had stayed a night with friends in Salisbury. "We have someone who wants to work at Mandea," said our host. "Her name is Lisa Teubes. Would you like to contact her?" This seemed too good to be true, so I rang a priest-friend who knew Mrs Teubes well. "A fine person," he said. "A youngish widow with three children of school age. It would be marvellous if she could come." After a further telephone call Lisa Teubes was with us. She was a biggish person with dark hair and an infectious laugh: a qualified secretary and nurse. There were problems to be

160

resolved about her children's education, but within an hour it was settled that she would come. She was at Mandea to receive us, with Carol and Jojo and William, when we returned to the mission at the beginning of 1964.

At Christmas in England we received a rather touching letter from the Africans at Mandea, which said simply: "Please come back." However things were going so well at St Peter's that we were left in no doubt about the power of prayer and with no false notions of our own importance.

This state of affairs was largely due to Father Elijah Chirimuuta, the African priest who had taken my place and who now stayed on as assistant. The diocese had long accepted that the spiritual work of the mission had grown to a point where it could no longer be done by a white priest alone.

Father Chirimuuta (affectionately called Father Chiri) had amazing drive and initiative. He had covered the whole area while I was away, and he needed no prompting now. A man of strong opinions and personality he was accustomed to getting things done. In the pastoral work which was his only concern, he inevitably had a vast advantage over me, with his command of the language and his familiarity with the people. He had nine children, and a tenth was on the way. This made the accommodation of his family something of a problem. A further difficulty was that his wife knew little English, and English was widely spoken by the staff on the central mission.

Father Chiri had become accustomed to sharing the Landrover only with Ray, but now he had to share it with Lisa and me: and we all frequently needed to trek at the same time. Appearing in my office one morning he said: "I need a car."

"So do we all," I replied. "But we don't have the money."

"It's not practical to walk," he said, "because no one will carry anything. And I can do no good staying at home."

This was entirely true. In fact, Chiri was an indefatigable walker in the areas where motorised transport was impracticable and carriers were still obtainable.

"We could think about a motorbike," I said.

"You can't carry much," he said.

161

He was too courteous to say what was really in his mind. He had no driving licence, and depended on others to drive him. And if teachers were sufficiently well-to-do to get cars, why should a priest suffer the lack of status — and the drenchings — which went with a motorbike? Chiri had a compelling case. I knew perfectly well that while a white priest needed no status an African priest's position was very different.

A few days later Chiri came along with the news that the headmaster of Nyatsanza, our biggest outstation, was selling his truck. Mr Jonah Borerwe was leaving the district to train for ordination. His vehicle, I knew, was in good condition, and would be a bargain.

"It will," said Chiri, "cost no more than a new motorbike."

"True," I replied. "But it will cost a great deal more to run."

"If the mission will buy the truck," he said, "I will get the local people to maintain it."

This was a perilous proposition. It would not be long before the truck, even if properly maintained, would be costing a fortune. If the local people found the money — which they would not — it would only be at the cost of their already exiguous giving to the mission. However the choice before me was between losing Chiri's friendship and letting him learn the facts of life the hard way — albeit at the mission's expense. I gave in.

The story of Chiri's truck would fill a volume. Chiri's driver had no more mechanical sense than had he himself, and the truck broke down time after time in remote places and at impossible hours. I lost count of the nocturnal SOSs which dragged me to the scene of one disaster after another. On one occasion there was nothing to do but to leave the vehicle on the roadside overnight; and by the morning it had been wrecked by vandals. It was painstakingly reconstructed over a protracted period, after which the driver drove it enthusiastically on a major trek without a drop of oil in the engine. Even Chiri realised he had reached the end of the road. He bore the disaster uncomplainingly, and travelled by begging lifts and clambering on ancient buses or simply by walking. He almost always got to his intended destination. However much he suffered, his work did not.

It was some time later that he dropped into my office again. "Did you," he asked nonchalantly, "once say something about a motorbike?" Poker-faced I replied: "I believe it was mentioned." Chiri soon had two wheels instead of four.

10. Success at Mandea

THROUGHOUT the 'sixties spectacular changes were taking place on the outstations of St Peter's Mission. There were eleven of these. Wherever we had started with a leaky thatched shelter and a handful of grubby children there were now a permanent church and school surrounded by gardens ablaze with flowers. The schoolchildren — by 1964 we had over 2,000 — wore simple uniforms and were clean, healthy and laughing. If Europeans sometimes questioned the value of missions the Africans were convinced by the evidence of their own eyes.

Many of the children and some of their parents turned to Christianity. Much as we wanted people to become Christians — that was what the mission was for — we exercised no pressure apart from the influence of Christian teachers. Of these we had fifty. A few were quite outstanding, most were good and conscientious, several were trouble-makers and a few did real damage. One young lady-teacher concealed her pregnancy to keep her job, and then threw the baby down a latrine. At a place called Makwara somebody burned down a teacher's kitchen. The incident had nothing to do with politics: it was the broadest hint that teachers should stop spoiling local girls.

Peter Mandimutsira, the head teacher of Makwara, was indeed a ladies' man, not without charm and a turn of humour.

"Why don't you marry?" I asked him after one of his escapades.

"Because," he replied, "to get married you need one

165

woman and lots of money. I've got lots of women and no money."

At last he turned up and announced: "I'm getting married next year."

"Good," I said. "Who is the lucky girl?"

"I have no idea," was his reply. "There are lots of girls."

The outstation at Katiu was perhaps my particular love, since I was the first priest to get there. Within a few years it became the attractive little mission of the Sacred Heart, with a dedicated teacher, a sprinkling of "hearers" and catechumens and one or two Christians. At Katiu we pioneered the growing of tea, the most suitable crop for the valley. There was much hostility at first, for people feared that if the tea were a success the Europeans would take over their land. What actually happened was that a big African tea-estate was started nearby, bringing the local population into the cash economy.

Visitors to Mandea (who by this time were coming even from overseas) did not usually get further than the central mission. One of them, however, ventured with me as far as Katiu, and was immensely impressed to find the children building their own school.

Fortunately it was on another occasion that, leaving Katiu, I found the Nyankombe river had risen fast and was flowing too swiftly for comfort. There was no other way home, so I took the plunge. Within moments the water was up to the floorboards of the Landrover and the truck was stuck on a rock in the middle of the stream. After a long struggle I managed to manoeuvre it clear, only to find I was being borne downstream. A tree brought the vehicle to a halt and swivelled it round, and in the end, with the aid of the populace, I was able to reverse it out on the homeward side. If the engine had stalled all would have been lost. After that I had a snorkel made to fit on the exhaust-pipe.

The story of the central mission, St Peter's itself, was one of both success and failure. The number of people who came to "church" on Sundays continued to grow, as did that of the baptised and confirmed Christians who received Holy Communion. At the great festivals — Christmas and Easter and St Peter's Day — huge crowds assembled, under the trees if it was fine and in the school and on its verandah if it was raining. It was extremely difficult for the priest to administer the Sacrament in such conditions (there might be up to 400 communicants) and we were alternately blistered by the sun and soaked by sudden downpours. Plans were afoot to build a big central mission church, but the cost of the simplest structure would be several thousand pounds, well beyond the reach of the local Christians. We appealed for help to the diocese and the Society for the Propagation of the Gospel as well as the mission's friends, and locally we collected as much money as we could. An architect was engaged and plans drawn up. The architect suggested there was no point in copying the traditional churches of Europe or the plain rectangular buildings common in Africa. His idea was an octagonal structure bringing the people close to the altar, without internal pillars and with a roof supported on a steel framework — something not unlike a glorified rondavel. But the project remained a dream.

Meanwhile trouble with the local population brewed, and our thoughts switched from the church to a threat which put the survival of the mission itself in jeopardy. The Honde Valley was changing rapidly. The bamboos had gone, cut down by the tea estates. The rain-forest was hacked down for cultivation, and in the wet weather hundreds of tons of irreplaceable topsoil tumbled down from the hills, silting up the streams. Somebody described the valley as "a population explosion in a dustbowl." Desperate for land (but ignorant of how to use it) the people cultivated on the steep hillside above the mission and on the banks of the stream which supplied our water. Cattle were driven through the basin where our supply originated. Mud came out of our pipes, and at times the supply dried up altogether.

The government agricultural officer did his best to help, but was powerless. "If they would accept our help," he said, "they could grow on four acres what they now get out of ten. Government assistance is to be had for the asking, but they are scared of the agitators. And if we use compulsion there will be an uproar at the United Nations."

I had long been negotiating with Chief Mandea and with the local headman, and a more or less satisfactory agreement was reached on several occasions. It was never implemented, and I realised I was wasting my time and breath. Land is the most explosive issue in Africa. We were therefore faced with a choice. Either we must capitulate and abandon the mission or I must fight and alienate our immediate neighbours. The African staff were helpless. I decided that in everyone's interests the mission must survive, and I appealed to the District Commissioner who called in officials of the Natural Resources Board. These were appalled at the state of the valley, but exercised extraordinary patience and understanding. They reasoned, held meetings, offered help, issued warnings: all in vain. After further fruitless efforts they summoned the police, and the worst culprits were hauled before the magistrate at Inyanga who fined them and gaoled one or two.

The mission was saved, but at a cost in bitterness even higher than I had anticipated. The church boycott which followed went on for weeks, with pickets at the end of the mission road and Christians threatened with being beaten up if they dared to come to church. And the political agitators seized the opportunity to try their intimidatory tactics on me.

In my occasional newsletter to friends — which was circulated and reproduced quite widely — I had recently explained that the new Rhodesian constitution admitted Africans to the franchise on the same terms as anyone else. This was patently true. However at the height of the boycott I received an anonymous letter in Shona saying I would be murdered if I repeated the statement. A further anonymous letter followed, this time in English, from somebody calling himself "The Flames of Zimbabwe." It started: "Dear Imperialist Lewis," and described me as a "stupid boer" with a "bitch wife." We were accused of living on money stolen from the Africans, and told that both we and our children were going to be burned to death. Gladys and I discussed these threats, but decided to continue sleeping with our doors unlocked.

In church we soldiered on week after week with skeleton congregations. Then, one night, the arch-organiser of the boycott was found rolling round his hut with severe abdominal pains. In increasing agony he was rushed to Gladys at the clinic, and she quickly fixed him up. The Christians (and everyone else) roared with laughter at this episode, and the people returned to church *en masse* the following Sunday. In time most folk came to realise that if I had not made a rumpus they would have lost the central primary school, the clinic and all our outstations, and I enjoyed a period of unprecedented popularity. The church council said "thank you," and the point was repeatedly made that the mission would need a white priest-in-charge for some years if only to stand up to the agitators.

Meanwhile money for the new church and the new permanent clinic was coming in. The clinic (in fact a small, fully equipped hospital with eight beds) was blessed by Archdeacon Pat Mason in November 1965. A few weeks earlier the telephone reached the mission. It came down the steep slopes of Mount Inyangani from Inyanga, and a ten-mile clearing through the trees had to be made to bring it to Mandea. We were the last of twelve subscribers on the party-line.

Owing to delays with contractors in Salisbury and Umtali the big octagonal church took two years to build. Concrete bases were sunk with voluntary local help, and the steel framework was up by the end of 1964. On it was mounted a louvred lantern, topped with an eight-foot white cross which dominated the valley. The rest of the building was completed, again with local help, by the following Christmas. We tried to make it indestructible. The walls were covered with grey rough-cast, the "pews" were of brick set in the concrete floor and the airy spaces between the walls and the corrugated roof obviated the need for windows that could be broken. The huge African crucifix carved by Job Kekana was hoisted above the altar just before Easter.

St Peter's Church was dedicated by the bishop on Whit Monday 1966, a cool sunny day, in the presence of an enormous crowd. The choir, accompanied by drums, cymbals and tambourines, produced a magnificent volume of sound which sent shivers of emotion down the spines of our European visitors. Anthony, now aged four, acted as boat-boy, carrying the incense-boat and holding his own among the adult altar servers. Afterwards Gladys organised one of her multiracial cocktail parties in the mission house while the feast and celebrations outside the church went on for the rest of the day.

What our visitors did not know was that we had prepared for the dedication of St Peter's Church by a "month of dedication" among ourselves, which the Christian people took very seriously. Still fewer knew that the Christian menfolk had got together, without any initiative from the mission, to hold an all-night vigil of prayer in the new church before its dedication.

The future of the mission seemed set fair, but with one big problem. Just before the dedication Lisa Teubes left the mission for the sake of her children. She had done a superb job over more than two years, looking after the schools and mowing down mounds of work in the office. Unless and until I could find someone else her job would fall on me.

*　*　*　*

In 1964 Ian Douglas Smith had taken over as Prime Minister of Southern Rhodesia. Little as we liked his right-wing policies we believed he was justified in asking for the independence from Britain which had so readily been granted to the more backward members of the now-defunct Central African Federation. (Britain had promised not to dissolve the Federation without the consent of all its members, but had reneged on its promise in 1963.) Nyasaland and Northern Rhodesia were already Malawi and Zambia. Under the new multiracial constitution of 1961–1962 Southern Rhodesia was entirely capable of running its own affairs, and the constitution guaranteed increasing African participation leading to African predominance.

The demand for independence on the new constitution came from all races in Rhodesia. In 1964 it was demonstrated by a referendum of the multiracial electorate and a traditional *indaba*, at Dombashawa, of the African tribespeople who adhered to more ancient ways.

Britain refused independence, insisting that Rhodesia must

be run as a colony. Pleas and negotiations were alike in vain, and the prospect of a Unilateral Declaration of Independence became real. Rhodesians felt that no self-respecting people could agree for ever to be ruled from a distant land by politicians most of whom had never seen Africa. Particular anger was aroused by the British Prime Minister's use of the monarchy as a tool to subjugate Rhodesia to his political will.

On Thursday, November 11th, 1965 Gladys and I were having lunch in the mission house with Lisa Teubes, who was still with us. On the radio we heard Ian Smith making Rhodesia's Unilateral Declaration of Independence — independence from the government of the United Kingdom, *not* from the British Crown. His final words were: "God save the Queen."

The British Prime Minister, Mr Harold Wilson, called in the United Nations which, in breach of its own charter, imposed sanctions. "Five principles" (ultimately six) were imposed on Rhodesia as a pre-condition of recognition, principles which no state had ever implemented in the history of mankind. The Archbishop of Canterbury Michael Ramsey, the British Council of Churches and the missionary societies all lined up with Britain against Rhodesia. The archbishop outdid even Harold Wilson, proposing that Rhodesia be invaded. Thereafter he was frequently referred to as the "arch-bomber."

Rhodesia, meanwhile, was completely peaceful, the government having, we thought mistakenly, imposed a state of emergency before UDI. A preacher in Westminster Abbey (I have forgotten who) declaimed: "End violence in Rhodesia!"

Sanctions soon made themselves felt. Rhodesian independence postage-stamps were treated as invalid. Petrol was rationed. English funds for missions were cut off, and cheques from our friends could not be cashed. I put out an urgent appeal to our white Rhodesian supporters, who responded magnificently but could only partially close the gap.

Our daughter Margaret, now aged six, was due to go to boarding school in January, since Gladys could no longer teach her at home. We drove the 200 miles to Salisbury at 40 mph to save petrol, and there was a tearful farewell. The headmistress of Bishopslea told us privately that a bursary from England had been blocked by the British authorities, but said we were not to worry. (Bursaries for black children, we learned, were allowed through.)

Early in 1966 I protested in the London *Times* about the cut-off of funds to missions, and a relaxation was announced. In the news media I got much undeserved credit for this. The real work had been done by the missionary societies and the bishops who were not best pleased by my bursting into print.

In February I received an urgent call from Chavanga, where the school faced a crisis. The menfolk were back from the towns, thrown out of work by sanctions. Of the eighty or ninety new children registered for the beginning of term only thirty-five had turned up. The parents could not afford the fees and the books, though our charges were minimal. Happily the mission's friends rallied round to help them, and the problem was soon solved.

The difficulties of Rhodesia were compounded by the extraordinary venom of the British Broadcasting Corporation, whose overseas broadcasts were controlled by the British Foreign Office. We were prepared for bias, but not for the reporting of apocryphal events such as the shooting down of Rhodesian 'planes by African nationalists! (That happened more than a decade later.) I picked up one BBC news transmission whose first item was the Rhodesian government's refusal to recognise the royal prerogative: later, way down the list, was a mention of twelve million people facing starvation in India. British propaganda broadcasts were beamed into Rhodesia from Francistown in Botswana and from Zambia, and a new transmitter was erected by British technicians on the Rhodesia-Zambian border at Livingstone. Zambian broadcasts frequently urged black Rhodesians to murder whites. On the night of May 16th–17th 1966 Rhodesian terrorists from Zambia crossed the border and murdered the Viljoens, a white farming couple living in the north of the country.

Gladys and I had not voted for Ian Smith's Rhodesian Front government, and were in no way committed to UDI. However, the fury and the folly of the British reaction — and the malice of the church leaders — made it well nigh impossible to sympathise with the British standpoint. We were aware of the failings of Rhodesia, but were convinced that they were not greater than Britain's and that their remedy lay in Salisbury rather than Westminster.

In July 1966, during a brief visit to Britain for family reasons, I spoke for Rhodesia in the Albert Hall in London. However, shortly after returning to the mission from England I was involved in an unexpected political clash with the Rhodesian government. It centred on the African tribespeople at Taungwena in the Inyanga area. In that wild and chilly country we had what was now our remotest outstation, three hours' hard climb above Chavanga. And there, amid hills and streams of breath-taking beauty, Chief Kinga and his Taungwena people had their home and their lands.

At least, they thought they had. But it turned out that these were on a 45,000 acre European ranch bought in the thirties for (it was said) half-a-crown an acre. The government announced that the people must move, though the owner of the ranch had not known where his boundary lay.

Repeated interviews with the Ministry of Internal Affairs were in vain. I suppose I was written off as just another clerical do-gooder, and of such the Rhodesian authorities had had a bellyful. The Minister of Lands, on the other hand, was helpfulness itself, visiting the people by helicopter and offering excellent alternative land and plenty of it. Understandably, however, the people would not move. The European owner was prepared to sell, and it appeared there were overseas trusts which would put up the money. But the government insisted the land was "European," and could not become "African" without an amendment to the Land Apportionment Act, which it would not contemplate. To my mind this was both wicked and foolish, and I said so loudly in the press. However, what I wrote was repeated in the British media and, inevitably, used as a stick with which to beat Rhodesia.

The government remained pig-headed to the end, and did immeasurable damage to the country and to its own cause. Chief Kinga was succeeded by the highly political Chief Rekai, who was helped by Guy Clutton-Brock's friends on the neighbouring Nyafaru Farm. It was not long before the televicon cameras arrived, and the whole thing became an international *cause célèbre*. All a mission priest could do was to make the best of a bad job: to build a little church and school outside the disputed area and help to find homes for some of the people who were scattered.

My faith in Rhodesia was shaken. But I could not believe that a single act of inexcusable folly justified the far greater folly of a British Prime Minister bent on the subjugation of the whole country and the imposition of external rule. However I made up my mind that somehow, some day, I would try to have a say in the affairs of Rhodesia.

At the end of 1966 Ian Smith met Harold Wilson on HMS *Tiger*, but no agreement was reached: what Britain offered was not independence. In 1968 similar talks were held on HMS *Fearless*, with similar results — and for the same reason Mr Smith was an honest man, and Rhodesia paid dearly for his honesty. He turned down, with the assent of his government, two offers which in practice he could have accepted and progressively disregarded. There were further terrorist raids from Zambia, but most of the infiltrators were handed over by the local population to the Rhodesian security forces.

In 1969 Rhodesia proclaimed itself a republic, with a tougher constitution and a new flag. By then fourteen white priests had left or were about to leave the diocese of Mashonaland. With increasing strain men were cracking up and packing up.

*   *   *   *

At Mandea petrol-rationing meant that many journeys had now to be made by motorbike, with increasing physical exhaustion. By late 1966 (after we had returned from England) my additional job as Archdeacon of Inyanga had begun to involve me in long treks to lonely African priests on remote missions.

At St Peter's I had time for little but administration. Years ago our Anthony, when he began to talk, had said: "Why does Daddy always go away?" In 1967, as he entered the mission school, he was overheard asking a playmate: "Does

174

your Dad work in an office like mine?'' And people outside the office would say: ''Father doesn't have time to talk to us any more.'' It was, of course, the writing on the wall.

Relief came with the arrival, at the end of 1966, of a helper from England. Miss Ann Hadley — yet another answer to prayer — took over the office and schools and climbed mountains like her predecessors, but obviously had not their African background. She was very lonely. But she stayed more than a year, long enough to train a highly qualified African teacher to take over the supervision of the schools. Unhappily, and quite coincidentally, St Peter's went through its worst period after Ann's arrival.

For years I had been battling, at the instance of the local people, to get a secondary school for Mandea. The thirst for education was insatiable. At last, before Christmas 1966, permission from the Education Department came through. The very reasonable stipulation was made that a new and separate site should be provided. You could not have an eighty-acre secondary school on a hundred-acre mission where there was not enough flat land for a football-pitch. In any case I myself was unwilling to have the mission transformed (as had happened elsewhere) into a merely educational institution which would relegate the evangelistic work to the position of a sideshow.

One Sunday morning in January, after church, I announced what I thought was the good news about the secondary school. The expected delight was not forthcoming. Indeed some of the menfolk got up and walked out. Later a delegation of men, most of them the usual trouble-makers, came to see me and said the secondary school MUST be on the mission. The local folk were not prepared to give up any more land, nor were they willing to do any more building. All the work must be done by the mission.

The group became increasingly bellicose, announcing that if I did not capitulate at once on all issues they would drive me out of Mandea and demand a priest who would ''work with the people.'' I indicated that I wanted my lunch, and left the men still prophesying. Subsequently the non-politicised majority proved vastly more reasonable, and dozens of meetings were held to find a site for the school. But the Chief and the headman said "No more land," and I had no choice but to respond: "No land, no secondary school." The district was once more in turmoil. Troubles, however, did not come singly.

The new deacon sent to us by the diocese turned out to be a major headache. His ordination had been postponed owing to personality difficulties, and I soon knew why. Returning from Samtete one day he waded the river and found that Ann Hadley was not, as arranged, awaiting him with the car. He was many hours late, and Ann had reasonably waited till dark and concluded that he would not return that day. However the deacon was livid with anger and went about like a man demented for the next month. His frenzy had not abated when the Mothers' Union worker came from Bonda to hold a meeting of MU members. This he proceeded to wreck by organising the women to carry Mrs Chirimuuta's mealies — the sabbath notwithstanding! The situation was a public scandal. But it got worse.

Father Chirimuuta had done excellent work. He had twice kept the mission running efficiently while I was overseas and had coped with other longish absences of mine. But now a grave quarrel broke out between his family and the Jaris next door. What it was about I never knew, but it went on for months. To the best of my knowledge the Jaris had always behaved as good neighbours. Both of them were jolly and good-natured people with whom it was not easy to quarrel. Mrs Chirimuuta, however, was very different. Her outbursts increased in scope and magnitude and reverberated far beyond the mission. Though at times she could be charming and helpful she was the living embodiment of a principle which, I had long ago discovered, operated at Mandea if nowhere else. It did not take two to make a quarrel. As our deacon had just demonstrated, a quarrel could be initiated, maintained and escalated almost indefinitely by one person.

Father Chiri, meantime, was to a large extent running the mission, and became less and less happy about having to work under a priest-in-charge. This seemed to me natural. With Chiri's agreement I had advised the bishop that he was entirely ready for a post of independent responsibility: but

176

nothing was offered him. Then I inadvertently made a minor decision about a building which in effect countermanded a prior ruling of his. Nothing of any consequence was involved, and if anyone had pointed out the problem a few minutes' discussion would have sorted it out. I was quite unprepared for the eruption of Chiri's anger which followed. This was Vesuvian in its ferocity, and subsidiary eruptions emanated from Mrs Chirimuuta and the deacon. The real source of the anger, however, soon proved to be something quite different: it was my refusal to have the secondary school on the mission. However, no one was prepared to talk, and the mission was engulfed in yet another open scandal — clergy at loggerheads. The fact that I myself had nothing to quarrel about, and was more than willing to apologise for my mistakes, made not a ha'porth of difference.

It happened that at the time I was physically exhausted by much travel and by the problems of other missions in the archdeaconry. Not trusting myself to act wisely I talked the thing over with Gladys and we decided on a short holiday in the cottage on the Vumba Hills. I reasoned that I would be the better for some sleep and some prayers, and the furore must surely have quietened down by the time of our return.

What actually happened was that Chiri and the deacon went off to Salisbury to complain about me and my stand on the secondary school: and Chiri got his transfer on the spot. He did not return to St Peter's. There were none of the decencies of farewell, and there was no gathering to wish him Godspeed and to thank him for the quite admirable work he had done.

So what we found on our return was yet another full-scale church boycott, in twofold protest against the manner of Chiri's leaving and my failure to agree to a secondary school on the mission. Pickets manned the end of the mission road, notices were put up threatening beatings and Mrs Chirimuuta (who had remained behind because of her crops) was going from village to village telling people to stay away from church.

In the middle of all this, in May 1967, the Archbishop of Central Africa and our own bishop came to pay the mission a formal visitation. They knew perfectly well what was going on, but tactfully feigned ignorance. They could hardly do otherwise for the church was packed to the doors, and beyond, with Christians from the outstations. Douglas Dzimunwe, now headmaster and choirmaster, coaxed from his children harmonies of unprecedented magnificence, and the drummers excelled themselves. What was more important, it was impossible not to be impressed by the devotion and loyalty and friendliness of the Christians from throughout the district. The feast afterwards was marred only by the absence of *maheu*, the light local beer usually brewed by the women of the local Mothers' Union. These latter were on strike as part of the boycott, and dared not come near the mission. We drank tea instead.

After this the annual church meeting, representing the whole district, was held at Nyatsanza, our biggest and most successful outstation. I repeated what I had told church meetings ever since our arrival. "I am ready to make way for an African priest at any time you suggest. My wife and I are here simply as stop-gaps, to get the mission on its feet." The response was emphatic and unanimous. "Stick it out. This foolishness does not come from the ordinary Christian people. If you run away no successor of yours will have a chance." The point was repeated that if and when we felt we really had to move on ("which we hope will not be yet") there would still be a need for a white priest for a few more years.

Six weeks later the boycott fizzled out, it being apparent to the most hardened trouble-makers that nothing was being achieved and that popular feeling was turning against them. Intimidation and fear are the most powerful forces in Africa, the primaeval witchcraft of centuries having eaten into the African soul. But just occasionally, with God's help, the worm turns. I abandoned the proposed secondary school, and nothing more was said or heard of it. It was more trouble than it was worth.

The Christian revival which took place at Mandea after the boycott is difficult to describe. It manifested itself in ever bigger crowds in church and an overwhelming friendliness on the part of ordinary folk enjoying a new freedom. But it went far deeper than that. Many people were really striving to *be* Christians. You could go into church at any time and

178

there would be men and women on their knees praying. People tried to sort out their marriage problems, and there were more and more Christian weddings in church. The ideas of monogamy and fidelity were sinking in, and with a deep and sincere Christianity came a new happiness for many. Nor was this any flash in the pan. The change had come to stay.

On September 28th 1968 St Peter's Mission celebrated the tenth anniversary of its foundation by Father Mason. The festival proved to be the most spectacular in the mission's short history. It was prepared for by much prayer and attended not only by bigger crowds than ever (and European friends from many parts of the country) but by the new Head of State of Rhodesia, Mr Clifford Dupont. The latter was one of the 500 communicants at the tickets-only Solemn Eucharist. The service was partly in English and partly in Shona, and the dramatic harmonies of Douglas Dzimunwe's choir were both European and African.

No one failed to notice the unassuming nature of Mr Dupont's visit and his easy mixing with the people. He arrived with the District Commissioner, his own aide-de-camp and a single security officer, apparently unarmed. Many visitors remarked that there was probably no other country in Africa whose president could travel with so little fuss and mingle with the multitudes with so little protection.

Gladys put on her usual magnificent spread at the mission house, the chiefs and headmen had their own special feast and the rest of the folk consumed three oxen and a great deal else. Sports in the afternoon were followed by a huge bonfire and a firework display at night. Nobody got drunk and there was no trouble. The upheavals of the past were buried and forgotten.

One day shortly after this I was alone in the chapel in our house, quietly reading Evensong. I think I had got to the Magnificat when I realised the distant telephone was ringing two shorts and two longs — our call on the party-line which clamoured all our waking hours. I hesitated, but there was no one else to answer and I put down my book and went along to the office.

It was "Sam" Wood in Salisbury. Since Bishop Alderson's

death he was acting in his place as Vicar General of the diocese.

"Arthur," he said without preamble, "are you and Gladys going to stay at Mandea for the rest of your lives? Or do you want a change?"

"I had better talk with Gladys," I said.

"Fine," was the reply. "They are asking for both of you at Rusape."

That meant not St Faith's but the neighbouring farming parish centred on Rusape town. As we talked about the matter that night Gladys said: "It is time we thought more about the children. We have done what we came to Mandea to do." She was, of course, entirely right. Anthony, aged six, was about to go to his prep. school at Marandellas, only an hour's drive from Rusape. And Margaret, aged nine, was definitely a person in her own right, thinking about the future. "Mummy,"she had said to Gladys recently, "I don't like mini-skirts. Do I have to become a teenager?"

The church council asked us to stay at least another year or two, and when I said this was not possible ultimately requested me to look for another white priest. In the appeal I circulated I wrote: "Of the hundreds of priests who profess a deep concern for Rhodesian Africans, is there not one willing to live and work with them?" There was no volunteer: a fact which helped to shape my own future thinking on the value of contemporary ecclesiastical "liberalism." Fortunately it mattered little. Father Oliver Mandihlare had arrived at Mandea some months ago as assistant. It was better that Africanisation should come earlier than later.

One big surprise awaited us as we prepared to leave Mandea the following year. Gladys and I, of course, had a deep affection for the African people we served. We would not have been at Mandea otherwise. But it had not occurred to us that the ordinary folk might have any reciprocal feeling for us. However farewell journeys to the outstations turned into something a bit like royal progresses, even though the Land-rover sank with all its axles deep in the mud. At Nyatsanza and Mandea there were big parties with speeches and presentations.

180

But these things were not the surprise. What moved us was the almost endless stream of visitors with gifts over the last two months before we left: eggs and chickens, rice and nuts, fruit and home-made pots and basins and small sums of money which the givers could certainly not afford. The women turned up to sing us a hymn, but gave up after a verse, said "Thank you" quietly and ran away.

As we finally drove from the mission and the crowds began to thin out two old women knelt in the road and we stopped. They were unknown to us and were not Christians. If we had ever done anything for them it was long forgotten. But they clapped their hands and gave us their gift. It was a fortune — sixpence.

11. Whites are People Too

RUSAPE was a growing little town surrounded by undulating plains and the strange granite domes and balancing rocks which were so characteristic of Rhodesia. The trees were a bright green in the summer rains of January; but in the African autumn, before the rains started again, the ubiquitous loquats (*musasa* trees) would, by some miracle of nature, blaze in the dry land into a spectacular riot of reds and pale greens and russets.

The town was the centre of a thriving farming industry. It thrived not because of any special fertility of the soil but because the white farmers — educated, hard-workers all — were, with their wives, as rugged and as rooted as the rocky kopjes which broke up their lands. Most of them were Afrikaners who attended the Dutch Reformed church with its white clock tower and its sonorous bell.

There were only 150 Anglican families in the whole parish. Their church — our church now — was dwarfed by its big Calvinist brother, and worshipped in English. It, too, had a white tower, more picturesque perhaps, but less imposing. It was certainly much less wealthy. The rectory, a simple single-storey house with a wide *stoep* or verandah and a big garden, was within the church grounds.

It was in a subdued mood that Gladys and I arrived at our new home. We had, after all, reached the end of an era, and had little experience of working among white people. But we need have had no fear. Our welcome at Rusape was as warm as our farewell at Mandea. The larder was full and the refrigerator stuffed with goodies. And it was glorious to have electric light again and to be able to chat easily in English.

"We don't bite," said one of the churchwardens, "even though we are not black. Whites are people too!" We knew from our time at St Faith's that these people were, most of them, far from being reactionary or anti-African.

Within days I was up to the eyes in parish work: visiting in the town and on the farms, preparing services, teaching in the school, instructing confirmation candidates young and old and trying to help people with their manifold problems. Church council meetings ran smoothly. The council included representatives of the two daughter-churches, at Headlands and Inyazura, each of them half an hour away on a good tarred road. On the few occasions when consensus was not quickly reached a simple vote settled the mattter, and we were away in little over an hour. It was a change from the contentious three or four hour marathons to which I had become accustomed.

The pay, as always, was less than lavish, and Gladys got a part-time job at Rusape hospital to help out. Indeed Anglicans were so thin on the ground that the parish was for practical purposes joined up with the independent chapelry of St Catherine at Inyanga, some seventy miles to the east in the hills. On Easter Day I celebrated the Eucharist in the morning at the parish church and at both daughter-churches before driving to Inyanga for a service in the afternoon.

Inyanga was a joy. The little stone church was high in the hills of Inyanga Downs, with a clear glass "picture window" beyond the altar overlooking the distant mountains of Mozambique. The Downs themselves, with their settled European population and their holiday cottages, were largely the work of a handful of pioneers who arrived in the nineteen-thirties. Major McIlwaine and the Hanmer brothers found bare windswept hills, planted trees (especially pines which spread like wildfire) and ended up with another Scotland, complete with man-made lakes and waterfalls and trout-streams. The steep and winding lanes were often shrouded in a Scotch mist.

Of course, I was already familiar with Inyanga, which was the centre of the archdeaconry for which I was responsible. In addition to my other jobs I had been made priest-in charge of St Catherine's while still at Mandea, and had taken occasional services there. But, above all, Inyanga Downs was special to Gladys and me because it was there that we had built our little cottage. The heat and the strain at Mandea had sometimes led to total exhaustion, and we had longed for a place of our own among the cool hill-tops.

For years the cottage had remained just "our pipe-dream." But as we had begun to make white friends at Inyanga they had implored us to build a place where we could rest. Some of them gave us sums of money. Ken Gamble of Inyanga Sawmills said: "It is a must. I will transport the materials free, and supervise the work when I can." We employed an African builder called Jana, whose fondness for the bottle proved vastly in excess of his enthusiasm for his work. He tried the patience even of the good-natured Ken, and on the few occasions when I could oversee the work myself drove me to distraction. "I'm off to the store for a pound of nails," he once told me. It was a fortnight before he staggered back. But the job was finished at last, and our cottage, with its bulging walls, looked a hundred years old when we first entered it. We called it "Ravenshaw," after a childhood haunt of mine in Warwickshire.

To this haven we fled on the rare occasions when we could get away, and here we brought the children during the school holidays. In the sunshine the brightly coloured sunbirds perched on the fuchsia bushes outside the windows, and yellow lilies sprouted through our bumpy new-made lawn. We would climb the hills and swim in the River Tsanga below a big waterfall on the property of our friends and neighbours, the Murrays. At nights, and on days when the rain poured and the mist descended, we read *Alice in Wonderland* and C. S. Lewis's Narnia stories to Margaret and Anthony or played games to the hiss of the pressure-lamps. The log-fire blazed (and smoked) and we were very cosy.

However, Ravenshaw had to serve as more than a holiday home and a centre for my work in the Inyanga chapelry. It was destined to do duty as a convalescent home too. As the reaction to the years at Mandea set in I was compelled to go into hospital several times for various kinds of patching-up, on each occasion being ordered a period of rest afterwards.

Because of the bad roads, Petronella the boneshaker (and the motorbike to which I was again reduced by the petrol-shortage) had wrought such damage to my spine that at one stage it appeared I would have to give up driving, and Africa, for good. From that fate peace and quiet at the cottage — and the patience of my parishioners — happily delivered me. Back at Rusape, too, there was always a little stream of African priests to visit me, with their sympathy as well as their problems.

Had I known to what extent the terrorists were building up their forces across the border, almost under our noses, recuperation might have been more difficult. The Portuguese were losing interest in their war with FRELIMO guerrillas in Mozambique, their conscripts from metropolitan Portugal having little concern but to get back to their homes in one piece. FRELIMO offered almost unlimited hospitality to the Rhodesian terrorists of ZANLA, the guerrilla wing of Robert Mugabe's ZANU (Zimbabwe African National Union).

Meanwhile Rhodesian politics gave us no respite. Mr Smith's government became increasingly exasperated with what it saw as the intransigence of the British Labour leadership, and particularly with Harold Wilson's use of the monarchy as a tool to subdue Rhodesia. It proposed a republic and a new, right-wing constitution, including the contentious Land Tenure Bill to divide the country equally into white sections and black. This was an attempt (misguided, many of us thought) to face the undoubted fact that if the entire land-surface of Rhodesia had been made over to the Africans land would still have run out within a lifetime owing to the skyrocketing population-explosion. In the meantime the (white) goose which laid the golden eggs would have been killed.

The church leaders, including our new bishop from England, virtually told us to vote against the republic and against the proposed new constitution. In church, of course, I said nothing about either. Our people were perplexed and divided. A referendum of the electorate was held on June 20th 1969, and both republic and constitution went through with large majorities. The new dispensation came into effect in March

186

of the following year, and the green-and-white Rhodesian flag, without the Union Jack, flew for the first time in Cecil Square in Salisbury and throughout the country.

Earlier in 1969, in a newsletter to friends, I had written of the shattering of my own illusions about Britain as throughout Africa it precipitately handed over power to the incompetent and the avaricious, sometimes to chaos itself. I wrote of Britain's "howls of wrath against this one small country with the courage to brave the world and fight for the civilisation and standards which once made Britain great." But I added: "The tragedy is that in the sheer bitterness of reaction Rhodesia, which claimed (in its Declaration of Independence) to have struck a blow for Christianity and civilisation, is now adopting policies which can be squared with neither."

Our new bishop, Paul Burrough, came from England and had been enthroned in Salisbury cathedral, Rhodesia, on the same day that Mandea celebrated its tenth anniversary, September 28th 1968. (The Mandea celebration had been arranged a year in advance, and could not be altered.) While we were receiving Mr Clifford Dupont, who had replaced the British governor as Head of State, the anglophiles in Salisbury towed Bishop Burrough off to Government House to advertise to the world that the Anglican Church supported the *ancien régime*. The former governor, Sir Humphrey Gibbs, was still in residence since he enjoyed enormous personal respect both among those who supported him and those who could in conscience do so no longer.

Bishop Burrough was unknown in Rhodesia at the time of his appointment, which caused some anger since it was believed Rhodesians were being passed over and Rhodesia was being treated as a colony ecclesiastically as well as politically. It was felt that the Church was becoming an ancillary of the British Foreign Office.

Before the new bishop had left England he was visited by diocesan representatives from Salisbury and briefed on his forthcoming responsibilities — from the "liberal," pro-British standpoint. In a broadcast interview he was even persuaded to say that the views of the Archdeacon of Inyanga were "somewhat extreme." Since at that stage he had seen neither

187

Africa nor me I did not know whether to laugh or cry. During the next few months Bishop Burrough was busy and so was I. It was no one's fault that we had little contact.

Before Christmas the bishop held a confirmation at Rusape. It was a lovely service and a fitting climax to much devoted preparation by the candidates. But my private interview afterwards was unhappy, and reminiscent of the bad old days. The bishop's manner was brusque: I did not realise that he himself was ill at ease. "I do not want you as archdeacon next year," was the gist of what he said. "In fact I am abolishing the archdeaconry of Inyanga altogether. My advisers tell me you are unpopular with Africans, and I have to win the confidence of the African clergy."

I was dumbfounded. Here was a man who owed his authority entirely to his position, talking to a priest who had lived among Africans for twenty years in lonely situations where survival itself depended on ability to get on with them. What I had not realised was the power of a small group of African nationalist clergy in Salisbury in alliance with the white "liberals." The bishop went on to add: "I am afraid I must tell you there may not be a place for you in this diocese much longer."

Clearly the "liberals" and the nationalists were angered by my contributions to the English and Rhodesian press in defence of Rhodesia. Their authority to speak for the Church might not, apparently, be challenged, and this was their revenge. It was intended to hurt and humiliate, and it did both.

The next day I had to go into hospital for a spinal operation, but was on my feet again for Christmas. It was after the festival that the news broke in the press and on the radio and television. "Inyanga Archdeaconry Abolished," the headlines shouted. "Controversial Cleric Loses Archdeaconry." The public rumpus which followed was as regrettable as it was unavoidable. Ultimately the bishop said he would "roust around" to find me work in the diocese, but the folk of Rusape and Inyanga insisted that I stayed put.

It was not long before I could laugh at this absurd storm-in-a-teacup. The new archdeaconry of the Eastern Highlands was much the same as the old archdeaconry of Inyanga, and its incumbent was none other than my good friend, Anselm Genders, of the Community of the Resurrection. His outlook differed little from mine, though he was less inclined to write in the press. By common consent I was asked to continue to keep a watching brief on Mandea Mission.

By this time I suspected that there was little future for me in the Anglican Church. However, I was not going to commit moral suicide by toeing the "liberal" political line, which could only mean handing the African people over to a Marxist government. But, equally, I was determined not to leave the Church or consent to be pushed out. I would stay in and, if necessary, fight. I still had a pen, and would wield it more often, not less. It was shortly after this that a leader-writer in the *Rhodesia Herald* described me as the church leaders' "hair shirt!"

* * * *

Rhodesia's republican constitution came into force on 2nd March 1970. A general election followed in April, and the Rhodesian Front once more swept the board. The Land Tenure Act became law, and missions working in African areas were required to register with the authorities as "voluntary agencies" — bringing them into the government's overall scheme of things. The church leaders publicly condemned the act and said they would not obey it. Bishop Burrough asked for our support and implied that without the backing of the whole diocese he would resign.

In this matter I had much sympathy with the bishop, though I did not think the question was quite so simple as he maintained. Some missions were already involved in subversion — something which, surely, no government could be expected to tolerate. Devout and sincere Christians were in fact divided, and many felt it was in any case useless to lament retrogressive legislation when in fact every attempt to move in a more progressive direction had been blocked by Britain.

The members of the Rusape church council were inevitably

divided. There was a pro-government majority which would nevertheless back the bishop in the event of official interference and an anti-government minority which supported him to the hilt anyway. All of them were good and faithful churchpeople who, it seemed to me, were entitled to their opinions. None of us would have dreamed of discussing such a question in the church council had we been free agents. However, we were required to discuss it, and we submitted.

A council meeting early in July was as heated as I expected, debating conflicting motions. There was no possibility of agreement. Some resolution had to be formulated, however, to put before the annual meeting of the whole parish later in the month. It was this which would return our reply to the bishop. Finally I proposed a compromise: that we should give our support to any approach by the church leaders to the government requesting that the Act be amended by the deletion of the clause on missions. This was passed *nem. con.* by a show of hands, and we all breathed a sigh of relief. I looked forward to piloting the same resolution through the annual parish meeting.

It was not to be. Gladys had accompanied me to Inyanga for the monthly services there, and after our arrival we were both laid low by a local influenza epidemic. It would have caused huge inconvenience to alter the date of the parish meeting, so I sent a message to Rusape suggesting that the meeting carry on without me. A competent lay chairman was elected, but he was faced with a highly-charged and stormy meeting. Not only did the pro-government section win the day: it went on to condemn the church leaders roundly for interfering in political affairs. We heard about it on the radio.

This development, of course, was a recipe for disaster. At the next council meeting four of the opponents of the government, having seen the bishop, submitted a prepared statement dissociating themselves from the resolutions of the parish meeting — and, unjustly, associating me with these resolutions. They took the opportunity to condemn my "political" activities (while approving the bishop's) and even deplored as "political" a meeting I had had with a government minister to back the bishop's objection to the registration of

190

missions! They then resigned and walked out. It was little consolation that the remainder of the councillors (more than three-quarters of the total) went on to pass a unanimous vote of confidence in their Rector.

I was deeply saddened by this split, though the dissidents did not let it interfere with their churchgoing. They had hitherto been good-humoured about their now "anti-church-establishment" Rector. After all I was one of very few priests publicly to dissent from the line of the hierarchy, and they were tolerant men normally willing to acknowledge the existence of two points of view.

But my sadness went deeper than this. These councillors were deeply devout and sincere people, who tried to practise their Christianity in every aspect of their lives. Even now I remember Rijk Fischer of Wakefield Farm and his wife Maymie: later I was to minister to Rijk in his last days. Both they and their friends were true Christians, and I as their priest had no business to let anything come between us.

It was to the credit of the other members of the council that they approached the dissidents privately, as of course I did myself, expressing regret at the turn events had taken and asking them to reconsider their resignations. In the end the government took the heart out of the row by announcing that the missions would be "deemed to have registered" without any action on their part!

It was in March the following year that Ferdie Fischer, Rijk's brother, was killed in a gun accident. Ferdie was universally liked, and at his requiem the local chapel at Headlands was so crammed with his family and friends that the Africans could only gather outside. The service, of course, was in English.

When it was finished the Africans came to me and said: "Can we have a service for Ferdie too?" I started again, this time in Shona.

Ferdie's death brought us all together, and at the parish meeting in April the men who had resigned were re-elected to the council as if nothing had happened, and quietly resumed their seats. If memory serves me, it was Rijk who led his friends back.

* * * *

Shortly after the Rhodesian election of 1970 the British had an election too, and the Conservatives ousted the Labour Party. It was commonly thought that they were more sympathetic towards Rhodesia than their opponents. People in Salisbury sang "Tory, Tory, alleluya," and hopes of a settlement with Britain were high.

In November 1971 Sir Alec Douglas-Home, the new British Foreign Secretary, arrived in Salisbury and within a few days he and Ian Smith hammered out an agreement. It softened the harshness of the new republican constitution but offered more to the Rhodesians than Britain had previously conceded. Reconciliation was in sight, and our problems seemed at an end. Champagne corks popped.

However, the ever hostile British Foreign Office had its torpedo ready. There had to be a "test of acceptability" among the Africans. It was perfectly true, of course, that the Africans had not been consulted. But the object of the agreement was to ensure that *they had a full say in all future decisions.* In December 1971 the Methodist bishop, Abel Muzorewa, set out to wreck the settlement with his new African National Council. It seemed that the Churches were lining up on his side.

As early as September the Synod of the diocese of Mashonaland had refused to vote on a resolution "that the problems of this country are capable of solution without bloodshed." In November the "Christian Council of Rhodesia" (a subsidiary of the World Council of Churches, 97% financed by that body) resolved to support the WCC's "Programme to Combat Racism." This was the programme which began in 1970 to fund every revolutionary movement in Southern Africa, including the ANC.

Before Christmas the "Christian Council of Rhodesia" had two visitors from overseas. One was the Reverend Elliott Kendall, the "Africa Secretary of the Department of International Affairs of the British Council of Churches" — a known ecclesiastical radical. The other was Canon Herbert Sydenham of the United Society for the Propagation of the

Gospel, now acting for the British Conference of Missionary Societies. This was none other than Sorbo Syd, whom I had known of old in the Universities' Mission and who had changed with the changing times. Following this visit the "National Affairs Committee of the Christian Council of Rhodesia" put out a statement condemning the settlement proposals *even though the Council had not met!* I published my own reply through the news media, pointing out that all these grandly named folk spoke for themselves: most Christians in Rhodesia had never heard of them.

After Christmas the "Christian Council" actually met, and the settlement issue was hotly contested. However, the Council's benefactor, the World Council, made available substantial funds for African schooling, and a majority against the settlement was therefore a foregone conclusion. (Vastly greater government funds for African education were forgotten!) The most notable event of the meeting was Bishop Burrough's vote *for* the settlement and *against* the majority, which he himself publicised.

This marked the end of the bishop's apparent tutelage to the "liberal" circle in Salisbury. Bishop Burrough was a big man, both physically and morally: and henceforth (it seemed to me) he did his thinking for himself. He was far too wise to change sides; but he strove honestly and courageously to be fair. His integrity was demonstrated by the fact that he was not infrequently attacked from both political wings.

Early in January 1972 a Commission headed by Lord Pearce arrived in Rhodesia to carry out the British "test of acceptability," and ultimately it claimed to have made some sort of contact with 6% of the African population. It was greeted with demonstrations and riots which led to loss of life — events which, in those days, were new to the Rhodesian scene.

The Commission's itineraries were widely advertised, and Bishop Muzorewa and his ANC merely bussed their agitators from town to town to urge Africans to reject the settlement. Paul Moorcraft wrote in his book on Rhodesia *A Short Thousand Years*. "Most (Africans) were ignorant of the details of the

193

settlement and some were even unaware that UDI had been declared.''

The story of the Commission's visit to a remote African tribe on the Zambezi is perhaps apocryphal. The commissioners, who arrived by boat, were received by the local Chief and his people with every courtesy. The tribespeople were asked, through an interpreter, whether they considered the settlement proposals were a satisfactory solution to the dispute with Britain. Their reply: ''What dispute?''

It need hardly be said that the Commission found that the settlement proposals were unacceptable to the African people — though no Commissioner knew either of the African languages! — and this, of course, effectively destroyed the hope of reconciliation. ''A group of foreigners stumbling around,'' commented Ian Smith. However, he continued to pursue the ''first prize'' of a settlement with Britain. This policy in practice gave the African nationalists a permanent veto.

The Prime Minister made it plain that there could be no question of unilateral implementation of the settlement proposals. However a number of people, including myself, made personal approaches to him on the question of racial discrimination. Here Africans still had real grounds for complaint. A Commission on Racial Discrimination was appointed, which took time but led to substantial practical improvements.

Soon after the Pearce Commission had arrived in Salisbury it happened that the clergy of the diocese of Mashonaland were having their annual retreat at Peterhouse, a church private school near Marandellas. At the end, when the silence was broken, half a dozen of us met to consider means of resisting the political hijacking of the Churches. We formed a small watchdog body to challenge, publicly, revolutionary statements made in the name of Christianity. Our principle was ''reconciliation not revolution.'' We called the new organisation the Rhodesia Christian Group, and I was chosen as chairman and scribe and Father John Gardiner, principal of Daramombe Mission, as vice-chairman.

The Rhodesia Christian Group rapidly grew in strength and influence, and became a force to be reckoned with. Even the church leaders had to take notice of us, and found their every political utterance subjected to public scrutiny. We were soon joined by influential lay Rhodesians, including a senator and a former Director of African Education. Shedding our Anglican character we became an interdenominational body with branches in all the major centres. Our newsletter found its way to most countries in the western world, and we discovered friends and supporters — hundreds of them, and later thousands — first in Rhodesia and South Africa and then in Britain, America, continental Europe and Australasia. We tried and failed to influence the Pearce Commission, but regarded this as only the beginning of the fight. Soon we had access to the news media in all the countries where we had friends, including some beyond the English-speaking world.

The snag was, of course, that I was a full-time parish priest. There could be no thought of neglecting my primary job, however long the hours that had to be worked. But actually there was no escape from politics, no possibility any longer of submerging oneself wholly in the simple pastoral work which had given me so much joy. "Politics," the courageous Hungarian Cardinal Mindsenty said of communist Eastern Europe, "can overturn the altar and imperil immortal souls." That was already beginning to happen in Southern Africa, a fact which forced some of us to follow a course we would never have chosen willingly.

At the diocesan Synod the previous year (the one which would not condemn violence) I had been nominated for various diocesan offices and elected to none. Clergy were elected only by clergy, and some felt I was ploughing too lonely a furrow. There was just one election in which lay people could vote for a priest — that to choose representatives on the Christian Council of Rhodesia! In this I romped home. My election took effect in the new year, after the Council's rejection of the settlement proposals, but at least it enabled me to make friends with some of the African nationalists. It was the CCR which had in fact been midwife to Muzorewa's new ANC.

At my first CCR meeting in February 1972 well-dressed and bespectacled youngsters prophesied eloquently against the iniquities of the whites. One young man declared: "I have been terrorised every day of my life for twenty-two years." Another spread his arms and said: "For eighty years we Africans have hung on the cross." Yet another dismissed, with magnificent oratory, a plea for sacrifices all round in order that reconciliation might be attained: "Sacrifice!" he proclaimed. "The British people must sacrifice. The white Rhodesians must sacrifice. But the Africans never. We have sacrificed too much already." After the meeting they sped away, some of them in expensive cars. But not before they had rejected a resolution that "the Christian Council of Rhodesia cannot support, either morally or materially, acts of naked terrorism."

*　　*　　*　　*

By this time Gladys and I were due for six months' overseas leave, and we set off with Margaret (now twelve) and Anthony (ten) to visit our families in England. The British consul in Pretoria — there was none in Salisbury — made difficulties about our Rhodesian passports, insisting that they be replaced by British, and there was a delay while we wrote off to England in search of documentary evidence that we had been born and married. We had to prove, too, that we were the parents of our children, for parentage was not normally included on Rhodesian birth-certificates.

My youngest brother Cecil was at Heathrow airport waiting for us: he had met me every time I returned from Africa since the 'fifties. We had a delightful time with our friends and relatives, and the children loved it. The United Society for the Propagation of the Gospel was helpful, but gave me little to do. It knew well that I would say the wrong things! I took the opportunity to visit supporters of the Rhodesia Christian Group and to address Rhodesian meetings, including a big one in the Caxton Hall, London. It did not take me long to discover that some English politicians, Conservative and Labour, were far more approachable than the churchmen. Members of Parliament listened carefully at a gathering I

196

was asked to address in a committee room in the House of Commons.

In London, too, I visited the British Council of Churches and the Reverend Elliott Kendall (of its Department of International Affairs) who had interfered so gratuitously in the affairs of Rhodesia. Mr Kendall made no secret at all of the unscrupulous methods used to promote revolution. I mentioned a recently published report which explicitly condoned physical violence in Southern Africa, and added: "It is good to read that the British Council of Churches would not endorse that." He replied, "My Department tends to be cautious. Members take time to absorb new ideas, and one has to bring these things back time and again. The report would certainly be endorsed now."

At Cambridge we punted on the Cam and visited King's College Chapel. The chapel was as lovely as ever, but I was told that what the chaplain preached about Southern Africa was indistinguishable from bloody revolution. At Great St Mary's (where I had preached years ago) the first leaflet I picked up was entitled: "Missionary Go Home."

My last meeting was at the Anglican cathedral in Liverpool, which was said to be a stronghold of the ecclesiastical left. The chairman mentioned that previous speakers in the series of meetings had included Bishops Huddleston, Ambrose Reeves and Skelton — all well-known for their radical political views. However, I received much sympathy, and the only outright opposition came from a canon who referred to the earlier speakers. "These bishops are great and holy men," he said. "They cannot all be wrong." (I had mentioned none of them.) A young priest jumped to his feet and said: "Mr Chairman, I understand that the leaders referred to are all in England, and the speaker is returning to Africa. I will listen to the man who is going back." The uproar of applause which followed brought the meeting to a close.

Gladys and I and the children did indeed go back to Rhodesia: we intended to live there as long as there was a Rhodesia to live in. It was our home. But the storm-clouds were already gathering. At the end of the year we were to witness the beginning of the terrorist war in earnest.

Just before Christmas 1972, ZANLA terrorists crossed Rhodesia's north-eastern border and attacked Marc de Borchgrave's Altena Farm in the Centenary District with rockets and grenades. The telephone wires had been cut. De Borchgrave ran the two miles to the neighbouring Whistlefield Farm to report the attack and get help for his family. He dare not use his car for fear of an ambush, and his forethought saved his life. The terrorists had fled and there was no ambush; but they had left a landmine in the road which would have proved as fatal. Shortly afterwards the attack was repeated on Whistlefield Farm and there were more casualties. These included a young white girl and members of the security forces, coming to the rescue, whose vehicle exploded another landmine.

Many horrific incidents followed. A parishioner of a member of our RCG committee was murdered and her husband wounded. A pregnant Rusape woman lost her husband in an ambush. Beatings and murders of black people were reported, and there were abductions and rapes and gang-rapes. The nationalists now were not the urbane people I had met: they would stick at nothing.

There had been sporadic terrorist incidents during the 'sixties, but the local tribespeople had quickly reported them to the security forces who seldom failed to round the attackers up. But now there was a change of policy. The insurgents realised they would never win the peace-loving rural people to their side without intimidating them as well as the whites. The witch-doctors and spirit-mediums were drawn into the struggle to inspire fear; political indoctrination sessions took place at night and at gunpoint. We did not know it at the time, but the theory came from communist China. The guerrillas had to melt into the local population, like fish in the sea.

The practical planning was done in Lusaka, Zambia, apparently by Herbert Chitepo, Rhodesia's first black barrister. He said later: "After politicising our people, it became easier for them to cooperate with us and identify with our programme." That programme had nothing to do with the ordinary African people, who were its victims. It was with stark horror that some of us began to realise that it was backed by some of the

most influential leaders in the main Christian Churches —
and partially paid for out of the collection plates.

12. The Gospel of the Gun

O UR Rhodesia Christian Group committee lost no time in studying the activities of the World Council of Churches in Geneva as well as the local Christian Council of Rhodesia. Most of our Churches belonged to both. There was dismay when it transpired that the CCR was not only almost entirely financed by the World Council but was required by the latter's constitution to implement its programmes, including the "Programme to Combat Racism." The local Council did not even have a vote in the decision-making processes of the WCC.

The General Secretary of the World Council had until recently been Dr Eugene Carson Blake, holder of the Lenin Peace Prize. Now his office was filled by the West Indian Dr Philip Potter, who used his 1972 Christmas message to extol the "liberation movements."

The "Programme to Combat Racism" or PCR turned out to be anything but what its name claimed. It had little to do with racialism and much to do with communism. Planned by a gathering of WCC radicals at Notting Hill, London, in 1968, it condoned terrorism. To finance it an initial sum of US $200,000 had been transferred from the general and other funds of the WCC (that is from the contributions of the member-Churches) without consultation with the donors. The first grants to the African revolutionary movements, in 1970, totalled US $130,000.

"The basic underlying concept of the Special Fund to Combat Racism," it was stated in an offical document (Utrecht, Netherlands, August 1972) "is that of a re-distribution of power, economic, political, social, cultural, ecclesiastical."

This was to be brought about by "a transfer of economic resources to undergird the redistribution of political power."

In March 1971 the WCC published the so-called "Declaration of Barbados" on Latin America. "We conclude," it stated, "that the suspension of all missionary activities is the most appropriate policy." This was followed by the WCC's 1973 conference on "Salvation Today" at Bangkok, Thailand, which issued a call for a "moratorium in sending missionary personnel and funds to the Third World." (The suggestion was made that the money saved might be given to the "liberation movements.") Professor Peter Beyerhaus of Tübingen University was present at the conference, and in his book *Bangkok '73* described the processes used in this "masterpiece of manipulation" to obtain the conclusions which had been reached before the sessions began. These included the weighting of the conference with a multitude of official consultants and advisers, the prevention of open debate and the refusal to bring a dissenting motion to a vote.

We in the RCG could scarcely believe that the documents we studied were genuine. It appeared to us that the WCC was dominated by officials who purported to countermand Our Lord's commission to go into all the world and preach the Gospel to every creature. Yet most of our Churches were not only deeply involved in the WCC, but actually subscribed to it. And at a later meeting of the Christian Council of Rhodesia at which I was present it was freely admitted that PCR funds, though intended for humanitarian purposes, might end up in communist arms factories. The WCC Utrecht document stated unambiguously: "The grants are made without control of the manner in which they are spent."

The Anglicans among us faced a special difficulty. The two Rhodesian dioceses of Mashonaland and Matabeleland were only part of what was officially called the Church of the Province of Central Africa, the ecclesiastical ghost of the now defunct Central African Federation. The province included Zambia, Botswana and Malawi: its archbishop in practice always lived in one or other of the uniracial black countries, never in multiracial Rhodesia. It was this agglomeration which belonged to and contributed to the WCC, not the individual dioceses which had to pay up and could not opt out. In practice this meant that white Rhodesians, who were finding about 80% of the money, were indirectly contributing to the destruction of Rhodesia and probably to the murder of their countrymen both black and white. Writing of the World Council the Central African archbishop, Donald Arden, stated bluntly: "The Province has no intention of withdrawing or dissociating itself from it." Debate was not tolerated.

"The first thing to do," it was suggested by our RCG committee, "is to make the facts known." I was asked to produce a booklet putting the case for Rhodesia — reconciliation not revolution — and pointing out that churchpeople were in fact financing revolution. The booklet, published in 1973 and called *Rhodesia Live or Die*, went through several editions, selling 10,000 copies. It was re-printed in Australia and translated into French and German. *Rhodesia Live or Die* made an impact, and contributed to a growing demand for secession from the WCC. Parishes threatened to cut off financial support from their dioceses, and priests inclined to sympathise with them received diocesan warnings about possible loss of leave and pension rights.

This was not the first crack of the whip. As early as May 1972, before the booklet was mooted, Father John Gardiner had tried to propose in the Provincial Synod a token reduction of the Province's contribution to the WCC. However the archbishop (who lived in Malawi) had vetoed his motion in advance.

The Anglicans in the Rhodesia Christian Group tried to bring some realism into the situation by proposing a separate Rhodesian Province. This would still have a large preponderance of Africans, but would not annihilate the influence of the white Christians on whom the Church depended financially and who in any case were entitled to a place in the sun. This proposal was ferociously resisted by the "liberals." The result was an appreciable exodus from the Church of ordinary white Anglicans, tired of being used as financial milch-cows and denied any effective say in the running of their Church.

It was the purpose of the RCG to keep Christians in their Churches, in spite of abuses, not to drive them away. We had, therefore, to move carefully and to avoid mere agitation A further reason for care was that the Rhodesian bishops, unlike the archbishop, shared our concern about the WCC, and Bishop Burrough of Mashonaland was prepared to examine the evidence we had collected. Both he and Bishop Wood of Matabeleland made repeated protests to the WCC in Geneva against its support for terrorist organisations. "Nothing here," they said, "can logically or morally call for acts of sheer terrorism against the civil population, and no such acts can conceivably lead to eventual justice." The bishops were ignored. So were those from South Africa who went to Geneva in person to make a similar protest.

The RCG was forced to recognise that the Rhodesian bishops could not in practice pull out of the Christian Council of Rhodesia in order to register their protest. That would have torn the Church in two on racial grounds. The unhappy truth was that because the WCC had a financial stranglehold on the Africans it had a stranglehold on most of the main Churches in the country. When in October 1973 I proposed in the CCR that it repudiate the "Programme to Combat Racism" I was tilting at windmills. The meeting, predictably, resorted to the old dodge: it voted to "proceed to the next business"!

Meanwhile a new ecclesiastical foe of Rhodesia appeared on the horizon in the form of the "All Africa Conference of Churches," an offshoot of the WCC which also funded "liberation movements" — and in which the Churches in Rhodesia took part. In July Canon Burgess Carr, its Liberian General Secretary in Kenya, stated that its purpose was "to harness the potential marginal groups . . . for agitation and restructuring society." "This is how we perceive the meaning of evangelism and salvation today." In May 1974 he announced that the "liberation movements . . . have helped the Church to discover a new and radical appreciation of the Cross. In accepting the violence of the Cross, God, in Jesus Christ, sanctified violence into a redemptive instrument for bringing into being a fuller life." It seemed that the Church was being hijacked by a gospel of violence remote from the teachings of its Founder.

The Roman Catholic Church did not belong to any of the "ecumenical" organisations, but its leadership was as extreme. Bishop Donal Lamont of Umtali condemned as inadequate every practicable step-by-step advance, and was reported as stating in New York in 1974 that the Rhodesian government authorised summary executions and torture and was comparable with that of Nazi Germany. If the report was true, he was lying.

In the Rhodesia Christian Group newsletter of June 1974 I wrote: "Is it surprising that a few days after this latest episcopal outburst the African National Council rejected further settlement proposals worked out by the Rhodesian Prime Minister and their leader, Bishop Muzorewa? Do not blame the ordinary African people for intransigence. It is those who claim to speak for the Churches who are poisoning their minds." Ultimately Bishop Lamont reconsidered his position, but by then the damage was done. In the meantime the only two Roman Catholic priests who had joined the RCG were moved out of the country.

Of course, at no stage did we suggest that the WCC and the Christian Council of Rhodesia were wholly bad. In my own experience Mr Percy Mkudu, the president of the local Council, was the bright spot, and our personal relationships were always good. He was a devout and urbane Anglican and a Member of Parliament. "White Christians and black Christians will just have to differ about the Programme to Combat Racism" was his line.

In December 1974 the various nationalist organisations got together at Lusaka, Zambia, in a reorganised African National Council under Bishop Muzorewa. An agreement followed with Mr Ian Smith which led him to announce that terrorist attacks would cease, detainees would be released and a constitutional conference be held. (By this time the South African Prime Minister, Mr John Vorster, was leaning heavily on Mr Smith.)

The nationalists did not honour the ceasefire, and nothing happened except the release of detainees. In the Christian Council this generated both good humour and goodwill "Let us give credit where credit is due," said Mr Mkudu.

205

Unfortunately I found neither good humour nor goodwill at the CCR's meeting in April 1975. It was held at Epworth, the Methodist theological college outside Salisbury. On my arrival a large student placard was thrust in front of me: "GET OUT OF THIS PLACE YOU DOG LEWIS." I smiled and gently worked my way through the throng. At lunch-time the budding theologians threw earth and water over both my food and me and waved another placard: "FOOD FOR THE C.C.R. BUT NOT FOR FATHER LEWIS." Having got the message that I was to have no lunch I retired to the quiet of the chapel where I felt I could spend the time profitably. But there were placards here, too, all round the walls. The one on the communion table read: "GO HOME AND BE MERRY IN HELL." My attempt to say some prayers was less than successful since the students crowded into the chapel and someone broke an egg over my head from behind. The principal of the college and the chairman of the meeting were alike quite helpless. When I finally escaped into the sunshine Salisbury was going about its business as usual and the Africans in the streets seemed as happy and smiling as ever. Of course, the press got hold of the story and the newspapers had a field-day. To the police I said: "Please forget it."

Less than a year later the World Council of Churches held its fifth World Assembly in Nairobi, Kenya. It welcomed members of several bodies committed to terrorism: the ANC, the South West African People's Organisation, the Palestine Liberation Organisation. The so-called "Programme to Combat Racism" was again approved, and non-violence specifically voted down. A daring attempt was indeed made to condemn communist oppression: but it was thwarted by the expedient of re-opening on another day a debate in which the official line had been defeated — and then engineering a contrary decision! Church of England delegates protested against the dominance of unelected and unrepresentative "super-numerary persons." The Bishop of Truro led a walk-out in protest against official pressure.

*   *   *   *

1974 saw the event which tilted the scales against Rhodesia. In Portugal General Spinola inspired a *coup d'état* which overthrew the government in Lisbon and led to the country's withdrawal from its overseas provinces. The new leaders, abandoning promises of free elections, announced their intention of handing Mozambique over to the Marxist guerrilla movement FRELIMO. Rhodesia had lost a good friend and would find itself with a long and indefensible eastern border through which ZANLA guerrillas would pour.

Gladys and I determined to pay one last visit to the Mozambique in which we and the children had enjoyed several happy seaside holidays. It was school holiday time, and our holiday time too. We collected Anthony from his prep. school at Marandellas — after watching him as a pirate in "The Pirates of Penzance" — and took him off to Inyanga. A week later term ended at Marandellas High School and the three of us picked Margaret up and made for Salisbury airport.

Our trips to Beira on the Mozambique coast had always been by car or train, but by this time FRELIMO (another recipient of largesse from the WCC) was blowing up trains and setting ambushes on the road. So this time we flew. The night 'plane to Beira turned out to be one of Rhodesia's newly acquired sanctions-busting Boeing 720s. The next day our adventurous friend Tony Waite, who frequently dropped in at our Inyanga cottage, turned up at Beira having driven down alone and unscathed from Umtali.

The sea and the beach were as lovely as ever, and the bazaars as fascinating. But the Portuguese army had been withdrawn from the countryside into the towns in preparation for its final evacuation to metropolitan Portugal. There was an uneasy and unnatural gaiety about the city. The shrill laughter of the crowds suggested apprehension as well as an obdurate hoping-against-hope. The cinemas and street-cafés were still thronged, but the carefree Rhodesian holiday-makers were missing and Swahili had joined the babel of languages. Tanzanian communists outnumbered Portuguese in our hotel. Communist slogans filled almost every available wall-space in the city, though we had never seen graffiti there before. But some of the inscriptions had been defaced. "VIVA FRELIMO" had become "FORA FRELIMO," "fora" meaning "out." In one place FRELIMO had been ingeniously truncated to LIMO, "scum."

On the sea-front I chatted with a Portuguese as the children played in the sand. Each of us had only a smattering of the other's language, but it was enough. I heard of the bitter strain on the local whites, who had known no other home, as they saw their lives' work and their families facing ruin. I learned of the nervous and mental breakdowns of many whose world was collapsing around them. Yet these people were as "colour-blind" as any Europeans in Africa.

The rest of the story told itself. The Portuguese who were able to do so were leaving as fast as they could for a Portugal many of them had never seen. The country folk, their farms pillaged, were flocking to the towns for safety. No glimmer of hope showed on the faces of the indigenous Africans for whom "freedom" (and starvation) waited round the corner.

Our friend, Tony Waite, visited Beira again a few months later, and found a different scene. There was little laughter now. He climbed to the top of his hotel and as he looked round he heard only one sound — hammering. The Portuguese who had built the modern city in a malarial swamp were packing up the few possessions they hoped to take with them if and when they could escape. Less than three years later another friend of ours visited Beira, via South Africa. He found a phantom city. We had little doubt as to what was planned for Rhodesia.

*   *   *   *

As the months passed we in the Rhodesia Christian Group became increasingly alarmed at the part the Churches were playing in the betrayal of both Christianity and civilisation in Africa, a betrayal which was driving back to barbarism the ordinary Africans who wanted the good things which white Christians had brought — not least Christianity itself. The Anglicans in the Group were particularly dismayed by what was happening to our missionary society, the United Society for the Propagation of the Gospel. Of the Marxist takeover of

Mozambique *Network*, the magazine of USPG, stated simply in 1975: "Mozambique is free."

Earlier *Network* had openly supported Maoist communism. The December 1973 issue headlined across its centre pages "Magnificat Now," and suggested that the Magnificat or Song of Mary was a "revolutionary document making the Communist Manifesto look meek and mild." Two pages were then devoted to political poetry and prose, much of it African nationalist in flavour, i.e., "Our Lady who is altogether black;" "Sing we a song of high revolt;" "Let us not dismiss them too easily as misguided terrorists."

Perhaps the most extraordinary *Network* article on Rhodesia appeared in October 1973. The anonymous author was described as "one of the few white clergy in a 'bridgepoint situation,' moving in both black and white groups." This raised howls of laughter in Rhodesia where, of course, dozens of priests were in such situations. What was more astonishing was that no priest any of us knew had ever heard of the author. Ultimately we discovered that he was an inexperienced youngster who had worked in Matabeleland briefly, proved a misfit and disappeared from the Rhodesian scene.

This, however, was not the worst. USPG had failed signally to find a mission-priest for St Peter's Mission, Mandea, in spite of the urgent pleas of old Father Mandihlare and his people. Father Mandihlare had long been a sick man, ageing fast. But he would not give up, and he had died of heart-failure on April 21st 1971, shortly after the Easter which it was beyond his strength to celebrate.

Had USPG even tried to find a mission-priest to replace him? Speaking in St Paul's Cathedral, London, on May 12th 1974, the Very Reverend Allan Shaw, Dean of Bulawayo, asked whether it was the intention of the Church of England to abandon the Anglican Church in Rhodesia. He quoted the case of a young priest he had wanted to appoint to his cathedral to fulfil a multiracial ministry and who himself wanted to come: yet every obstacle had been placed in his path. Nor was this an isolated instance. A priest hoping to work in Mashonaland and for whom a place was waiting was discouraged by an officer of USPG. He was told that in some people's eyes he would be going to strengthen the community of white settlers in a black man's land, and that his children might be regarded as those of an enemy whose life would be expendable.

A number of urgent approaches were made by USPG missionaries in Rhodesia to the Society in London to protest against its manifest political bias. All were entirely futile. It was plain that neither the supporters of the Society nor its missionaries had any effective say in its policy. A few of us decided it was time to act.

In the middle of December 1974 Father John Gardiner and I spent a couple of days at Inyanga putting together a pamphlet on USPG called *Propagation of the Gospel?* Father Gardiner's approach was perhaps more scholarly than mine, and the result was nothing if not factual and restrained. But it was hard-hitting and did its job. The pamphlet was highlighted on the front page of the English *Church Times*.

More than a year was to pass before Bishop Burrough, during a visit to England in 1976, preached a Sunday sermon at St Paul's Cathedral, London, attacking both the WCC and the Church of England for backing tyranny and economic chaos in Rhodesia. He did not need to mention USPG by name. It was an extraordinarily courageous address, which hardly made him popular in high ecclesiastical circles.

* * * *

After the publication of *Propagation of the Gospel?* I turned my attention to finding out what was really happening at the "sharp end," the war-zone in north-eastern Rhodesia. The news which reached us over the local radio and in the newspapers was only occasionally falsified but often doctored. British broadcasts were partisan in the opposite direction, and even less trustworthy.

In the middle of 1975 I was able to make two trips by light aircraft into the troubled areas. The achievement of the authorities in building protected villages for the tribal Africans was spectacular. In the Chiweshe Tribal Trust Land there had been a spate of 25 murders by terrorists before the establishment of the protected villages. Since then there had been one.

We flew over vast areas of irrigated land in which 40,000 Africans now lived in 21 protected villages, each with its own fortified "keep" or patrol-base, its water-supply and a school. The largest village housed 4,000 tribespeople whose lives had indeed been disrupted but who now dwelt in comparative safety. Wherever we touched down the guards, mostly black, were happy and friendly, as were the people themselves.

In my second trip I was flown to Mrewa, where the District Commissioner (a youngish man called David Mirams) was responsible for 150,000 people, only a handful of them white. He was helped by nearly 200 very cheerful black District Assistants. "We have had ten people murdered recently," he said. "Two District Assistants were killed last week. Four other people were battered to pulp, including two pregnant women."

After both these trips we returned to base at the airstrip at the little town of Bindura, and on both occasions, I was shown round the hospital by the doctor. I dare not try to describe the limbless horrors, the broken and tortured bodies of the victims of terrorist landmines and hand-grenades. It was difficult not to be sick on the spot, and even harder to talk with the tormented men and women and children who so recently had been innocently tilling their land. Nothing that had been broadcast or printed in the papers had prepared me for this carnage.

Could any cause justify such barbarism? Until recently Rhodesia had been as happy a country as any in Africa, and had indeed enjoyed half a century without a shot fired in anger. Now an unholy alliance of western governments, foreign-backed "nationalist" movements and communist weaponry was returning its simple people to something worse than the savagery from which Christian missions and the founding of Rhodesia had rescued them. To suppose that this could be condoned by Christians on Christian grounds was, it seemed to me, a wicked nonsense. As horrific as the murders and mutilations was the large scale abduction of school-children who, taken over the border for guerrilla training, sometimes never saw their families again.

But what could a small "conservative" Christian group *do*? What could a tiny minority of working priests *do*? It seemed we could only strive to alert Christians in Rhodesia and overseas to the true nature of the struggle. There was no need to idealise Rhodesia. The Marxist alternative was manifestly and palpably evil. Yet the Africans were so mesmerised by the fate that was to be thrust upon them, or so terrorised, that it was difficult to gain their co-operation. They knew that we could run away. They could not. I set to work writing more pamphlets, more newsletters, more press-statements for local and overseas publication.

Meanwhile the South African Prime Minister, Mr John Vorster, was scared stiff by the collapse of Mozambique, and saw "black majority rule" as inevitable in the whole sub-continent except South Africa itself. He was pressed, too, by Britain. Together with President Kaunda of Zambia he brought Mr Ian Smith and the nationalist leaders together at the only venue acceptable to both sides — a railway coach in the middle of the bridge between Rhodesia and Zambia over the Victoria Falls! The Rhodesian delegation remained in Rhodesia, and the nationalists in Zambia. This comic-opera conference, on August 25th 1975, continued until midnight. No progress was made, since Bishop Muzorewa demanded the immediate handover of the country. It was agreed to meet again the next day, but the Africans did not turn up and Mr Smith and his friends went home. My family and I were having a short holiday at the time with a relative from England, and we flew to Victoria Falls on August 27th. The politicians and the journalists had gone, and the train (which we saw) had been shunted off the bridge. The hotel was in a bit of a mess, but the elephants still strolled gently across the road, the Falls were as magnificent as ever and the cruise up the Zambezi was as breath-taking. This time, however, a soldier rode shotgun on the gunwale of the boat.

Christmas 1975 we spent at Inyanga Downs, and it was a poignant one. It marked the end of our dream of peace at Inyanga, just before the incursion of terrorists into the beautiful hill-country. I drove the family up to the cottage several days beforehand and returned to Rusape for the Christmas Eve service at Headlands. (This year a friend was to take the Rusape services.) The little church at Headlands, ablaze with candles, was packed to the doors, and the spirit of Christmas prevailed over the anxieties of the time. After the service the Salisbury road was crowded with traffic, but that to Inyanga was almost eerie in its loneliness. The darkness seemed impenetrable, and I was driving through torrential rain and a dense mist. The earth road which spiralled up to Inyanga Downs was a nightmare, but at last the lights of the cottage gleamed through the downpour. Inside the log-fire roared and the pressure-lamps were bright, and Gladys and the children had decorated the Christmas tree with tinsel and unlikely snow. The presents were piled under the tree.

Next morning St Catherine's was fuller than I had ever seen it, and the carols echoed among the pine-trees under a cloudless sky. After I had shaken hands with the congregation and we had exchanged Christmas greetings I tackled the perilous journey down the muddy roads to Inyanga proper, where I celebrated the eucharist again in the Rhodes Hall. (Soon there was to be a beautiful church nearby, but we had not started it yet.) The crowd here was even bigger. As I drove back up to the cottage the rain poured down again, and we spent a traditional indoor Christmas. But in the following days we walked in the hills and swam in the sunlit river. The children had the time of their lives, and so did we.

Within a few months the cottage had been broken into and looted, and though we re-stocked to the best of our ability the same thing happened over and over again. The thieves came from over the Mozambique border, their task to supply the ZANLA terrorists from the holiday cottages. Many of these later fell into disrepair, and visitors became fewer and fewer.

The security situation deteriorated rapidly in the new year. Trains from Salisbury on the Beira line now terminated at Umtali, and night trains to Umtali were discontinued for fear of terrorist attacks. It became unsafe to travel on the roads at night. In the south of Rhodesia road ambushes compelled the formation of armed convoys between the main centres.

The Rhodesia Christian Group committee now met frequently in Salisbury, determined to work for the survival of the country as the guerrilla war hotted up. We met groups of Africans from time to time, including nationalists, in a search for understanding and to encourage some of the more courageous. There were a few black groups parallel to the RCG, but we could not join up with them publicly since our high profile would have meant death to their members. Only one African actually joined our committee, Ndabazinhle Musa, perhaps the bravest man I have known. He was determined that black and white should work together. A one-time terrorist himself, converted at an evangelistic meeting he was sent to wreck, he would carry out lonely evangelistic and relief missions in remote and dangerous places. He was the sort of black man who got invited to tea on Afrikaner farmsteads. ''Ndaba,'' as we called him, was quite fearless.

By this time it was apparent to me that I was not devoting enough time to my two parishes and to my primary job. But, our committee pointed out, there were virtually no parishes left in either Mozambique or Angola: the overall Christian task now was to resist Marxism. The proposal was made that I should devote myself full-time to organising the RCG and writing and speaking for a Christian Rhodesia. This would not have involved my ceasing to live and work as a priest, and I was prepared to consider it. In the end it fell through, but it led to something else.

My support for Rhodesia had not silenced my public criticisms of the government where its racial policies still discriminated against Africans. One or two people sounded me out as to whether I would be prepared to join Rhodesia's multiracial Senate as an independent. ''You could criticise to your heart's content,'' one friend told me, ''and not damage the country. And you would carry some weight.''

I thought about this. I was no politician, and had no wish to become a politician. But how else could I work for genuine co-operation between the races, and get to know the people in power and perhaps exert some small influence with them?

214

What else could I do to help save a country which was probably Africa's last hope of a multiracial, power-sharing society? There was, of course, also the questionable thought at the back of my mind: "You will never get anywhere in the Anglican Church. If the chance comes elsewhere, why not seize it?"

The RCG committee and most of my friends were enthusiastic about the idea. The Senate was not a full-time job, and it would leave time not only for taking church services but for RCG work and for writing. The pay was not large — it was a mere extra for the doctors, lawyers, chiefs and gentlemen farmers of whom it largely consisted — but it would be adequate. Members of our Group sounded out the bishop, who could not be expected to show enthusiasm but who was at least understanding. He anticipated no insuperable difficulty in replacing me at Rusape. When I saw him he assured me that I would be able to take temporary leave of absence, to remain a priest of the diocese and to return later to parish work. If the situation arose, he would give me a "general licence."

The biggest difficulty was in my own mind: I was not prepared, in any circumstances, to conduct a political campaign. There was indeed a vacancy on the Senate, but there would inevitably be other contenders and one would have to collect signatures, put down a substantial deposit, solicit support and face an election. I had no stomach for any of these things.

It was then that I received an oral message from the Prime Minister. "Will you," was the substance of the message, "criticise less and help more? Or, rather, will you criticise where criticism will do some good? We all want a fair, multiracial Rhodesia now. No one expects you to align yourself with a political party or obey a party whip. But if you stand the ruling party will put forward no candidate. I suspect no one else will either."

My friends were unanimous that I should say "Yes." The only opposition came from some of the establishment clergy, whose opposition could be taken for granted anyway. And from that moment matters were virtually taken out of my hands. A friend at Marandellas called Hamish Lumsden enthusiastically dealt with the practicalities, and in a day or two had got the fifty signatures for the nomination paper. "I could have got five hundred," he said. A senator friend put down the deposit. Nomination day, June 18th, came and went, and I was duly elected unopposed. Congratulations poured in, and for the first and only time in my life I made the main front-page headlines in the Rhodesian press.

Three days later Gladys and I attended the impressive ceremony of Beating of Retreat at Government House, where we met Mr Wrathall, the new President of Rhodesia. The outdoor ceremony (based on an ancient British one) included a magnificent parade by the police band, almost entirely African, and a muted and very moving rendering of "Abide with me." Finally, as the sun set, the green and white flag of Rhodesia was lowered to the accompaniment of a lone bugler. Then we all went indoors for a "sundowner" party. The cue to go home was the playing of the new Rhodesian national anthem which had replaced "God Save the Queen." We had been to this ceremony before, but tonight, as many people approached us with congratulations, we got to know men and women of influence whose acquaintance years ago would have been invaluable in our work among the Africans. There were still more white people present than black, but the disproportion was now much smaller.

The State Opening of Parliament took place the following day, and the Senate met briefly in the morning for my swearing-in. I was sponsored by my good Inyanga friend, Senator Carol Heurtley, and by an African chief, Senator Chief Musikavanhu. We then trooped into the House of Assembly to hear the President's speech which was to be debated during the following days. We missed the traditional pageantry outside Parliament in Baker Avenue, but saw it on television in the evening. Meanwhile Mr Ian Smith entertained some of us to lunch at his home, Independence. My maiden speech in the Senate took place two days later, when I spoke of the abuse of religion to promote revolutionary violence. The speech went down well enough, but there was no great scope for eloquence since one had to make frequent pauses

216

for the interpreters to put it all into Shona and Sindebele. Nothing would make my headphones work.

Gladys and I continued to live at Rusape until August, making frequent trips to Salisbury. We found a house to rent there and hunted for furniture, having none of our own. Hamish Lumsden lent us a car — hitherto we had only had parish or mission vehicles — and, almost miraculously, a new Renault 12 was subsequently given to the RCG for our use. To this day I do not know the donor. I only know that we were supported by the prayers and practical help of more people than we can remember. When finally we left Rusape it was with much goodwill and several exciting parties.

I had not expected goodwill in the higher echelons of the Church, but had hoped for some charity and tolerance. It was a fond hope. The bishop, who had promised me a "general licence," was subjected to intense pressure by some of his advisers. He had a duty to listen to these latter and had little choice but to go back on his promise — made, as he said, without advice. He was only a constitutional monarch! In due course he sent me a valueless scrap of paper giving me a "permission to officiate." In effect this removed almost all my rights as a priest of the diocese, including my freedom to return to parish work. As one friend put it: "They want you out, and this is their chance." However, the bishop soon found himself subjected to a battery of contrary advice from those who were not officially his advisers but who nevertheless could not be ignored. Then the Diocesan Chancellor, Professor "Dick" Christie, studied the Constitution and Canons — or whatever one studies on these occasions — and discovered that the bishop could only grant a "permission to officiate" to someone who did not live in the diocese. A resident priest had to be granted a full licence, or nothing.

Plainly a nasty row was brewing, and if all of us had not succeeded in keeping it out of the press it would have done the Church much harm. There were hundreds of Christians in Rhodesia who would not have stood by silently if a priest were turned out of his diocese for taking a stand contrary to that of most church leaders.

The situation was defused by Father Peter Grant, Rector of

Hartley, Chaplain of the Selous Scouts and a member of the RCG committee. "My church council," he said, "is asking the bishop to license you as assistant priest of Hartley. The job has no work and no pay, but it should solve the problem." It would have done. By this time, however, the bishop had granted me the "general licence" which was offered in the first place and which enabled me to assist anywhere in the diocese. My opponents could not resist church law.

In England the United Society for the Propagation of the Gospel, now moved to the far left, was not to be appeased. One morning I received a letter saying that my name had been removed from the list of the Society. That meant I was expelled, kicked out. Such a step was not normally taken without the consent of the bishop and diocese concerned: but in this case the bishop and diocese were not consulted and were not guilty. I was told there was no appeal, and was refused the names of the committee who made the decision. Clearly our pamphlet *Propagation of the Gospel?* had hit home and hit hard. Yet the gospel of violence was still very much in the ascendant.

13. Rhodesia Fights to Live

WHEN in 1944 I was ordained a priest of the Church of England we sang the hymn, "Bright the vision." The vision then, as with any young priest, was bright indeed, and it shone undimmed for many years. Africa, and the dream of a Christian Africa, made it brighter still, though some of those who controlled missionary work quickly shattered one's youthful illusions.

In Rhodesia in the mid-seventies, however, we faced another kind of vision: a vision of evil so intense that the persuasive tactics of the missionary were apparently of little avail. Whatever the wrongs in Rhodesia, nothing could justify the horrors of terrorism. If Rhodesia were targeted to become a Marxist state, then a priest could not confine himself solely to ecclesiastical functions — not if he intended to stay in the country and identify with its people. The exodus of white priests was indeed already well advanced.

In August 1976 a friend of ours, Anne Everitt, was one of those who felt the full impact of the invading terror. Anne was parish secretary at Rusape during most of my years there, and a stalwart helper of the Rhodesia Christian Group. John, her husband, was an honest doubter: too sincere to proclaim himself a Christian, yet far more Christian than many in his day-to-day conduct.

At the beginning of the month John was working in a remote area of the Makoni Tribal Trust Land with a team of African road-makers. His work was usually for Africans. He was, like most youngish men, a member of the police reserve, and armed with an FN rifle.

The terrorist attack was not expected, and came with breath-taking suddenness at first light. John reacted with phenomenal speed and courage, getting all his men to safety before, single-handed, trying to fight back. I was told later that he was shot while re-loading his rifle, but no one witnessed his struggle. All that can be said with certainty is that, with all the courage in the world, he had no chance. John's only crime was to be white and to be working for the African people.

His death sent shock-waves of horror and disbelief through every community at Rusape, for he was universally known and liked. I was in Salisbury at the time, and had to obtain leave from the Senate to go to Rusape to see Anne and her family and to conduct the funeral. A huge crowd was there, white people and Indians and Africans. Anger mingled with something close to despair; but with a determination, too, not to be defeated by such cowardly hit-and-run tactics.

Most of the victims of the growing terror were, however, black, not white. On the same day as John Everitt's death fifteen terrorists seized an African at his farm south-west of Zaka, in the Mushawasha Purchase Land, cut off his upper lip and right ear, forced his wife to cook the flesh, and compelled him to eat it. Only days later we received reports in the Senate, from the Minister of Education, of even more gruesome attacks. A black schools-supervisor had been doused with paraffin and set alight by a gang dancing to a radiogram. Another employee of the Education Department was tortured and literally burnt at the stake in front of his wife and the school staff. These were not manufactured atrocities of some propaganda-machine: they were rapidly becoming the daily acts of the self-styled "freedom fighters" determined to seize control of the country.

Inevitably the Rhodesian security forces strove not only to fight back but to eliminate the guerrillas in their camps outside the country. In mid-August 1976, following an attack on the Ruda police post in the Honde Valley, Rhodesian bombers penetrated deep into Mozambique, wiping out 300 of the terrorists in their bases. But there were plenty more to take their place. It was shortly after this successful military action, in September 1976, that Rhodesia suffered its biggest political and psychological reverse, a reverse far more damaging than any military setback.

September 12th was celebrated annually as Pioneer Day, commemorating the arrival in Fort Salisbury (as it was originally called) of the Pioneer Column which founded and opened up the country. It was on the Column's arrival in September 1890 that the British flag was first raised in what was to become Cecil Square in the centre of the modern city, outside the Parliament Building.

In 1976 September 12th fell on a Sunday, so the commemoration was postponed till the following day. For the first time Gladys and I were able to be present at the flag-raising ceremony. A big crowd was present and the day was cloudless with a light wind. As the green-and-white Rhodesian flag fluttered in the breeze Mr Ian Smith, the Prime Minister, stepped forward and laid the first of the wreaths in memory of the Pioneers.

Shortly after the ceremony Mr Smith drove to the airport and flew to Pretoria to meet Dr Henry Kissinger, the American Secretary of State. We in the Rhodesia Christian Group were dismayed at the prospect of this visit, and had done what we could to suggest to the Prime Minister that Kissinger was utterly to be distrusted. The American State Department in general and Henry Kissinger in particular had proved themselves the implacable foes of Southern Africa. Smith, however, had some regard for Kissinger, saw it as a privilege to meet him and was convinced that American involvement might mean a political breakthrough which could not be won from Britain. He seemed oblivious of the fact (plain to lesser mortals) that what Kissinger wanted was a dazzling diplomatic *coup* to boost his failing reputation and to secure votes for himself and his President in the November American elections. No foreign policy achievement could do more to secure black votes in America for Mr Ford than the end of white power in Rhodesia.

Paul Moorcraft wrote truthfully that Kissinger "would employ his usual tactics of evasion, compromise and plain lying, garnished with his effortless intellectual superiority." This is precisely what he did. He had prepared the ground by seeing Mr Vorster, the South African Prime Minister, both in Germany in the European spring and in South Africa later. Oil and arms gave him enormous leverage over the South Africans. Kissinger also saw various African presidents and external Rhodesian black leaders — but not Rhodesia's.

Ian Smith, the rugged, honest farmer, was undoubtedly overawed by Kissinger, and Kissinger himself was taken aback by a phenomenon he had seldom met, an *honest* politician. But business was business. The diplomat immediately established rapport with the Rhodesian by a caustic comment about the British, and went on to show him three sets of intelligence reports, all of which predicted the imminent collapse of Rhodesia. Smith knew he was not (at this stage) bluffing, for all the cards were in the hands of the Americans and the South Africans, who could strangle land-locked Rhodesia at will. The South Africans were prepared to join in the strangling of Rhodesia if that were the only way of saving their own country from being strangled by the United States.

Kissinger proposed a package deal: "majority rule" in two years; a transitional government; the end of sanctions and the cessation of terrorism. This, he assured Smith, had the approval of South Africa, America, Britain, France and the presidents of the black frontline states. These latter, of course, would control the guerrilla leaders operating from their territories. It seems that so far as the black presidents were concerned Kissinger was lying through his teeth: but no one was to know this since the rest of his facts were clearly established. The offered alternative to submission was that "the world" would bring Rhodesia to its knees.

As an insurance, in case the plan did not work, Kissinger promised *a hundred million dollars* for the resettlement of Rhodesians who might feel they must uproot themselves and their families and go elsewhere. The money never existed outside Kissinger's fertile imagination, but the offer was taken seriously by Rhodesians.

Smith discussed the proposals with the cabinet ministers who accompanied him, and yielded the same evening. The Rhodesians believed they simply had no option, and that by giving way now, under protest, they would avoid a holocaust and bring about some sort of peace backed by the international community. Smith wrung vital concessions from Kissinger, and stipulated that the package must be non-negotiable. There were to be no alterations, and in no circumstances was the package to become the starting-point for further demands and concessions. (That, of course, is exactly what happened.) Nothing, however, could turn defeat into success, though even Kissinger was impressed by Smith's dignity.

On the following Thursday we in the Senate were briefed on the developments by Desmond Lardner-Burke, the Leader of the House. They had already been accepted by the caucus of the ruling Rhodesian Front Party. The Senate carried on with its business staunchly after the briefing, but it was all shadow-boxing.

The next morning I flew to Pretoria for a religious conference which had been planned some time before. So it was in South Africa that I heard the broadcast of Smith's "surrender speech" on September 24th. The pill was well coated, but not the pleasanter for that. "The American and British governments," said Smith, "together with the western powers, have made up their minds as to the kind of solution they wish to see in Rhodesia and they are determined to bring it about. The alternative to the acceptance of the proposals was explained to us in the clearest of terms, which left no room for misunderstanding . . . Sanctions will be lifted and there will be a cessation of terrorism. Dr Kissinger has given me a categorical assurance to this effect and my acceptance of the proposals is conditional upon the implementation of both these undertakings." He ended with the words of Churchill: "Now is not the end; it is not even the beginning of the end; but it is, perhaps, the end of the beginning."

I was soon back in Salisbury, where the RCG committee was busy issuing statements and sending communications to Smith and to Kissinger. But our minds were almost numb. "Majority rule," so called, could only be a disaster. All of us had indicated as far back as the early sixties that we were more than willing to work with Africans and, in a short space of time, under an African majority government. The "majority rule" to which we objected   and which Smith had so long resisted — was a government by African terrorists armed from the Soviet Union and Communist China and master-minded by Solodovnikov, the Soviet arch-conspirator in Lusaka, Zambia. This is what "majority rule" meant now: rule by the men with the guns who were determined, with western as well as communist help, to seize power. The ordinary Africans had no means of making their feelings felt in the face of this sort of "majority rule."

From this point our committee no longer enjoyed quite the unity it had had in the past. Our Vice-Chairman, Father John Gardiner, felt that Smith had sold us out and that Rhodesia was probably finished. Most of us took the line that the Prime Minister had yielded to irresistible duress, and had in effect run away to fight another day. We all agreed, however, that a psychological dam-wall protecting Rhodesia had suffered a major and alarming breach.

My own reaction to the débâcle was a determination to write another topical booklet. I could not fight with guns, but would fight harder with my pen. The idea of the pamphlet came to me as I was walking through Salisbury, ablaze with purple jacaranda trees, when the children were coming out of school. I had spent much of my ministry working for black school-children, but here were hundreds of white school-children making their way home on foot or by bicycle. *They* were Africans too, and like the black children had no home other than Rhodesia. What was to be their fate, white children and black alike? It depended on our rescuing something from the calamitous determination of overseas powers to subdue us, in deference to political dogma and careless of its effects on the common people of the country.

Gladys and I went up to Inyanga Downs, to get away from the clamour of the RCG office. We travelled in broad daylight because ambushes were already commonplace at dusk. The cottage had been repaired after several further break-ins and was tolerably habitable. We had no security fencing, and no "agric-alert" or radio warning system. However, we invested in a battery-operated siren, which could be set off from our bedroom and which emitted a fearsome wailing.

No sooner had I sat down at my desk than the title of the

new booklet came to me: *Rhodesia Undefeated*. "The moral justice of Rhodesia's case is, of course, one thing;" I wrote, "her ability to survive is another. The Unilateral Declaration of Independence provided a breathing-space: without it we would have trodden the path of the black African states prematurely given 'independence' with massive 'aid' and waste-paper-basket constitutions. But no one could foresee the ferocity and vindictiveness of the British reaction."

I went on to list the atrocities of the terrorists and the financial aid given to them by the World Council of Churches. I quoted the hate-filled poem, "White Whore," published by the WCC, and argued that the struggle against such evil was one which Christians could and must win — however superhuman the effort:

> You!
> White whore,
> with your colonial coloured styles,
> how, you
> have turned me
> into an expatriate-bourgeois-playboy . . .
> Just you wait,
> till the moon is ripe,
> when my black and brown
> ancestral spirits
> rise up in anger,
> to wrinkle
> your white-starched soul
> with justice.

(WCC's *Risk* vol. 12 no. 1, 1976)

Rhodesia Undefeated was published by the RCG and quickly went through five editions. Perhaps, because its appeal was specifically Christian, it gave courage to some. Rhodesia did indeed have claims to be Christian, though it would be foolish to exaggerate these. Throughout the seventies Presidents Dupont and Wrathall called periodic Days of Prayer, Penitence

225

and Fasting for the country, and there were observed with enormous fervour on ordinary working days, not Sundays.

Meanwhile, on November 2nd 1976, the American people rejected Mr Ford in favour of Mr Carter, and Dr Kissinger was out of office. Smith was still in power, and ready to implement the settlement agreement he had signed. But Kissinger's sleight-of-hand had been performed without the concurrence of the frontline presidents or the guerrilla leaders, and aimed little further than to break Rhodesia. There was no cessation of terrorism and no thought of ending sanctions.

The ball was back in Britain's court, and Britain called another conference, to be held at Geneva under the chairmanship of Mr Ivor Richard, a Welsh Member of Parliament. This became popularly known as the "Geneva Circus." How Richard succeeded in getting all the important people together was not apparent, but his achievement went no further. Smith attended, determined to implement the Kissinger package, but was soon back in Salisbury declaring the conference a waste of time. The Africans were frequently late, and showed no interest in the Kissinger plan except as a starting-point for further demands.

"The ANC," declared Bishop Muzorewa at the conference, "is not here in a spirit of give and take. We have come here only to take — to take our country." Robert Mugabe's ZANU had forged a marriage of convenience with Nkomo's ZAPU, called the "Patriotic Front." But Mugabe made no bones about his belief that you cannot gain at the conference table what you have not already won by fighting in the bush. Eddison Zvogbo, a Chicago law professor in the Mugabe faction, stated with less than academic finesse: "This conference is a load of crap."

The conference finally adjourned, ignominiously, on December 15th, never to meet again. One wag declared that the only agreement reached by the delegates was to the effect that Rhodesian beer was cheaper and better than the Swiss brew.

Acts of terror continued in Rhodesia throughout the conference. At the beginning of December a Roman Catholic bishop was murdered by guerrillas together with two missionaries.

226

The nationalists attributed the murders, incredibly, to the Rhodesian security forces!

I myself was shortly to witness at first hand an even worse act of terror. On the night of Sunday December 19th an appalling massacre took place near Aberfoyle Tea Estate in the Honde Valley. This, of course, was within my old mission-district, and I was able to beg a lift on a Dakota the following morning down to the new Ruda airstrip. We finished the journey in mine-proofed lorries.

The carnage was hideous. ZANLA terrorists from over the Mozambique border had force-marched the inhabitants of an entire Aberfoyle labour-compound to the lighted tea-factory at the neighbouring Eastern Highlands Estate: forty men and thirty women and children. Two men escaped by leaping into the river in the dark. The workers were then forced to lie down in the blaze of light and were raked with automatic fire before their womenfolk. (Their crime was that they had ignored an order from the guerrillas to stop working for white men.) The twisted and mutilated corpses were still lying there in pools of blood when we arrived, and the women were still wailing. I prayed with some of the women in their own language, but it was the hardest prayer I had ever prayed.

Shortly afterwards Patrick Dumba and his wife were murdered near Mandea Mission. Patrick was a storekeeper, and had been one of my churchwardens. He refused to hand over supplies to the terrorists in spite of his wife's pleas, and both were gunned down. Teacher Beaven Mabula was killed too, at his school at Pimai. This was the school we had built near the big rock where, in the early days, I had held services for a congregation containing more donkeys than people.

Less than a month later four hundred school-children were abducted by ZAPU to Botswana. Then seven white mission-aries were murdered by ZANLA at St Paul's Roman Catholic Mission at Musami. Again the security forces were blamed, but the truth was laid bare by ballistic experts.

And so the atrocities continued. There was another Honde massacre in April 1977, seven tea-estate workers being mur-dered at Pimai. In May of the same year St Peter's Mission, Mandea, was abandoned as being militarily indefensible, though Father Mashingaidze, the priest-in-charge, remained there for some time before joining his people in the protected villages. At Rushinga, near Mount Darwin in the north-east, twenty-three men, women and children were locked into a thatched hut which was set alight: all perished in the flames.

Not less horrific was the fate of some of the African school-girls who left their school at the Elim Mission north of Inyanga for the August holidays. The buses in which they travelled were destroyed by landmines, with frightening casualties. In a state of shock the pathetic remnant of the holiday party wandered for many hours before finding a telephone and calling for help. The security forces and local missionaries took them under their wing and gave them shelter until they could return to their families. Ultimately, after a stay in Umtali, their Elim mission school was re-located in the open uplands of the Vumba Hills. Here, at least, it was believed they would be safe: and so they were, until the middle of the following year. It was then that the Elim massacre of June 23rd 1978, by ZANLA terrorists, horrified the world. Nine British missionaries and their wives and children were beaten and bayoneted to death, the women being first sexually assaulted.

Against such terror as this the forces of law and order had a daunting struggle. But they had spectacular successes too. Some of these were military, both within the country and outside it, while others were concerned with winning the "hearts and minds" of the ordinary people. In October 1977, before the Elim massacre, I was able to visit the Honde Valley again. The valley was transformed. Gone were the scattered and vulnerable hamlets, replaced by large protected villages. The people I had known so well had gone through a shattering and traumatic experience, and were sometimes almost as frightened of the security forces as of the terrorists. Their traditional way of life had gone. But the slaughter in that part of the country had ceased at last and the army and the civil administration were now clearly on top.

Mandea was now in a "no-go" area, and news of the deserted mission's fate took time to reach us. We later disco-vered that the guerrillas had shot out the louvres of the great

228

lantern above the church, but could not destroy the white cross which dominated the valley. Everything within the church was wrecked, and Job Kekana's magnificent crucifix disappeared. However, the steel-and-concrete structure, built to be terrorist-resistant, survived unscathed. At one stage it was used as a cattle-kraal. The school was extensively damaged and the mission-house, in which we and our children had lived such happy years, was a burnt-out shell.

* * * *

Salisbury was a different world, almost an oasis of peace. There were indeed guerrilla attacks — a bomb at Woolworths in August 1977 killed eleven people and injured about seventy — but these were altogether unusual.

Long before this the Rhodesia Christian Group office had become a hive of almost fevered activity. Our secretaries despatched the correspondence at a rate of knots in the brief intervals when they were not answering the telephone, and there was an almost endless coming and going of voluntary helpers. I myself turned out a stream of newsletters which went far afield and were translated into several foreign languages. The most popular was called *Rhodesia Unafraid*. It told the story of a white farmer's wife who resisted a terrorist attack, aided only by her 13-year-old son who reloaded her rifles while she continued to fire. She went on firing until, exhausted, she could no longer hold a weapon. Then putting her arms around her two children she said: "We are all going to die tonight, but we must be very brave. No tears." She did not know till much later that she had won her battle and that the guerrillas had fled.

Outside interference in Rhodesia continued, of course, unabated, and the busy-bodies always came to Salisbury. (Fortunately a lot of overseas friends came to see us too.) Andrew Young, a black American ambassador, comported himself with almost unbelievable maladroitness. The *Rhodesia Herald*, which was not markedly pro-government, described him as "this strolling player from the Theatre of the Absurd." Doctor David Owen, the new British Foreign Secretary, also turned up, with yet another plan, and the two diplomate joined forces. Somebody said that the good doctor, having diagnosed Rhodesia's ills and prescribed a lethal remedy, felt bound to appear and take a quick look at the patient.

The visitors would have done better to stay at home, for by this time the Rhodesian Front government was having a serious re-think. The RCG committee discovered this when we had an interview with the Prime Minister as early as January 1977. We urged three things. First, no more concessions to outside pressure. Secondly, the rapid removal of all racial discrimination. And thirdly, action against security force brutality. We had Ndabazinzhle Musa with us to quote chapter and verse about this last. Mr Smith was surprisingly sympathetic on all three points.

Plainly the Prime Minister had already been thinking on similar lines. His party had realised that the swing to the right which followed UDI and the declaration of the Republic would have to be put into reverse to retain the goodwill of the moderate Africans. The virtual abandonment of the policy of separate development would restore the liberal Rhodesian tradition of the past. However, as a result of this shift of policy a dozen of the more right-wing members of the Rhodesian Front resigned and formed a new party. To me they posed a dilemma. They had an intense loyalty to the country, and would certainly not capitulate to external duress. On the other hand their predominant concern was with the whites, and they had no intention at all of repealing the country's surviving racial laws.

On Friday March 4th 1977 there was a battle royal in the House of Assembly, the lower house of Parliament, when the Land Tenure Amendment Bill came to its third reading. This dealt with the key issue — the abolition of restrictions on African access to land. The bill needed a two-thirds majority to become law, and the twelve dissenters voted against it. Ten African MPs abstained on the ground that the bill did not go far enough, leaving the government in real trouble. However, the African ministers supported the bill and carried three black MPs with them, just saving the day. I was told that somebody had to be pushed into the House in a wheelchair. We debated the bill in the Senate a few days later, and gave it an easier passage.

The opening of the next Parliament took place routinely on June 21st with a 21-gun-salute, an impressive fly-past and all the paraphernalia of tradition. A few days later, while we were debating the policy of the Ministry of Internal Affairs, I made a speech on the sufferings of innocent Africans in the tribal areas. Apart from what I could vouch for personally I had got my facts from Bishop Burrough, who went everywhere and was in regular contact with both black and white, and from Ndabazinzhle Musa. I praised both the officials of Internal Affairs and the security forces, who to my certain knowledge were doing a magnificent job. Nothing could alter the fact, however, that the people in the middle were getting "caught in the cross-fire," and there were frequent occasions when more care and humanity could and should have been used. It was for this that I appealed.

The speech got the mixed reception which I expected, with sundry dark mutterings and an attack from Senator Jack Brendon on my "irresponsibility" in quoting unsubstantiated reports by Bishop Burrough. However, in his reply to the debate the Minister, Mr Jack Mussett, was sympathetic. Senator Whaley congratulated me, Bishop Burrough was almost reconciled to my being a senator and the press had a free-for-all.

It was about this time that Mr Ian Smith finally lost patience with the endless attempts to organise the country from outside, and made up his mind to go for an internal settlement. He would sit down with any Africans who had a genuine constituency and — bypassing the British and the Americans and the United Nations — would try, with the black people on the spot, to work out a future for Rhodesia. But first he wanted a clear mandate from the whites. He wanted to be rid of the new white opposition; and with this in view he decided to dissolve Parliament and call an election on August 31st. My job as senator, of course, disappeared overnight. But Mr Smith got his mandate — all fifty white seats in the House of Assembly.

The RCG made contingency plans for me to work full-time

231

for the Group, but advised me to stand for the new Senate anyway. Once again there was no campaigning and all the formalities were taken care of by friends. Within a few weeks I was back again in my old seat.

The British, of course, did not give up, and by November the unsmiling Lord Carver, their "Resident Commissioner Designate," had arrived with more proposals. The "Patriotic Front" turned him down, with his plans, in advance. Even the new and moderate ZUPO (Zimbabwe United People's Organisation) pelted him with tomatoes. Chief Chirau, the organisation's leader, explained that the tomatoes were few only because most of them had been eaten by the demonstrators in their buses on the way! Meanwhile Mr Smith (not always the soul of tact) was watching cricket and had no time to see the noble lord until his fifth and final day in the country.

Mr Smith was, however, very much in earnest about his internal settlement with the Africans, and sat down with Bishop Muzorewa (United African National Council or UANC), the Reverend Ndabaningi Sithole (Zimbabwe African National Union, ZANU) and Chief Chirau (ZUPO). (At this point there seemed to be two ZANUs, ZANU Sithole and ZANU Mugabe.) Nkomo and Mugabe refused to join in and would settle for nothing less than the armed takeover of the whole country.

The "Salisbury Agreement" of March 3rd 1978 resulted from these talks. On March 4th the "Patriotic Front" set off bombs in Salisbury to indicate its disapproval. The agreement could have worked if Britain had given its blessing: but Britain would not undertake to recognise the internal leaders even if they organised a credible general election with universal adult suffrage — which by this time Ian Smith had accepted. Commonwealth pressure and Nigerian oil meant more to the British government and British business than the fate or the freedom of the people of Rhodesia. Britain's famous "six principles," long ago fulfilled by Rhodesia, were conveniently forgotten. After every concession the goal-posts were moved further away.

232

*   *   *   *

With the implementation of the Salisbury Agreement in 1978 Rhodesia was ruled by a Transitional Government headed by an Executive Council (EXCO) consisting of one white (Smith) and three blacks (Muzorewa, Sithole and Chirau). The feelings of our Group about the new set-up were summed up in a newsletter entitled *One Cheer for the Settlement*. It was the best that could be done in the circumstances, and as such most of us would back it.

Meanwhile, with the help of the Group, I myself brought out my slender *magnum opus*. This time it was not a pamphlet but an in-depth study of our situation from a conservative Christian standpoint. Called *Christian Terror in Southern Africa* (or *Christian Terror* for short) it had an arresting cover by my friend Cyril Hartley, showing the face of Christ on the Cross blotted out by the red star and hammer-and-sickle of Communism. The announcement on the cover summed the study up: "Christ is crucified by those who claim to act for His Church while His people are murdered in His name." We printed 5,000 copies, but encountered endless difficulties and delays because of call-ups among the printer's staff. When the edition was nearly sold out we sent the typescript and art-work to a printer in South Africa, who lost the lot. The demand continued, but the book has remained out of print ever since.

Our Group decided that the best way for me to spend the Easter parliamentary recess of 1978 was on a speaking tour in England. Gladys accompanied me, and our son Anthony, now sixteen and studying for his O-levels. (Margaret was nursing in Salisbury.) I spoke from pulpits and platforms up and down the country, confining myself to Christian issues in the pulpit and defending Rhodesia unashamedly on the platforms. At public meetings I encountered everything from sympathy and critical questions on the one hand to heckling and downright hostility on the other. During a meeting at Cambridge I spoke on "The Strangling of a Christian Land," and found as many foes as friends. Unbeknown to me it was one of the former who asked with apparent innocence where else I would be speaking. I fell into the trap, hostile messages

233

were sent to other universities and an "alert" was proclaimed at seats of learning I had no intention of visiting! A local Cambridge rag called *Stop Press* came out with a headline: "Apartheid Priest in Cambridge." Back at my brother Cecil's in Warwickshire, Tom Lawler of the Anglo-Rhodesian Society rang me up: "The Anti-Apartheid Movement is after you."

At Bristol I was due to speak at a lunchtime meeting at the University Union, in the Winston Theatre, on May 5th — the 160th anniversary of Karl Marx's birth! I did not know that an enterprising young lady student called Jo Roberts had rung up the police to say it was suspected I had entered the country illegally, having somehow "got through the immigration net." A plain-clothes immigration officer and a member of the Special Branch duly turned up to question me. I explained to them that I was English by birth, held a British passport (which I produced) and had entered the country at Heathrow in the normal way after a direct flight from Salisbury, Rhodesia. The officers, courtesy itself, withdrew, wishing me luck. Only later did I learn that a Labour MP, Robert Hughes, Chairman of the Anti-Apartheid Movement, was already busy approaching the Home Secretary, Mr Merlyn Rees, demanding my immediate deportation from the country. He, too, had no success.

Meantime, in the Winston Theatre, there was an excited crowd of about 400 students, most of them obviously interested and prepared to listen. I asked if I might open the meeting with a prayer, when an enormous caterwauling began at the back of the hall which made it impossible to proceed. A couple of dozen youngsters then set up a deafening cacophony which lasted for the next hour, to the manifest exasperation of the majority. They included members of the Anti-Apartheid Movement, the British Anti-Nazi League, the Socialist Workers' Party and sundry Trotskyites. Some of them produced an enormous banner, which quite blotted out all of us on the platform.

There was nothing to do but to sit patiently until finally everybody went away. This provided plenty of time for the local television folk to get hold of the story, and when I emerged from the hall with the platform party a camera team

234

was there waiting — ready to walk backwards in front of me as if I were royalty. It was a publicity bonanza.

The Organising Secretary of the Bristol Anti-Nazi League, a certain Colin McGregor, wrote a letter to the *Western Daily Press* of which a copy was sent to me later. It was headed: "This is why we kept Mr Lewis quiet . . . This man is a supporter of the Nazis," he wrote. "If Mr Lewis was to be given freedom to speak, then so should everyone else — at the same time."

A few days later we flew back to Rhodesia. On the way we squeezed in a little holiday at Athens. I had leisure to wonder what the original democrats would have made of our contemporary attempts at democracy, whether British or Rhodesian. The British government (without any mandate from its people) had persuaded the United Nations to condemn Rhodesia as "a threat to world peace." No democracy there. Could we in Rhodesia achieve a genuinely representative government? And, if we could, what chance was there that "the world" would accept it?

14. The Beginning of the End

THE Mission of Christ the King, Daramombe, had a history going back to the early days of Rhodesia. It was wholly dedicated to religious and educational work among black Africans. Canon John Gardiner, Vice-Chairman of the Rhodesia Christian Group, was the last of a distinguished line of Christian educationalists who had served there, and on the one occasion I visited him on his home ground I was struck by the respect and affection in which he was held. He had been head of the mission and principal of its secondary school for fifteen years.

I was stunned therefore to learn, on my return from England, that Daramombe Mission had been attacked by terrorists of Robert Mugabe's ZANLA. Perhaps I ought not to have been; for I knew that the previous Christmas guerrillas had hacked to death John's African churchwarden, Mr Edson Muzerurwa, and his huge congregation had dwindled.

The terrorists reappeared on June 6th 1978, armed to the teeth, while the school-boys were in hall eating their supper. "At dawn you will leave," they said. Soon afterwards the only sign of life was the looters, one-time Christians who had succumbed to the pitiless intimidation and village-to-village indoctrination of the armed insurgents. The mission and church were left a ruin.

John Gardiner, thank God, was in Salisbury at the time, and his life was spared. His house was wrecked and he lost everything except his books. A great work had, for the present, come to a tragic end. The only marginal consolation was that John, now living and working in Salisbury, could devote more time to the RCG.

After my return from Britain — and after I had seen John — I myself plunged immediately into the work of the Senate. President Wrathall, in his speech at the Opening of Parliament, urged us to make the internal agreement work. In the subsequent debate Senator Doctor Barnard, realising our days were numbered, quoted the cry of Suetonius' gladiators to Claudius: "Those who are about to die salute you." My own speech argued that the Salisbury agreement of March 3rd was the limit of concession and compromise, and the time had come to stand firm. I was wasting my breath, for our new leaders were subjected to remorseless and escalating pressure from a British government which, though all its stipulated conditions had been met, was determined to maintain sanctions and exact vengeance for UDI. It was impossible for the new Rhodesian government to fulfil its promises or to end the terror which was destroying both the country and its people. Britain, for all practical purposes, was siding with the terrorists.

It was at this point, that the Elim massacre of June 23rd 1978 occurred. The Secretary General of the Anglican Consultative Council stated that the massacre was "exceptional," and the United Society for the Propagation of the Gospel, realising that its friends had gone too far, expressed condolences. In July the Lambeth Conference, the ten-yearly world assembly of Anglican bishops, reiterated its approval of the WCC, Elim notwithstanding. The following month the WCC registered its approval by sending a further US $85,000 to the Patriotic Front, despite loud protests from Bishop Burrough of Mashonaland.

With international and ecclesiastical backing the terrorists became ever bolder. On Monday September 4th near Kariba they brought down an Air Rhodesia civilian airliner, the *Hunyani*, with a Soviet Sam 7 heat-seeking missile. Joshua Nkomo cackled his glee over the radio. (I heard him.) Of the 56 people on board 18 survived owing to the outstanding skill of the pilot. Of these ten were shot by Nkomo's men on the ground. Dismay and anger spread among the Rhodesian population, and something like despair when it was realised that the world community did not care.

At least, however, Dean da Costa's "deafening silence" sermon, preached from the pulpit of Salisbury's Anglican cathedral, echoed around the world:

Are we deafened with the voice of protest from nations which call themselves 'civilised'? We are not! . . . One listens for loud condemnation by Dr David Owen, himself a medical doctor, trained to extend mercy and help to all in need. One listens and the silence is deafening. One listens for loud condemnation by the President of the United States, himself a man from the Bible-Baptist belt, and again the silence is deafening. One listens for loud condemnation by the Pope, by the Chief Rabbi, by the Archbishop of Canterbury, by all who love the name of God. Again the silence is deafening.

Rhodesia's friends world-wide began to be more than alarmed. And the RCG's supporters in South Africa, realising that their own country was next on the list, determined on immediate action. Some of them proposed and financed an expedition to Britain and the United States to try to get our message through to opinion-makers. They invited both me and Ndabazinhle Musa to join them. Ndaba was a fluent speaker in English, and his presence would emphasise the multiracial future we all envisaged. The first of many snags we encountered was Ndaba's banning from Britain by Dr David Owen, Foreign Secretary in that country's Labour Government. Both Mr Patrick Wall MP (later Sir Patrick) and I challenged Owen from the platform of the Caxton Hall in London, though Mr Wall warned me: "The Foreign Office is gunning for you next." But it was a white party, apart from one South African Indian, which flew from London to Washington DC.

Here, because of the time difference, it was lunch-time when it felt like evening: and here we encountered our second snag. We were required to register with the Justice Department — the first Christian group ever to be subjected to this demand. In vain we protested that terrorists such as Nkomo were welcomed with open arms and without any

239

registration. *They* were invited, we were told, while we had come of our own initiative. The officials dispensed charm and Pepsi-Cola, but were adamant. We must register as "agents of a foreign principal." They were not amused when I said "God?"

The Criminal Department then proceeded to harass our American friends who were offering us platforms and pulpits and TV and radio slots, insisting that they register too. Some of our plans had to be abandoned and there was much last-minute improvisation. But one friend, the Reverend Colonel Bob Slimp, came to the rescue. He refused to submit to the demands of the Criminal Department and set lawyers on to it. After that it left us alone.

Shortly afterwards another acquaintance, a clerical journalist, secured an interview with a spokesman of the Justice Department and posed the question: "If Jesus Christ came to speak in the United States, would He have to register with the Justice Department?" The answer was "Probably." You may look it up in the Congressional Record of October 7th 1978.

I myself lost no time in trying to get into the State Department, and I asked for an appointment with Anthony Lake who was some sort of VIP — I have forgotten what. To my surprise the interview was granted. Friends warned me, however, that it would never materialise, and that I would be at the receiving end of an Official Snub. This is what happened; I was fobbed off with a young lady called Marianne Spiegler who vouchsafed me thirty minutes of her time. She had the complete "answers for Africa." No, she could not promise an end of US sanctions against Rhodesia in return for the majority rule which the US had demanded. If the whites were sincere they would hand over the country to the blacks in any case in spite of sanctions, which they had got used to. No, the members of the Executive Council could not be admitted to America, for that would be to break sanctions.

We got an entirely different welcome in the office of Senator Jesse Helms, a long-time friend of Rhodesia, though unfortunately the senator himself was ill at the time. At the American Security Council we argued for the admission to the US of

240

the Rhodesian leaders, and were sympathetically received. From these very satisfactory meetings we went on to a most unsatisfactory one at the Methodist Centre, where we had an encounter with a certain Reverend Timothy Howland Smith. This exalted personage was Director of the Inter-Faith Centre for Corporate Responsibility of the National Council of Churches of America. He was a boor. He listened to us (when he was not talking) with his feet on the table and laughed outright when I described the torments of the African people at the hands of terrorists. "Go and tell that to the American people," he said. "They will laugh in your face." Most of our subsequent experiences contradicted him, and it was with some relief that we later discovered that he himself was not an American.

From Washington our group split up to speak in many of the main centres of the US. In North Carolina two of us had to abandon a proposed symposium at Duke University since the organiser was threatened with a riot. In South Carolina we got a hearing wherever we went, finding the churches friendly and radio talk-shows especially useful. Everywhere our message was the same. We were not in the US to defend particular governments in Southern Africa but to defend our countries from Marxism. We were Christians who would support any government, black, white or brown, which would do that. But Southern Africa needed the sympathetic understanding of the American people, and above all of American Christians — not the hostility of the US government or the bigotry of the news media.

At Phoenix, Arizona, the waitresses at the Big Apple restaurant wore revolvers. We took time off to look at the Grand Canyon and arrived at Las Vegas after dark. The neon lights were so bright that you could get a daylight reading on a light-meter. The wedding-chapels announced "Happiness Begins Here" and we were told the divorce offices were round the corner. We visited Los Angeles (where the atmosphere was unbreathable and the night as bustling as the day), Dallas (Texas), Denver (Colorado) and Chicago. When we left New York at the end of October for London, Johannesburg and Salisbury we were totally exhausted.

241

From Salisbury, on behalf of the Rhodesia Christian Group, I at once sent a cable to Mrs Margaret Thatcher, Leader of the Opposition in Britain, in advance of the annual debate on sanctions in the House of Commons. Our appeal was simply to a Christian political leader to use her influence to stop the persecution of Rhodesia, which now made no sense at all even in terms of Britain's own demands. The Commons voted to continue sanctions.

I do not know how much influence our American expedition had in getting Mr Smith and the three black members of EXCO into the US. But on this point the American government relented. The Rhodesian leaders were popular in the US and effective on TV, and they were received at the State Department. But Carter's Secretary of State, Cyrus Vance, was unyielding. The final abandonment of statutory discrimination in Rhodesia made no impression on him. Nor did the offer of an all-party conference without pre-conditions.

The Rhodesian cause was not helped in America by the fact that the security forces were fighting tooth-and-nail to destroy Nkomo's Zambian camps. Nkomo himself was the hero of the American establishment. The latter was not pleased at the famous "Green leader" raid into Zambia, when, on October 19th, the Rhodesians took over Zambian air-space and air-control and destroyed Nkomo's military base outside Lusaka. Smith and his friends met Vance on October 20th.

* * * *

It was early in December that Salisbury experienced the biggest fire in its history. Insurgents of the Patriotic Front attacked the fuel storage depôt in the industrial area with rockets and tracer-fire, and the resulting blaze took nearly a week to put out even with South African help. The depôt had been guarded by five Africans with truncheons. That the fire did not spread and that lives were not lost was due to the extraordinary courage of the Rhodesian firemen, white and black. "We prayed," said a senior officer, "and our prayers were answered."

The pall of smoke which hung over the capital for days

242

reflected the gloom which prevailed in it. The country had lost a third of its precious oil reserve — precious because Britain was still blockading Beira harbour and supplies could only come through South Africa. The financial loss was between four and five million Rhodesian dollars.

It was at this point that I had a private interview with Ian Smith, who said that Rhodesia was surviving on two-monthly loans from South Africa strictly on the condition that it toed the line. The particular point on which I initially went to see Mr Smith concerned the proposed new constitution and the Dedication to Almighty God which had begun every Rhodesian constitution. *The British wanted this out*, and the RCG wished to know whether it was retained in the new majority rule constitution to be submitted to the electorate. Smith assured me it was definitely in, and he personally would have nothing to do with any constitution from which it was deleted.

Christmas that year was as prosperous and brilliant as ever. The Christmas lights in First Street and Salisbury Gardens seemed even brighter, and the crowds denser for the late night shopping and the carols in the streets. On Christmas Eve and Christmas Day the church services were packed. After my church duties on Christmas morning Gladys and I and the "children" celebrated at home, though the nursing members of the family — Gladys and Margaret — had to nip off to work at odd times. Anthony was home from Marandellas after successfully completing his O-levels.

After the festival Gladys and I and Anthony went up to Inyanga, driving in the middle of the day for fear of ambushes. Our cottage was intact, though there were thieves all around and our friends, the Storrers, had just been attacked. The home and farm of other friends, the Swire-Thompsons, was mortared and largely destroyed one night during our stay. Fortunately the family was away. St Catherine's church was full for the Christmas service on the Sunday, but the congregation consisted chiefly of visitors. The local population was much diminished.

At the end of January the promised referendum of the electorate was held on the proposed one-person-one-vote constitution which was to usher in new elections and an

African government. The country was to be called Zimbabwe-Rhodesia, which was no clumsier than Sierra Leone or Saudi Arabia, and the constitution attempted to enshrine the ideals of all parties. Everybody knew that if we did not vote for this constitution South Africa would abandon us. In a 71% poll 85% said "Yes." The proposals were made palatable by the expedient of reserving 28 of the 130 seats in the House of Assembly for whites, thus ensuring them a place in the country and a voice in Parliament. This was gladly conceded by a large number of Africans, who knew that the presence of the whites was essential for the prosperity of the country. It was rejected by the Patriotic Front, which made it abundantly plain that it would settle for nothing less than the armed takeover of Rhodesia and its metamorphosis into Zimbabwe under its own rule. Meanwhile whites were streaming out of the country and Smith was quietly negotiating with Nkomo to see if any compromise with the Patriotic Front was possible.

Early in February Gladys and I took a short holiday at Lake Kariba. The vast man-made lake on Rhodesia's north-western boundary provided hydro-electric power for both Rhodesia and Zambia. On its southern border was the thriving new town of Kariba, which soon became a popular holiday centre — the nearest approximation to a seaside holiday resort that land-locked Rhodesia could offer. We flew from Salisbury in an Air Rhodesia Viscount and stayed at the Cutty Sark Hotel. It was very hot, and when we were not at the swimming pool we got about by hired car or by coach.

One day we went to Caribbea Bay, a large lake-side complex where crowds of Rhodesians were enjoying themselves with a number of visitors from other countries. In the late afternoon we jumped on to the airport coach which would drop us off at our hotel on the way. There was a slight delay because a little girl was crying for the loss of her doll, left behind in the hotel. I believe she was Australian. The courier was patient, though she had a 'plane to catch, and the girl's mother dashed into the hotel and retrieved the doll. The little girl was all smiles and it was a laughing coach-load which set off for the airport.

Gladys and I got off the coach at the Cutty Sark and shortly afterwards changed and went in to dinner. Suddenly the music broke off and an announcement was made — an announcement which horrified Rhodesia and the world. The *Umniati*, the Viscount which had just left Kariba airport, had been brought down by another Soviet Sam 7 heat-seeking missile with the loss of all 59 people on board. Once again Joshua Nkomo claimed responsibility, but this time there were no survivors for his men to massacre on the ground. The little girl and her parents were among those who perished, as was a new black air-hostess.

Rhodesia was numb. The Rhodesian airforce mounted a spectacular and highly successful revenge attack on Nkomo's base in Angola, 1,000 kilometres from Rhodesia's borders. But even this brilliant and daring move, with ageing aircraft, did little to raise flagging spirits. Smith's negotiations with Nkomo came to an abrupt end.

Gladys and I flew out of Kariba three days later in another Viscount which climbed to 15,000 feet above the lake before heading for Salisbury, avoiding as far as possible the terrorist-infested tribal lands. There were only nine passengers on board. We spiralled down over the city from a great height before coming in to land at Salisbury airport. The previous day's aircraft had arrived with three holes in its tailplane.

It fell to me to conduct a memorial service in the police chapel for four women who had died in the crash. Their husbands had travelled from Kariba to Salisbury in mine-proofed vehicles, but had sent their wives on by air which they thought the safer way to travel. They showed great courage. "What we are fighting is evil," one of them said to me afterwards. "We must just keep going."

The following month David Frost, the television interviewer, got together Smith, Nkomo, Harold Wilson and Andrew Young in a TV satellite link-up. The British studio audience cheered its approval when the bringing down of the Viscounts was mentioned.

*   *   *   *

Meanwhile I had my own troubles, though they were minor

245

compared with those of the country at large. About the middle of January 1979 I received a letter, dated the 3rd, from a certain R.W. Barnett of the Foreign and Commonwealth Office in London. The nub of it was that my British passport had been invalidated and I could no longer enter the Britain of my birth or travel anywhere outside Southern Africa. I had "furthered and encouraged the unlawful actions of the illegal régime." (The "illegal régime" was, of course, our new multiracial Transitional Government!) I might make an appeal to the Advisory Committee on Rhodesian Travel Restrictions, the body which had recommended the ban in the first place. This move was plainly Dr David Owen's vengeance for my challenging him on the banning of Pastor Musa and for resisting his policy on Rhodesia. He either could not or would not understand that my opposition to British policy was on religious, not political, grounds. I stood for a Christian Rhodesia, not a Marxist one.

I knew well the consequences of trying to enter Britain in the face of such a ban. A British-born Rhodesian acquaintance of mine had been thrown into a cell at Heathrow airport and deported on the back of a lorry with a group of illegal Pakistani immigrants. I wrote back to Mr Barnett, requesting chapter and verse of my transgressions of English law. He replied that he regretted it was not possible to supply me with the details I had requested, but it was believed that I had written articles and made speeches sympathetic to the régime and had played "an organising and leading role" in political meetings which supported it. In vain did I point out that I had not attended a political meeting since I came to Africa in 1947 and that my activities were "political" solely in the sense that they were pro-Christian and anti-Marxist.

Barnett made matters worse by writing: "I should point out that, while the action against you was taken on the basis of the belief that you have in the past been involved in these activities supporting or encouraging the régime, the likelihood of your engaging in them in the future would be relevant to any reconsideration of your case." Be a good boy, don't do it again, and we may let you in! My reply was that I was uninterested in the Alice-in-Wonderland "justice" which

246

required me to address an appeal to a body which was prosecutor, judge and arbiter in its own cause. Even aliens and convicted murderers had a right of appeal to a superior court — why not a British citizen in Rhodesia? I stated that I was prepared to receive an unconditional revocation of the order, which should be in my hands by Easter if the matter was not to be referred to the English courts. A legal opinion I was given was that "the entire Star Chamber apparatus set up by the Foreign Office in 1968 is *ultra vires* and could be attacked in the courts of England."

Bishop Burrough, while not necessarily committed to my own stand, came to my help very courageously on the grounds of a Briton's right to freedom. He wrote to the Archbishop of Canterbury, Dr Coggan, asking him to make representations to Owen. "It is the inalienable right of every British subject to express his political views freely . . . A Briton can freely and openly join the Communist party . . . It is a totalitarian act, unprecedented in the past 200 years, if a British subject is to be deprived of his citizenship and passport because of his political views." Bishop Burrough repeated these views in the *Church Times*.

When Owen's action became publicly known, there was uproar. Relatives in England and friends worldwide wrote to British Members of Parliament as well as to the Foreign Office. Mr Patrick Wall tabled a question in the Commons, and was fobbed off by Mr Ted Rowlands, Minister of State in the Foreign Office. There was a petition to the Queen, which was passed on to the same Office. A demonstration outside the British consulate in Toronto took place at a temperature of minus 30°C.

Mr Ronald Bell QC MP, a brilliant English barrister, hit on a particularly telling device to challenge Owen's decision. On March 5th 1979 he introduced into the Westminster Parliament a private member's bill, a quaintly named "Outlawries Bill," for "the better prevention of clandestine outlawries." This was supported by a number of influential MPs, including Mr Enoch Powell and Mr Patrick Wall. It was only a gesture — there was never any hope of its being granted parliamentary time — but it attracted considerable attention.

On March 27th a Rhodesian meeting was held in the Caxton Hall, London, to protest against Pastor Musa's banning and my own. The speakers included Mr Patrick Wall, Mr Bernard Smith of the Christian Affirmation Campaign and an African nationalist politician Mr Wiseman Zengeni — and myself. I had my say by dictating to a tape-recorder over the telephone from Salisbury! "In asking you to insist that the Foreign Office ban on my entry to Britain be unconditionally revoked," I said, "I am asking you to defend what is left of your own dwindling freedoms."

Owen ignored all protests. But the Labour government fell in April and Mrs Thatcher and the Conservatives came to power in May. The ban on myself was lifted on July 16th.

I retain still a letter from Mr Ronald Bell which shows how close Rhodesia came to winning its long struggle and how justified it was in holding out apparently against all odds. The letter was dated July 23rd 1979. "I am relying, fairly confidently, on the firmness of Mrs Thatcher to hold firm on the present course, which is that we shall not renew sanctions in any circumstances and will recognise the Rhodesian government by the autumn. That is the intention of the Prime Minister and the main body of the Conservative Party in Parliament, but the Foreign Office ministers are being dragged along reluctantly."

*   *   *   *

The Senate was busy during the early part of 1979, but largely as a rubber stamp. We scrapped the controversial Land Tenure Act with the appropriate majority and, after the referendum, passed the Zimbabwe-Rhodesia Constitution Bill to prepare for majority rule elections. It included the Dedication to Almighty God. Minister Hilary Squires gave us a briefing on the security situation, saying there were now 10,000 terrorists in the country.

On March 1st the Rhodesian House of Assembly met for the last time after 55 years. Ian Smith showed rare emotion as he denounced the treachery of a Britain which, having neither built the country nor helped it on its way, made demands that had been imposed on no other colony and continued to refuse recognition when every condition had been met. The Senate adjourned the following day. There was provision in the new constitution for a Senate of Zimbabwe-Rhodesia, but since this was to be party-political there was no question of my standing for it.

The five-day common-roll election was held in April, for the most part in a carnival spirit. There was a general call-up of the whites on Maundy Thursday (the Thursday before Easter) to provide the necessary security, and never did a white minority take more prodigious pains to ensure that a black majority had a fair chance to express its will. Everybody knew that if power-sharing did not work in Zimbabwe-Rhodesia now it would never work anywhere.

On Good Friday I was busy preaching the Three Hours Devotion in the parish church at Marlborough, a Salisbury suburb. At the same time the security forces were taking energetic steps to ensure that the Patriotic Front could not wreck the election. Following a daring series of air-raids on terrorist camps in Zambia a rapid ground attack was launched on Nkomo's headquarters in Lusaka. The forces were in and out before the Zambians knew what was happening, leaving Nkomo's house a ruin. The corpulent leader was said to have made his escape through a lavatory window, an event which became the subject of much ribald mirth. It is not impossible that a Rhodesian "mole" gave advance warning of the attack and deprived the forces of the ultimate prize of Nkomo himself.

The election itself began on Easter Tuesday. Bishop Abel Muzorewa stood as a man of peace. He was the undoubted favourite, because peace was what the Africans — and everyone else apart from the Patriotic Front — wanted above all. Gladys and I voted at the Catholic Hall in Pendennis Road, where much good humour and all the excitement of the hustings was in evidence. The African electoral officer sent us home to find some proof of identity, but after that we dipped our hands in the tasteless fluid which prevented multiple voting and cast our vote in the ordinary way. (One uncharitable wag said the fluid was Rhodesian wine!)

Throughout the country there were huge queues at schools and halls and makeshift polling booths, and people travelled long distances in remote areas to vote.

When the polling was over more than 63% of the electorate of Zimbabwe-Rhodesia had voted: 1,869,077 people. And the little Methodist bishop was the big winner. His United African National Council won 51 of the 72 common-roll seats. Sithole's ZANU got 12, Chief Ndiwenis's United National Federal Party 9 and Chief Chirau's ZUPO none. Muzorewa complained that he had not made the clean sweep he expected, and Sithole proved a very bad loser by alleging vote-rigging.

This latter charge was simply not true. The vast majority of the 340 pressmen who covered the election, and who could go where they wanted, pronounced the voting free and fair — and convincing not only by African but by European standards. The 65 foreign observers, including the British, agreed. The PF made extraordinary efforts to disrupt the election, without success. But there were some poignant tragedies. On the second day of the poll our young friend Gerald Ross was shot dead: at 27 he was the youngest Rhodesian District Commissioner ever. Four Africans were killed by a landmine on their way back home after voting, and 38 were injured in the same incident. One survivor lost both legs.

At the end of May Mr Josiah Gumede was sworn in as President of Zimbabwe-Rhodesia and Bishop Muzorewa as Prime Minister. On May 31st we went to bed in Rhodesia and on June 1st woke up in the new state of Zimbabwe-Rhodesia. A new flag was ceremonially raised. Before the change-over a farewell to the past took place at a "Beating of Retreat" ceremony at Government House, when representatives of both the old order and the new met under the benign gaze of the Acting President, Lieutenant Colonel Everard. After "Abide with me" the green-and-white flag came down for the last time as the lone bugler wailed in the setting sun.

The RCG committee was meeting, in sombre mood, at the time the election results were announced. Most of us (with the exception of Father John Gardiner) felt we had to make the best of a bad job. Muzorewa was weak, but he had some excellent men. And the new system of joint-ministers, one white and one black, could have worked admirably for a transitional period. But events were soon to suggest that John might be right. President Carter of the US announced that he would not lift sanctions.

The Group found the money to keep the work going while we planned our course into an uncertain future. For my own part I was busy writing morning, noon and night — writing in the hope that we might still save a Christian country from a Marxist takeover. In addition to a booklet *Liberation in Africa* — on the consequences of such takeovers — I produced a series of leaflets and newsletters: *Dry your Tears for God's Country; Unbroken by the Storm; Say No to the Crocodile,* and *The Killing of a Christian Land.*

Whenever possible Gladys and I escaped to Inyanga, I to write without interruption and she to type my manuscripts. People said we were mad to travel on such dangerous roads and to sleep at so lonely a spot as Ravenshaw, our cottage, but we survived. We believed we would be protected as long as God had a job for us. On one occasion we forsook Ravenshaw in order to guard the home of our friends Ivor and Chris Ramsay, enabling them to get a break in Salisbury. The agric-alert gave us no peace. There was the usual "phase two red alert" and we had to answer the roll-call at 6.45 every morning. One night we heard the activity following the murder by terrorists of a resident in the lonely Cumberland Valley. An ambush was reported the same night.

On the Sunday I took the service at St Catherine's, baptising two young children. It was hours later that we learned we were all lucky to be alive. Early that morning the army had lifted a landmine from the road near the church. At the christening party at Troutbeck Inn, newly re-opened after several guerrilla attacks, I felt I faced death again: for what seemed to be a snake dropped from nowhere and slid inside the neck of my white cassock and down my back. I shot to my feet and disrobed with alacrity — to roars of laughter from all sides. The "snake" was an ice-cube slipped down my neck by one of the children I had baptised. "You poured water on me!" he exclaimed.

251

Bishop Muzorewa was a poor leader. He had claimed to be able to bring peace and call back the guerrillas from the bush. But he had no such ability. Under pressure he agreed to the abandonment of the "Rhodesia" in "Zimbabwe-Rhodesia," breaking faith with the Europeans and many of the more moderate Africans. But even if Muzorewa had been a good leader he still would not have had a chance. As long as Britain and "world opinion" backed the Patriotic Front in its bid to seize power at gun-point he could not bring peace. He could and did meet all the conditions Britain imposed, but neither he nor anyone else could make Britain keep its promises. We could only trust in the good faith of the new British Conservative government. And this proved a broken reed. British concern was with Nigerian oil and the pressures of a predominantly black Commonwealth. The British Council of Churches joined the clamour for continued sanctions.

The Parliament of Zimbabwe-Rhodesia met at the end of June. Early in July the Commonwealth Conference opened in Lusaka, Zambia, under the Soviet Solodovnikov's nose. The RCG had sent another cable to Mrs Thatcher appealing to her to take the pressure off Zimbabwe-Rhodesia and at least to make no further demands. She did the opposite. Herself under pressure from Lord Carrington (the new Foreign Secretary) and the Foreign Office, she capitulated to the Commonwealth demand for a further Rhodesian conference, another constitution and new elections.

We could hardly believe our ears. Here was the clearest possible breach of a promise clearly given. The Marxist plan for Rhodesia was plainly on course. The goal-posts had again been moved, and it was obvious that there were going to be conferences and constitutions and elections until the winners lost and the guerrillas were in power. The absurdity of having two one-man-one-vote elections within months of each other was evident, but this was what the Foreign Office demanded. And the Conservative Government, so far from dragging the Foreign Office along with it, was itself dragged along by the Foreign Office.

The Lancaster House Conference in London began on September 10th. Short of staging a military *coup*, which would have lost the country even South Africa's support, the Rhodesians had no choice but to attend. This time Nkomo and Mugabe were there, having been given the assurances they demanded. This Conference proved as cynical an exercise in political horsetrading as history affords. Within days the constitutional conference was widened, at the insistence of Carrington, to include all the demands of the Patriotic Front. The hotel rooms of the delegates were bugged and every delegation — almost every delegate of consequence — was privately told a different story. Each was going to come out on top. Only too late did most realise the gigantic hoax which had been perpetrated upon them.

Carrington astutely divided the whites in Muzorewa's delegation and isolated Ian Smith. Muzorewa was talked into abandoning all safeguards for minorities, even though his request for an end of sanctions was rejected. Perhaps he was not entirely at fault: self-seekers and turncoats among the whites cut the ground from under his feet. Nobody at all noticed that in Rhodesia the Patriotic Front had just murdered the country's most heroic and saintly Christian missionary, John Bradburne. As a Roman Catholic ascetic, he lived a solitary life in extreme poverty tending Rhodesia's few remaining lepers. Robert Mercer, Anglican Bishop of Matabeleland, said of him: "If anyone should have been left alone it was he."

The visit which Gladys and I paid to Britain from the end of September was not intended to have anything to do with the Lancaster House Conference. My brother Cecil invited us over and paid our expenses to demonstrate that I was no longer a prohibited immigrant. Cecil met us at Birmingham airport. At Solihull parish church, where I had been brought up, Canon Raymond Wilkinson and his clergy and people gave us a particularly warm welcome. They and the priests of the local deanery, like hundreds of other Christians in England, had worked hard for my freedom.

By October 1st, however, I was on the platform at another Caxton Hall meeting in London, speaking on "Zimbabwe-

Rhodesia Betrayed?" A crowded and enthusiastic audience passed a resolution, for the forthcoming Conservative Party conference, supporting Zimbabwe-Rhodesia — a resolution which the conference ignored.

In the middle of the month my wife and I were staying with friends at Grimsby in Lincolnshire when the telephone rang. The voice at the other end said: "This is Ian Douglas Smith." I had known that the former Prime Minister was at the Lancaster House Conference in London, but had hardly expected to hear from him. "If you happened to be in London tomorrow," he said, "you might be able to help."

I made it my business to be in London the following day, at the Carlton Towers Hotel where some of the delegates were staying. I saw the procession of VIP cars returning from Lancaster House at lunch-time, and waited while Smith extricated himself from the people buzzing around him. We went straight to his room, where he turned the TV on full blast to beat the bugging devices. "Carrington has got me completely isolated," he said, "and I don't know which of my colleagues I can trust. I wonder if you would take a message to 10 Downing Street?"

Within a little over an hour I was there with two messages for Mrs Thatcher, handing them over to Mr Ian Gow, the Prime Minister's Personal Private Secretary. What was in Ian Smith's message I do not know. My own, on behalf of the RCG, was another straightforward Christian plea to a Christian Prime Minister not to hand us over to a Marxist government. Mr Gow was very friendly but said: "The British government will never return to the Salisbury agreement between the whites and the blacks in Rhodesia."

By the end of the month Muzorewa had been persuaded that in a second election he would get an even bigger majority and had agreed to step down and accept the whole paraphernalia of British rule — and this in spite of the fact that sanctions were to continue. I was told by a leading Conservative Member of Parliament that this pathetic climb-down was totally unnecessary. There were enough Conservative MPs ready and willing to defy even a three-line whip to save Zimbabwe-Rhodesia.

254

By November I was back in Salisbury, briefing the RCG committee and making plans to advertise the enormity of what was happening in London. Our scheme was to insist that any agreement must be fully debated in the Salisbury Parliament. Meanwhile in England the Lancaster House conference continued in bitterness and acrimony for another month. Ian Smith reported later: "At the end of the game I was left alone on the field, and the referee had blown the whistle."

The conference ended in double tragedy: with the defeat of all moderate hopes and with the mysterious death of Mr John Giles, the constitutional adviser to the Zimbabwe-Rhodesia government. Such evidence as there is suggests that Giles may have discovered the fatal flaw in the new British constitution for Zimbabwe and its attached Bill of Rights, and might have been about to speak. A new Zimbabwe government could (as it subsequently did) nullify the Bill of Rights by the simple expedient of declaring a state of emergency.

John Giles was a happy and out-going man. On that fateful Thursday he spoke to his wife in Salisbury on the telephone and bought Christmas presents for her and for their children. He showed no sign of mental disturbance. The next morning he was found dead, having apparently jumped from a first-floor window. Maybe he committed suicide. Maybe he did not.

From Lancaster House the African people of Rhodesia got one clear and unambiguous message: "Last time you voted for the wrong people. Now vote again, and this time vote for the men with the guns." The following February they proceeded to do just that.

15. Say not the Struggle Naught Availeth

IN mid-November 1979 Gladys and I got away from the RCG office, which was pouring out statements and protests, to Inyanga. Beyond Rusape the road was lined with wrecked homesteads and burnt-out stores and farms. Pulling in at a little African "business centre" we found one or two shops were still open, though we missed, as we had missed for over a year now, the smiling face of Basil Nyabadza. It was from Mr Nyabadza, a local Christian leader, that we used to buy our meat. Some said he had been killed by terrorists because he had not paid his protection money. Others said the security forces had had a hand in his death. We never knew the truth, though we felt that in Basil's position the Archangel Gabriel would not have known what to do.

At Juliasdale the Montclair Hotel had obviously been attacked again. This must have been the third time. We went in and spoke with the proprietress, Mrs Ann Lount, who was visibly shaking as we talked with her. She had rolled under her bed as two rockets landed in her bedroom, and when it was all over had counted 173 bullets. How she had survived I cannot pretend to know, but she was not thinking of closing down. Others had suffered more than she. The previous week Chris Ross, whom we knew, had been killed as, unarmed and alone, he resisted the guerrillas who were trying to kidnap him. They all but blew his head off. The young Dunley-Owens, former parishioners of mine, had been attacked again the night before but were still alive.

As we hurried on before dusk to Inyanga and our cottage

we saw clouds of drifting smoke to the north. The fruit factory at Claremont had come under attack during the night, and was still burning. However, we could not pause. It was becoming dangerously late to travel, but fortunately we reached Ravenshaw without event. On the Sunday morning there was only a handful of people in church, and among the people there I found more courage than hope. During the service rifles, as usual, were stacked in a corner at the back of the church.

Back in Salisbury one had an increasing sense of being imprisoned in the city, and there were fewer and fewer places to which I could drive to conduct Sunday worship. However, invitations continued to come in from lonely farming areas such as Mrewa and Mtoko, and I always accepted them. The farmers would send a truck to collect me (or, usually, both of us). These trucks were invariably bristling with protective weapons, but mercifully we never had any occasion to use them.

Meanwhile in London, in the middle of November, the British Parliament passed another Southern Rhodesia Act, to enable it to by-pass the Salisbury Parliament. This reduced Zimbabwe-Rhodesia to the status of a crown colony. We were beginning to realise that ever since Muzorewa's election victory in April Britain had been under increasing economic pressure from oil-rich Nigeria, from the black Commonwealth and the US Carter administration to oust our multiracial government and to install a black nationalist one. She had neither the will nor the courage to resist, and moral considerations were simply ditched.

The RCG agitated loudly for a sight of the new constitution which was to be imposed upon us. Our present constitution guaranteed a minimum period of thirty days for public discussion of any proposed constitutional change, but under pressure from London the House of Assembly voted to rescind this provision — thus making it possible to push through the Lancaster House constitution unseen by the electorate. The reasons for the pressure and the haste soon became plain. Not only was the name "Rhodesia" to be totally abandoned, but so were many important safeguards. In any new elections we would not be able to vote for an executive subject to the law or for an army, judiciary and public service independent of the politicians.

The feeling of most of our group was that it would be better to let Britain impose its will by duress rather than to give it a semblance of constitutionality by putting it through a puppet Parliament. The government decided otherwise, wishing to avoid a dangerous precedent and the further loss of life which might have been occasioned by delay. Maybe it was right.

On Tuesday December 11th Mr Denis Walker, then Deputy Minister of Mines and Works, called on me at breakfast time to discuss a matter which even in those days of parliamentary turmoil could hardly be thought trivial: the Dedication to Almighty God in the Preamble to the Constitution. This said simply: "The peoples of Zimbabwe-Rhodesia acclaim the supremacy and omnipotence of Almighty God and acknowledge the ultimate direction by Him of the affairs of men." (Previously it had read "The peoples of Rhodesia . . .") It was this which the British were determined to delete, presumably believing it was their own prerogative to direct the affairs of men!

Denis Walker then went on to Parliament where, again under pressure from London, both houses proceeded to adopt in a single day the British constitution for Zimbabwe of which the electorate had still had no sight. The Parliament of Zimbabwe-Rhodesia then voted itself out of existence. Its last act, before its dissolution, was a plea to the British government to restore the Dedication to Almighty God in the constitution. This was proposed in the Assembly by Mr Walker and in the Senate by Senator Carol Heurtley, and carried unanimously in both houses. It was the last gesture of a subject people.

Lord Soames, appointed governor by Britain, arrived the following day. President Josiah Gumede handed over his office, the first popularly elected African leader to submit to a white colonial governor. The new flag was hauled down, and the Union Jack hoisted in its stead. Soames refused to see Mr Walker on the matter of the Dedication, and ignored the unanimous representations of the Heads of Churches. He put in a formal appearance at Salisbury Anglican cathedral,

259

but his true feelings were shown later when he went to Inyanga. He passed the church, where Bishop Burrough was taking the service, to go trout-fishing! To this day there is no Deity in the constitution of Zimbabwe.

To us in the Rhodesia Christian Group the British occupation seemed the end of our dreams. We had lived and worked and fought for a free Christian Rhodesia in which all races could play a part, and seldom had a small country put up so brave a struggle. Yet our new colonial masters were determined to wipe Rhodesia off the map, and to exclude God and Christianity from the very title-deeds of their new state.

Britain had neither colonised nor built Rhodesia — that was the work of Cecil Rhodes' Pioneers and their successors — and had given it virtually no help. Its claim to legal responsibility for the country rested on the free decision of the Rhodesian electorate in 1923 to offer allegiance to the British Crown rather than neighbouring South Africa. But politics knows no gratitude.

In the new circumstances the committee of the RCG continued to meet and to offer our friends and supporters what guidance it could. But we ourselves were perplexed, and sometimes divided. *Dying and Behold we Live* was the title of our Advent newsletter, and we knew that however just our cause had been the future struggle would have to be on very different lines. Our task now was to recall Christians to prayer and to help the victims of the tragedy. Already many white people were abandoning their homes and possessions and leaving the country with the pittance allowed them, while the blacks had no choice but to make what terms they could with the new order. It is true that they turned out in huge numbers to welcome the nationalist leaders when they returned to the country. What else could they do?

Gladys and I had necessarily to think of the future of our own family. Anthony, now nearly eighteen, left Marandellas High School at the end of November, having gone as far as the school could take him. The deputy headmaster, whom we knew well, had just been murdered, leaving a widow and young children. Anthony was due to go on to Mount Pleasant High School in Salisbury to take his A-levels in a year's time,

260

but we all agreed it would be wise for him to continue his studies in South Africa. Margaret, now twenty, was about to qualify as a State Registered Nurse at the Andrew Fleming Hospital in Salisbury, and felt that she should bide her time. She had a boy-friend, so that settled that.

The Christmas of 1979 was not a happy one. Once again the lights were bright in First Street and in Salisbury Gardens, but the roar of jet engines overhead drowned the carols as the British occupying forces were flown in with mountains of equipment. The polyglot crowds in the city streets — British, Nigerians, Fijians, Kenyans, Australians, New Zealanders — left Rhodesians in no doubt about their subject status. The choir in the cathedral sang of peace and goodwill, but most worshippers went quietly home after the service and left the streets to the occupying forces. On Christmas morning I celebrated the eucharist in St Elizabeth's church, Belvedere, a Salisbury suburb, but just as we reached the climax of the service, the scream of British aircraft seemed to mock our worship.

At midnight on Friday December 28th the British declared a ceasefire. This had been signed by Nkomo, Mugabe and Muzorewa at the Lancaster House Conference on December 21st, precisely seven years after the attack on Altena Farm which had marked the beginning of the terrorist war in earnest. The ceasefire made no perceptible difference.

It was on the following Sunday that Ted Wright was killed. Ted was an adult confirmation candidate of mine while I was at Rusape, and he and his wife Mary became our good friends. They had a struggle to keep their farm going, and in the end they had to abandon it. The courage of neither of them wavered in the difficult times. Ted got a job as water bailiff at Lake Alexander near Umtali. Then Mary was crippled in a terrorist attack — she is still crippled today — and she was in hospital at Umtali over Christmas. Ted went to visit her on the Sunday afternoon, but was slightly delayed by some friends who wanted to entertain him. "Don't come, Ted," Mary had said over the telephone, "if it is after three o'clock." It was only a little later than three when he left for Umtali, and it was a bright clear day. But close to Penhalonga village

261

Ted saw a gang of guerrillas attacking and looting an African bus. He reversed with all speed, but not quickly enough. Moments later he was dead. It was said afterwards that the terrorists retreated to St Augustine's, the Anglican mission at Penhalonga run by the Mirfield Fathers.

I do not know if it was before or after the "ceasefire" that old Mr Guthrie Hall of Penhalonga village was murdered. He was over eighty and blind, and he lived alone. The terrorists beat him pitilessly before they bayoneted him. They, too, were commonly associated with St Augustine's Mission. In the Johannesburg *Star* of March 6th 1984 Father Prosser, the head of the mission, was quoted as saying that "Staying alive meant befriending and helping the guerrillas, letting their presence go unreported, giving them money and food and refusing to become part of the security 'agric-alert' system."

It is difficult to believe that Father Prosser was concerned only for the safety of his mission and his charges. The mission school's list of "old boys" reads like a "Who's Who" of the guerrilla leaders. It was reported that on one occasion when the security forces visited the school they ordered the students to put up both their hands. One young man — he may or may not have been a student — failed to do so because he was holding an AK rifle, and he paid the price. After the war a memorial statue of a guerrilla fighter was erected on the mission, leaving no doubt as to its wartime allegiance. But by then, of course, no one talked of "terrorists" any more. They were "freedom fighters."

*   *   *   *

The Rhodesia Christian Group came to the inescapable conclusion that its operations in Zimbabwe must soon be wound up. This would mean the end even of our Terrorist Victims' Relief Fund. The new régime would plainly countenance neither criticism nor opposition, for the freedom of the freedom fighters was freedom to conform. Father Peter Grant, chaplain of the Selous Scouts, was the first to suggest that we might investigate the possibility of continuing operations outside the country — in fact that the RCG might go into exile. There would be huge numbers of people needing help, while gaoled opponents of the new régime would stand little chance if they had no voice in the larger world.

It was Father Grant, too, who first said bluntly that my own high profile meant that I might have to leave the country. It was suggested that I pay a further visit to South Africa to consult with our friends there, and Gladys accompanied me. Meanwhile it was agreed that Ndabazinhle Musa should keep his ear to the ground to determine what continued presence, if any, we might have in the new Zimbabwe.

At the beginning of 1980 the guerrillas came flooding into the country, now legally, from the neighbouring territories where they had been based. The idea was that they would foregather in the Assembly Points set up by the British, where they would be supervised by members of the British Monitoring Force. Some 22,000 actually turned up at the Assembly Points, and of these many were indeed genuine guerrillas. What the British did not know, at least initially, was that many were not. Large numbers were merely *mujibhas*, youngsters who were no more than messengers or hangers-on. They freed the hard-core terrorists to remain at large to intimidate the civilian population during the election, roaming the countryside and establishing a dreaded presence in every village and kraal. Most of them were Robert Mugabe's men.

From the moment the election campaign got under way the immense scale of electoral intimidation was apparent. Only in the cities was there any semblance of free electioneering. In huge areas of the country no more than one party was allowed to campaign, and that party was Mugabe's ZANU. The populace was told in unambiguous terms that ZANU was going to win, and if it did not ZANU would start up the war again and the war would continue until ZANU was in power. A number of Muzorewa's election workers met a violent death, and Nkomo's fared little better outside Matabeleland. It was ZANU, not ZAPU or even the Patriotic Front, that was going to win. One of Nkomo's parliamentary candidates was murdered by a Mugabe supporter by having hot coals thrust down his throat. In the Fort Victoria area, where more than a million people lived, even the British election administrator openly admitted that no party other than Mugabe's was permitted to campaign.

Perhaps the most scrupulous witness of events in Zimbabwe at this time was an American politician who later became an Assistant Secretary of State, Dr Richard McCormack. He wrote: "It was obvious that the ordinary citizens of the war-weary land were desperately tired of death and disruption . . . Many people would undoubtedly have voted for Atilla the Hun if he offered the prospect of an end to the conflict . . ."

General Walls was the Commander of Combined Operations in Rhodesia's war and the man who more than anyone had denied Mugabe his hope of military victory. He summed up the situation tersely: "Intimidation is universally practised by African politicians. Mr Mugabe's followers' intimidation was a damn sight better than anyone else's."

Mugabe was undoubtedly the man most hated by the whites and most feared by the moderate Africans, and the British had given categorical assurances that they would police the elections strictly and would disqualify him if he attempted to intimidate voters. In the event they did nothing. Hundreds of affidavits on intimidation were submitted to Soames, who merely ignored them.

There may have been a certain cynical method in the policy of the British. It is thought they believed that in a fair election Muzorewa would again come out on top, and this plainly would not do. Nkomo was their man. He was more a national-ist than a Marxist, and as a member of the minority Matabele (Ndebele) tribe would only be able to rule with the co-operation of Muzorewa and Mugabe. Mugabe must therefore do reasonably well, and it would not be wise to put obstacles in his way. McCormack was convinced that this was the calculation of the British authorities, and that their plans went tragically awry.

The elections began on Wednesday February 27th 1980, and the enormous turn-out was itself a witness to the fear of the people. Every polling station was supervised by a British policeman, and it was no fault of the policemen that they were regarded as figures of fun. The British bobbies were hopelessly out of context and knew nothing of the Africans or their languages. They could and did ensure that there was no malpractice at the polling booths, but they did not know the significance of the people crowing like cockerels round the booths — the cockerel was Mugabe's symbol — or of the black boxes and other devices by which ZANU supporters purported to read the secret ballots of the voters.

2,702,275 African men and women cast their votes, or nearly 94% of the electorate. Even the British were shocked by the result, while Rhodesians were dazed and horrified. Mugabe had won 57 seats, Nkomo 20 and Muzorewa three. General Walls asked Mrs Thatcher to invalidate the result because of the massive intimidation, but it was said that his message was delayed by the Foreign Office. In any case it was ignored. Walls said there would be no white *coup* — that would have bedevilled matters still further — but many of the Europeans who could leave were already packing their bags. In the end 100,000 left, abandoning their homes and properties, their savings and their livelihoods. There were huge African rejoicings; but there was also silent African dismay and despair.

The RCG committee lost little time in putting its tentative plans into operation. Our work could not now continue overtly in Marxist Zimbabwe, but most of our members would remain at their jobs as long as they could. Father Peter Grant's chaplaincy of the Selous Scouts disappeared almost overnight, for this prestigious unit, much feared by Mugabe's men, was disbanded informally. (The Rhodesian Light Infantry had just time to be ceremonially stood down, laying up its standard in the Anglican cathedral.) We made arrangements to keep in touch with Ndaba, who would have to be very much a freelance — as indeed he always had been. My own commission was (if Gladys and I felt able) to go to South Africa, contact our friends throughout the world and urge Rhodesian organisations world-wide not to fold up but to keep going. There was work to be done, maybe more than ever.

Most of the British pulled out with all speed after the election. On April 18th the Prince of Wales lowered the Union Jack and Lord Soames departed. It was a coincidence that I had read recently a work by Mr Ivor Denoon which dealt

265

generally with British abandonments of colonial responsibilities. "Followed," he wrote, "in all the British territories, the pantomime of abdication: flags being lowered, a Royal Personage handing over the deeds and so on. The only truth behind this woeful pageant was that the black man was being handed back to slavery." Benson was describing the fate of Rhodesia.

Gladys and I did not see the end. We agonised for long days, and prayed for guidance. What *was* the right thing to do? To stay on, as so many must? Or to leave the country we loved so dearly, building up the RCG in exile and trying to help the refugees and those who would inevitably fall foul of the incoming Marxist leaders? Either way we faced a daunting and uncertain future. The final decision was taken as much by our friends as by ourselves. Head had to prevail over heart.

I could of course have got a job as an Anglican priest almost anywhere, but to take that course immediately would have been to run away from the crisis. The time for that would come soon enough. Of the need for Christian workers in the new Zimbabwe there was no doubt. Fortunately there were many such, quiet men and women who had not shouted the odds, who had taken no part in the struggle but who had tried to live Christian lives in the turmoil and to bring people to God. It was their turn now.

The RCG office was busier than ever during those last few weeks, and everyone was making plans for an uncertain future. People dropped in with unexpected little gifts. The telephone seemed to ring night and day. The prospect of leaving our home, with its garden and its books and its memories, became bitterer every day.

We never formally emigrated. On Thursday March 20th 1980 Gladys and I piled what we could into the car and began the two-day drive to Pretoria. We had managed to sell the cottage, but could not take the money with us. As we drove through the empty spaces south of Fort Victoria, making for Beit Bridge and the border, there were no terrorists. They were the rulers now.

Zimbabwe, of course, was to enjoy little peace. Apart from

266

the vast exodus of Europeans, which it could ill afford if it was to become anything but another begging-bowl state, there were horrendous massacres until the dominant Shonas had subjugated the Matabele minority. No one knows how many Matabele died, but the figure may have run into tens of thousands.

In my first newsletter from South Africa I wrote, under the title *By the waters of Babylon*: "No words can voice our sorrow for our lost and lovely land, the one African country where the non-racial ideal could and would have succeeded but for Britain. Yet, humanly speaking, our cause is defeated . . . Defeat, however, is not for ever. A battle has been lost. But the war was won on Calvary . . . Let no Christian who moves to South Africa think he faces anything but the same struggle. There is no hiding place."

Had Gladys and I done the right thing? It was only in 1983 that we became sure beyond all doubt. News reached us that our friend Ndabazinhle Musa was sick and in leg-irons in Harare Central Prison. (Salisbury was called Harare now.) He had been invited by friends to undertake an international preaching tour, but while in America was taken ill. Diabetes was diagnosed, and he was in an American hospital when his passport expired. After his return to Zimbabwe — no other country could receive him without a passport — an unsuccessful attempt was made to arrest him while he was in a hospital ward in a diabetic coma. His arrest finally took place after he was discharged, and he was sent, untried, first to the Central Prison and then to Chikurubi Maximum Security Gaol. He would have died for lack of insulin if his friends had taken no action.

First we organised, by inter-continental telephone calls, a world-wide chain of prayer. Then, with other well-wishers, we raised an agitation for him among British church and political leaders, American congressmen and sympathetic members of the German Federal Parliament. Ndaba was freed, and ultimately allowed to leave the country and continue his evangelistic work in Europe.

Our action for Ndaba merely repaid a debt. He had given us enormous support in the past. Of the hundreds of other

Rhodesians we and our friends were able to assist over the years few were known to us in the first instance. It was sufficient that they were Rhodesians, and that they were in trouble. Yes, with God's help we *had* made the right decision.

However on one count we were, thank God, proved quite wrong. In Angola and Mozambique as in the Soviet Union and China the ruling Marxists had closed and destroyed the churches, and persecuted and murdered Christians. This was not the pattern in Zimbabwe. Rhodesia had been perhaps the most prayed-for country in the modern world. God did not give us what we asked, for He does not overrule the freedom even of evil men. But He gave something not less precious — freedom to preach His Gospel where otherwise freedom was all but destroyed.

*   *   *   *

In the early days of Zimbabwe, before the revolutionary government was firmly in the saddle, it was still possible for opponents of the new régime to return to the country unmolested. In 1981 Gladys and I paid a final visit, and were able to get down into the Honde Valley.

The Virgin rocks still dominated the valley, as did, in a smaller way, the great white cross of St Peter's Church. The usual road to Mandea was completely broken up, but we were able to reach the mission by the long way round. The "road" might have been a dried-up river-bed, and the villages we had known so well were no more. We saw only charred ruins. But Father Gabriel Mashingaidze, the priest-in-charge, was back again from the now abandoned protected villages. The mission was overgrown with tall grass, which he was cutting down, and there was not a pane of glass left unbroken. Our old home was a burnt-out ruin, but the assistant priest's house had been made habitable. "I feel like Nehemiah," said Father Mashingaidze, "re-building the walls of Jerusalem."

There were 400 school-children, but only one trained teacher. I remembered David Mandangu well. "Come back, Father," he said, "and help us." I could not go back. It would never have worked. But what need? Father Mashingaidze was there, and doing a magnificent job. It was up to the Africans now, and they were not failing. We went into the shell of the church, from which the cow-dung had been removed. "We get a dozen in church on Sundays," said Father. "It is a start." St Peter's Mission was to rise again from the ashes, and the work of the past was not in vain. But that is another story — an African story.

*　　*　　*　　*

Too bright the vision? No. Our hope of a multiracial Rhodesia was dead, but our vision of a Christian Africa was like a flame which will not go out. For a few years the torch had been in our hands. Now we had no choice but to leave it in the hands of those who had listened to our message. But that was the object of missionary work anyway.

The bitterest blow was that soon we had to break off all contact with most of our African friends. Perhaps they thought we had abandoned them. The truth was that if we had maintained contact with them they would have suffered at the hands of the new rulers. For Zimbabwe was now a Marxist state where indeed the Gospel could still be preached but where letters were opened and telephones were tapped — and where the name "Rhodesia" might not be breathed.

But history does not stand still. Today Marxist states are toppling everywhere. And the vision of Christianity and freedom is still bright in the hearts of Christians. Perhaps decades must elapse before whites and blacks learn to live together in Africa without the one dominating the other. But that time must surely come.

Index

Dombashawa Indaba, 170
Douglas-Home, Sir Alec, 192
Dupont, Clifford, 179, 187, 225
Durban Castle, 72, 90
Dzimunwe, Douglas, 178-9

Eastern Highlands Tea Estate, 141, 227
Education Department, 97, 135-6, 139, 147-8, 175
Elections; Southern Rhodesia 1962, 159-60; Rhodesian 1970, 189, 192;
    Rhodesian 1978, 231; Rhodesian common-roll 1979, 249-50; Mugabe
    1980, 264-5
Elim massacre, 228, 238
Empire Windrush, 1, 2
Epiphany Mission, 100
Epworth Theological College, 206
Esther, Sister, 96, 103, 110, 114, 123
Everard, Lt Col, 250
Everitt, Ann, John, 219-20
Executive Council (EXCO), 233, 242

Fearless, HMS, 174
ffrench-Beytagh, Dean Gonville, 108
Fischer, Ferdie, Rijk, 191
Frank, Mwalimu, 30, 32
FRELIMO, 186, 207-8
Friends of St Faith's, 99
Frost, David, 245

Gardiner, Canon Arthur John, 194, 203, 210, 224, 237-8, 250
Genders, Archdeacon Anselm, 189
Geneva, conference, 226
Gibbs, Sir Humphrey, 187
Giles, John, 255
Goto, 114
Gow, Ian MP, 254
Grant, Rev Peter, 217, 262-3, 265
"Green leader" raid, 242
Green-Wilkinson, Archbishop, Central Africa, 177
Gumede, Josiah, 250, 259

Hadley, Ann, 175-6
Harries, Dr Lyndon, 61, 70
Hart, Miss Beatrice, 23-4

Hegongo, 5-6, 10, 15, 35, 52
Helms, Senator Jesse, 240
Heurtley, Senator Carol, 216, 259
Honde massacres, 227
Hugh, Mwalimu, 17-8
Hughes, Archbishop, Central Africa, 125

Inyanga, 168-9, 184-5, 188, 190, 212-3, 224, 243, 251, 257-8, 260;
    St Catherine's church, 184, 213, 243, 251
Inyanga archdeaconry, 126, 174, 188-9

Jackman, Ray, 148-51, 154, 160
Jari, Beaven, Lydia, 148-9, 154

Kapuya, John, 123
Kariba, 244-5
Kaunda, Kenneth, 212
Keltana, Job, 118, 123, 169, 229
Kendall, Rev Elliott, 192, 197
Kihurio, 37, 42-53
Kinga, Chief (Taungwena), 173
Kissinger, Dr Henry, 221-3, 226
Kiungani High School, Zanzibar, 59, 69
Kizara Mission, 19-35
Korogwe, 22, 30, 37-8, 40, 46, 49, 72, 87
Krapf, 5
Kwata, 22, 29-33

Lambeth Conference 1978, 238
Lamont, Bishop Donal, 205
Lancaster House Conference 1979, 253-5, 261
Land Appointment Act, 173
Land Tenure Bill/Act, 186, 189, 230, 248
Lardner-Burke, Desmond, 223
Laver, Tom, 59, 65-6
Liberation in Africa, booklet, 251
Liuli, 79-81
Livingstone, David, 1
Lount, Mrs Ann, 257
Lumsden, Hamish, 216-7
Lury, Rev Edward, 49, 52-3

Machiha, Nathan, 119, 121
Magila, Msalabani, 2-5, 9, 11, 16, 18, 34
Makoni, Chief, 101

Rhodesia Undefeated, booklet, 225
Richard, Ivor, 226
Robinson, Father John, 87–9
Rusape, 94, 96, 106, 183–4, 186, 188, 189–90, 213, 217, 219–20
Russell, Rev Neil, 37–41

St Catherine's church, see Inyanga
St Faith's Mission, Rusape, 88, 90, 93–127 *passim*
St Faith's Mission Farm, 88, 107, 113, 115–9
St Peter's Mission, Mandea, see Mandea Mission
Salisbury, Rhodesia, 91–3, 96, 108, 114, 120, 146, 169, 187–8, 192–4, 217, 223–4, 226, 229, 237, 242, 245, 248, 255, 258
Salisbury Agreement 1978, 232–3, 238
Salisbury fire, 242–3
Same, 38, 40–1, 49
Senate, Rhodesia, 214–7, 223, 231, 248–9
Shambala country, 19–21, 25
Sharpe, Canon, 56–7
Shaw, Dean Allan, 209
Shona, people and language, 91, 95, 102–3, 105, 217
Sithole, Ndabaningi, 232–3, 250
Sitwell, Dr Lesley, 87
Slimp, Rev Col Bob, 240
Smith, Bernard, 248
Smith, Father Harold, 22–3, 34
Smith, Ian Douglas, 170–2, 174, 186, 192, 205, 212, 215–6, 221–3, 226, 230–2, 242–5, 248, 253–5
Soames, Lord, 259, 264–5
Society for the Propagation of the Gospel (SPG), 90, 99, 167, 192, see also USPG
Solodovnikov, 224, 252
Southern Rhodesia, 87, 91, 100, 106
Southern Rhodesia Act, UK 1979, 258
South West African People's Organisation (SWAPO), 206
Spinola, General, 207
Stephens, Archdeacon, 10, 14, 52
Stowell, Rev Donald, 93, 96–7
Stradling, Bishop Leslie, South West Tanganyika, 70–3, 80, 86–7
Sudi, Agnes, 64
Sudi, Rev William, 64, 67
Swahili, 3, 7, 21, 33, 48, 56, 62, 69–70, 74, 207
Sydenham, Archdeacon Herbert, 37–8, 40–1, 52, 193
Synod, Diocese of Mashonaland, 192, 195
Synod, Province of Central Africa, 203

Tambo, Rev Cyprian, 104, 107, 115

Note on place-names in Zimbabwe. Salisbury (now called Harare). Umtali (now Mutare). Marandellas (Marondera). Inyanga (Nyanga).

Note on the pronunciation of Bantu names. Stress on last syllable but one. Vowels as in Italian. Initial M approximately "Um." G hard. Magila (Ma *gee* la). Msalabani (Um sa la *ba* nee). Same approximately *Sah*-may. Mutare (Moot-*tah*-ray).